YOUNG PEOPLE *and* SOCIAL CHANGE

Second edition

SOCIOLOGY *and* **SOCIAL CHANGE**

Series Editors: *Alan* **Warde,** *Nick* **Crossley, University of Manchester**

Published titles

Amanda **Coffey – Education** *and* **Social Change**
Gail **Hawkes –** *A* **Sociology** *of* **Sex** *and* **Sexuality**
Colin **Hay – Re-stating Social** *and* **Political Change**
Máirtín **Mac an Ghaill – Contemporary Racisms** *and* **Ethnicities**
Mike **Savage – Class Analysis** *and* **Social Transformation**

YOUNG PEOPLE *and* SOCIAL CHANGE

New Perspectives

Second edition

Andy **Furlong** *and Fred* **Cartmel**

Open University Press

Open University Press
McGraw-Hill Education
McGraw-Hill House
Shoppenhangers Road
Maidenhead
Berkshire
England
SL6 2QL

email: enquiries@openup.co.uk
world wide web: www.openup.co.uk

and Two Penn Plaza, New York, NY 10121–2289, USA

First published 1997
First published in this second edition 2007
Reprinted 2011

A catalogue record of this book is available from the British Library

ISBN 10: 0 335 21868 7 (pb)   0 335 21869 5 (hb)
ISBN 13: 978 0 335 21868 4 (pb)   978 0 335 21869 1 (hb)

Library of Congress Cataloging-in-Publication Data
CIP data applied for

Typeset by RefineCatch Limited, Bungay, Suffolk
Printed and bound in Great Britain by CPI Antony Rowe, Chippenham, Wiltshire

The McGraw·Hill Companies

Contents

List of figures

The authors

Andy Furlong is Professor of Sociology in the School of Business and Manage-
ment, University of Glasgow and Senior Honorary Research Fellow in the
School of Political and Social Inquiry, Monash University. He is editor of the
Journal of Youth Studies. Fred Cartmel is Lecturer in Sociology in the Depart-
ment of Sociology, Anthropology and Applied Social Sciences, University of
Glasgow.

Acknowledgements

The changes we described back in 1997 are still evident, but not all of the trends continued in the direction we had expected and situations have arisen that we had not thought of as significant enough to comment about in detail in the first edition. Since completing the first edition our interpretations have also developed, partly in response to the debates sparked by interest in the book, but also through engaging with ideas being developed by colleagues in the field. In writing this new edition we have taken the opportunity to draw on a wealth of new evidence on young people's experiences and to refine our interpretations of changes that have taken place. With the first edition having attracted an international readership, we have also attempted to source evidence from a wider range of advanced societies. This edition reflects the experiences of young people living in the developed world and we have attempted to highlight key differences between countries.

We would like to express our thanks to the many people who have engaged with us on the ideas presented in the first edition of this book at various meetings, conferences and workshops. We are particularly grateful to Andy Biggart, Helen Sweeting and Patrick West who worked with us on a recent project on transitions; Peter Kelly and Johanna Wyn for an introduction to recent Australian work; and to Akio Inui and his colleagues for sharing his knowledge about young people in Japan. We remain grateful to those who read and commented on drafts of the first edition and to Gerda Reith who pointed us in the direction of some useful literature for this edition.

Series editor's preface

In response to perceived major transformations, social theorists have offered forceful, appealing, but contrasting accounts of the predicament of contemporary Western societies. Key themes emerging have been condensed into terms like post-modernity, risk society, disorganized capitalism, the information society. These accounts have widespread ramifications for the analysis of many aspects of social life and personal well-being. The focus of this series is the critical appraisal of such general, substantive theories through examination of their applicability to different institutional areas of societies. Each book introduces current debates and surveys existing sociological argument and research about changing institutional arrangements.

In this second edition of their acclaimed *Young People and Social Change*, Andy Furlong and Fred Cartmel present a completely revised authoritative overview of the most recent sociological evidence about the contemporary transition to adulthood. They document some sharp and significant changes in the nature and experience of the transition which have occurred since the 1970s. As the duration of the transition has lengthened and the apparent alternative routes increased in number, the process has seemed to become more hazardous and uncertain. For the young people involved choices appear to have multiplied and the sense of responsibility for success or failure to have become even more a personal and individual matter. Yet objective constraints imposed by entrenched social structural divisions of class and gender operate much as before. The authors examine the new scenarios and old barriers operating in various spheres of social life, including education, labour markets, leisure and politics. Enriched by their own original research on youth, they describe the situation of young people while simultaneously critically evaluating influential theoretical accounts of the process of individualization associated with Beck and Giddens. A bold general thesis, supported by a wide-ranging review of current evidence, serves to distinguish the key elements of change and continuity.

Alan Warde

1 *The* risk society

Images of a classless society, a common way of speaking, dressing, and seeing, can also serve to hide more profound differences; there is a surface on which everyone appears on an equal plane, but breaking the surface may require a code people lack.

(Sennett 1998: 75)

Introduction

The life experiences of young people in modern societies have changed quite significantly. These changes affect relationships with family and friends, experiences in education and the labour market, leisure and lifestyles and the ability to become established as independent young adults. Many of these changes are a direct result of the re-structuring of labour markets, of an increased demand for educated workers, of flexible employment practices and of social policies which have extended the period in which young people remain dependent on their families. As a consequence of these changes, young people today have to negotiate a set of risks which were largely unknown to their parents: this is true irrespective of social background or gender. Moreover, as many of these changes have come about within a relatively short period of time, points of reference which, by serving as clear route maps previously helped smooth processes of social reproduction, have become obscure. In turn, increased uncertainty can be seen as a source of stress and vulnerability.

On a theoretical level, these changes have been expressed in a number of ways, with sociologists holding different opinions about whether they signify the beginning of a new era, just as significant as the transition from medieval to modern society, or whether they represent developments within modernity. At one end of the spectrum, post-modernists such as Lyotard (1984) and Baudrillard (1988) argue that we have entered a new, post-modern, epoch in which structural analysis has lost its validity. In post-modern societies it is no longer seen as appropriate to apply grand theories to the study of social life. Patterns of behaviour and individual life chances have lost their predictability and post-modernism involves a new and much more diverse set of lifestyles. The validity of a science of the social is rejected, along with the usefulness of key explanatory variables such as class and gender. As Lash and Urry suggest, for post-modernists, 'all that is solid about organised capitalism, class, industry, cities, collectivity, nation-states, even the world, melts into air' (1987: 313). Other theorists have been more cautious in their interpretation of the changes and have used terms like 'high modernity', 'late modernity' (Giddens 1990, 1991) or 'reflexive modernisation' (Lash 1992) to draw attention to the far-reaching implications of recent socio-economic change, at the same time as expressing the view that, as yet, these changes do not represent an epochal shift.[1] This is a view with which we concur.

There is little doubt in our minds that radical social changes have occurred, yet we are extremely sceptical of the validity of post-modernist theories and suspicious of a tendency among fellow social scientists to exaggerate change. Modernity has always involved differentiation, a plurality of life-worlds (Berger *et al.* 1974), a weakening of communal regulation (Elias 1978) and a sense of uncertainty (Durkheim 1947): indeed, the weakening of traditional ties, the depersonalization of relations and the growing obscurity of factors which structure patterns of exploitation in advanced capitalism were identified by the founding fathers of sociology. While structures appear to have fragmented, changed their form and become increasingly obscure, we suggest that life chances and experiences can still largely be predicted using knowledge of individuals' locations within social structures: despite arguments to the contrary, class and gender divisions remain central to an understanding of life experiences.

At the same time, we recognize that traditional ways of conceptualizing class are not well suited to the analysis and understanding of the distribution of life chances in late modernity. Employment relationships, which serve as a cornerstone for conventional class analysis, and the occupations that serve as proxies for class, have changed significantly. There is evidence that, for many, employment relationships have become more precarious and that individuals' skill in managing risk should be regarded as a significant resource. In the flexible workplace, having the resources to manage risk (and here we refer not just to financial resources but to capital in a broad social sense) underpins labour market security and the reproduction of advantage. Increasingly models of class must take account of agency.

Despite these reservations, in this book we provide empirical evidence to support the argument that concepts (such as social class) which have long been central to sociological analysis still provide a foundation on which we can develop an understanding of processes of social reproduction in the modern world. Nevertheless, we argue that some of these concepts need to be re-specified in ways suited to modern conditions. In this context, we suggest that writers such as Beck (1992, 2000), Giddens (1991), Sennett (1998) and Bauman (2001) have been successful in identifying processes of individualization and risk which characterize late modernity and which have implications for lived experiences and for the ways in which we represent social divisions. While we accept the main thrust of their arguments about individualization, we suggest that life in late modernity revolves around an epistemological fallacy: although social structures, such as class, continue to shape life chances, these structures tend to become increasingly obscure as collectivist traditions weaken and individualist values intensify. As a consequence of these changes, people come to regard the social world as unpredictable and filled with risks which can only be negotiated on an individual level, even though chains of human interdependence (Elias 1978, 1982) remain intact.

In many respects, the study of young people's lives provides an ideal opportunity to examine the relevance of new social theories: if the social order has changed and if social structures have weakened, we would expect to find evidence of these changes among young people who are at the crossroads of the process of social reproduction. One of the key aims of this book is to uncover evidence of the changing impact of social structures through the study of youth and young adults in modern societies. The central questions we seek to answer relate first to whether the traditional parameters which were previously understood as structuring the life chances and experiences of young people are still relevant. Second, we will examine the extent to which the terms 'individualization' and 'risk' convey an accurate picture of the changing life contexts of the young.

We accept that the experiences of young people have changed quite radically over the last three decades, yet suggest that in the age of 'high modernity' life chances and processes of social reproduction remain highly structured. We also agree that there has been a breakdown in 'ontological security' (Giddens 1991) which validates the claim that modernity, as traditionally understood, is changing.[2] It is possible to draw on a number of theorists within the 'late modernist' tradition to understand these changes (such as Sennett 1998 and Bauman 2001), but in our opinion, the ideas of Ulrich Beck put forward in his book *Risk Society* (1992) (and elaborated in *The Brave New World of Work*, 2000) and those of Anthony Giddens in *Modernity and Self Identity* (1991) provide clear statements about the nature of these changes and therefore a good base for the study of young people in the late modern age. We begin this chapter with a summary of the relevant ideas of Beck and Giddens and then start to identify some of the ways in which they can be applied to an understanding of young people in modern societies.

'Risikogesellschaft'

In *Risk Society* (*Risikogesellschaft*) Beck (1992) argues that the western world is witnessing an historical transformation. Industrial society is being replaced by a new modernity in which the old, 'scientific', world view is being challenged; predictabilities and certainties characteristic of the industrial era are threatened and a new set of risks and opportunities are brought into existence. Whereas modernity involved rationality and the belief in the potential offered by harnessing scientific knowledge, in late modernity the world is perceived as a dangerous place in which we are constantly confronted with risk. These risks include those stemming from the threat of nuclear war or environmental disasters, as well as other risks which have to be negotiated in day-to-day life. Indeed, according to Beck, people are progressively freed from the social networks and constraints of the old order and forced to negotiate a new set of hazards which impinge on all aspects of their day-to-day lives. Previous securities are broken and people's concerns start to centre upon the prevention or elimination of the risks which are systematically produced as part of modernization.

This is not to suggest that we have moved into a new era of classlessness or that people's structural locations have a limited effect on their life chances. Beck acknowledges that risks are unequally distributed within society and may be arranged in a manner which follows the inequalities characteristic of class society:

> Like wealth, risks adhere to the class pattern, only inversely: wealth accumulates at the top, risks at the bottom. To that extent, risks seem to *strengthen*, not abolish, the class society. Poverty attracts an unfortunate abundance of risks. By contrast, the wealthy (in income, power or education) can *purchase* safety and freedom from risk.
>
> (Beck 1992: 35, original emphasis).

Despite an unequal vulnerability to risk, Beck does suggest that class ties have weakened (at least in a subjective sense) and that in late modernity it is not always possible to predict lifestyles, political beliefs and opinions using information about occupations or family backgrounds. Indeed, Beck argues that 'people with the same income level, or to put it in the old-fashioned way, within the same "class", can or even must choose between different life styles, subcultures, social ties and identities' (1992: 131). These doubts about the validity of class and about the relevance of social structures that are elaborated somewhat cautiously in *Risk Society* are expressed more boldly in Beck's later work. In *The Brave New World of Work*, for example, he talks about a 'political economy of ambivalence' in which 'top and bottom are no longer clearly defined poles, but overlap and fuse in new ways', and where 'insecurity prevails at nearly all positions within society' (Beck 2000: 3–4).

Because individual behaviour and lifestyles can no longer be predicted using concepts like social class, Beck describes the new epoch as 'capitalism *without* classes' (1992: 88). Individualized lifestyles come into being in which people are forced to put themselves at the centre of their plans and reflexively construct their social biographies. Collectivities fragment as 'individuals are encouraged to perform as a "Me & Co.", selling themselves on the marketplace' (2000: 3). The workplace becomes less of an arena for conflicts, and ascribed social differences such as gender and racial inequalities come to assume a greater significance. In all aspects of their lives, people have to choose between different options, including the social groups with which they wish to be identified, and temporary allegiances are formed in respect to particular issues. People may join a number of social and political groups whose aims appear to clash – they may join a trade union, for example, and vote for right wing political parties – yet Beck regards these various allegiances as representing pragmatic responses by individuals in the struggle for survival in the risk society.

While we agree with Beck that subjective dimensions of class have weakened and that lifestyles and experiences in education and the labour market have become increasingly individualized, it is important to stress that we are not arguing that class has weakened as a predictor of individual life chances. It is also important to be clear about Beck's view of the ongoing nature of social divisions which continue to shape life chances: he is not suggesting that social inequalities disappear or weaken within the new modernity. Social inequality continues to exert a powerful hold over people's lives, but increasingly does so at the level of the individual rather than the group or class. Beck admits that within western societies social inequalities display 'an amazing stability' (1992: 91) and that empirical research is unlikely to uncover significant changes. 'Income inequalities, the structure of the division of labour, and the basic determinants of wage labour have, after all, remained relatively unchanged' (1992: 92), although there has been a weakening of class identities and the individualization of lifestyles.

The social processes identified by Beck have received broad support in the work of Anthony Giddens (1990, 1991), although there are significant differences which we highlight in the concluding chapter. Giddens argues that the age of 'high modernity' is characterized by a risk culture insofar as people today are subject to uncertainties which were not part of day-to-day life for previous generations. Within this risk culture, the self is reflexively created as people are forced to interpret a diversity of experiences in a way which helps them establish a coherent biography. Thus Giddens argues that people have to accept the central part played by risk in their lives which involves acknowledging 'that no aspects of our activities follow a pre-ordained course, and all are open to contingent happenings' (1991: 28). Furthermore, 'living in the "risk society" means living with a calculative attitude to the open possibilities of action, positive and negative, with which, as individuals and globally, we are confronted in a continuous way in our contemporary social existence' (1991: 28).

Unlike post-modern perspectives, the interpretation of high modernity presented by Beck and Giddens and their view of changes in the balance of the relationship between individual and society does not mean that people are free to re-create the world in increasingly diverse forms. For Giddens, modernity 'produces difference, exclusion and marginalization' (1991: 6). Diversification involves the emergence of new experiences and trajectories, but does not involve a process of equalization nor does it dilute the nature of class-based inequalities on an objective level. In this context we will argue that processes of diversification may obscure underlying class relationships and may provide the impression of greater equality without actually providing anything of substance: a process which we refer to as the epistemological fallacy of late modernity.

Thus while structures of inequality remain deeply entrenched, in our view one of the most significant features of late modernity is the epistemological fallacy: the growing disjuncture between objective and subjective dimensions of life. People's life chances remain highly structured at the same time as they increasingly seek solutions on an individual, rather than a collective basis. Beck argues that in late modernity, risks have become 'individualized' and people increasingly regard setbacks and crises as individual shortcomings, rather than as outcomes of processes which are beyond their personal control. Unemployment, for example, may be seen as a consequence of a lack of skills on the part of the individual, rather than as the result of a general decline in demand for labour. Similarly, problems faced by school-leavers in less advantaged areas may be seen as a reflection of their poor record of academic performance rather than as a consequence of material circumstances and the lack of compensatory mechanisms within the school. The individualization of risk may mean that situations which would once have led to a call for political action are now interpreted as something which can only be solved on an individual level through personal action. The search for solutions to entrenched inequalities tends to become focused on individual 'deficiencies' rather than social and economic structures. As a consequence of these changes, Beck argues that an increase in social inequality may be associated with an intensification of individualization as more people are placed in unpleasant situations which they interpret as being due, in part, to their own failures. In the risk society, individual subjectivity becomes an important force.

Social class and biography

The challenge to the validity of traditional ways of thinking about social class and the relevance of class for understanding the distribution of life chances in modern societies has engaged the imagination of a wide range of sociologists (e.g. Pahl 1989; Goldthorpe and Marshall 1992; Pahl 1993; Saunders 1995; Pakulski and Waters 1996; Sennett 1998; Savage 2000; Bauman 2001). Pahl has even gone as far as to suggest that class is 'ceasing to do any useful work for sociology' (1989: 710). Indirectly, social scientists studying youth have made significant contributions to this debate by looking at the new ways in which the lived experiences of young people are affected by class and by observing the ways in which processes of social reproduction unfold at this key stage in the lifecycle. A crucial issue here relates to the ways socio-economic divisions are re-created through the individualized experiences of young social actors and the processes whereby reflexivity is located in class relations. Reflexivity does not challenge the validity of class but is a central component of the dynamics of class. As Savage suggests,

> Reflexive modernization does not create the 'free' individual. Rather, it creates individuals who live out, biographically, the complexity and diversity of the social relations which surround them.
>
> (2000:104)

To understand the ways in which reflexivity contributes to social dynamics it is necessary to move beyond descriptions of biographies so as to understand the ways in which outcomes that individuals may attribute to personal agency or regard as deficiencies of skill or motivation are largely shaped by forces that can lay beyond the full comprehension of individuals.

Reflecting on the linkages between structure and agency in the context of youth transitions, Furlong and colleagues (2003) suggested that to secure any outcome, such as gaining an educational qualification or securing a particular job, an individual must mobilize structural resources (such as economic, social and cultural capital) as well as capacities usually regarded as indicative of agency (such as motivation and effort).

For Furlong and colleagues, the mobilization of resources can be either conscious or unconscious, although no individual is ever fully aware of the conditions under which they act, the resources they are utilizing and the constraints on their actions. However, individuals usually have at least a partial awareness of the resources available to them and of obstacles that they may encounter. Inevitably rationalization will involve some distortion as individuals seek to reconstruct events and biographies in ways which give their lives an overall meaning and consistency (Heinz 1991). In an individualized society, people may not be as aware of the existence of constraints as they are of their attempts at personal intervention, and therefore a process of rationalization may lead to an exaggeration of the role of individual action. It can also be argued that the relative weight placed on external constraints or personal action in explaining outcomes will vary according to the perceived desirability of that outcome. For example, individuals may be more likely to blame negative outcomes on external forces or conditions while giving themselves credit for achieving more favourable outcomes.

The issue of biography has occupied an important place in youth studies, especially among those researchers whose work is mainly focused on cultural dimensions of experience. Essentially biographical approaches have been used as a way of understanding how individuals make sense of their lives within the dynamic processes of transition and change. Biography, which can be seen as another way of talking about rationality or, more accurately, rationalization, helps us to understand agency and the ways in which individuals negotiate uncertainty and attempt to manage their lives. Used extensively in the German literature, a distinction is frequently made between the 'normal' biographies that are regarded as characteristic of the Fordist era and the (poorly named) 'choice biographies' that are seen as describing the experiences of significant numbers of 'trendsetters' (du Bois Reymond 1998a) in late modernity.

Methodologically biographical approaches are an effective way of learning about young people's interpretations of their experiences and of discovering the ways in which they attempt to plan their futures and put together the pieces of life's jigsaw. Theoretically, biographical interpretations may run the risk of underplaying the significance of structure and of taking young people's interpretations at face value. Du Bois Reymond (1998a), though, uses the concept as a way of highlighting tensions between the choices that stem from an increase in options and the need to adapt to circumstances over which individuals have little control.

> Adolescents and young adults develop life concepts and attempt to direct the content and complexity of their lives: at the same time, they are forced to adapt to the constantly changing demands of their environment (especially the labour market).
>
> (du Bois Reymond 1998a: 63)

Du Bois Reymond is also very clear about the extent to which these biographical 'trendsetters' are concentrated in the more advantaged social classes, representing what Lash and Urry refer to as 'reflexive winners' (1994: 143).

The use of biographical approaches within a framework that not only remains firmly in touch with the pervasiveness of structural constraints, but

which analyses the ways in which structures are recreated through the interpretations of social actors can be particularly illuminating. In the context of
young people, such an approach was pioneered by Paul Willis (1977) and
comes across particularly effectively in the recent work of Stephen Ball and
colleagues. Like du Bois Reymond, Ball and colleagues (2000) recognize the
advantages derived by those who are able to act as 'biographical engineers' but
also appreciate that some have limited 'coping resources'.

In a sense, part of the biographical project of youth relates to the construction of a sense of selfhood in which there is a reasonable degree of
congruence between objective and subjective experiences. While this reconciliation has always involved some tensions, in Fordist societies young
people were, to an extent, able to use the experiences of significant others
(especially family members or peers from the same class positions or with
similar educational attainments) to help them construct road maps. In late
modernity it is argued that rapid processes of social change and the fragmentation of experiences make it extremely difficult to plan for the future or
manage lives (subjectively or objectively) in a meaningful sense. As Sennett
puts it 'How can a human being develop a narrative of identity and life
history in a society composed of episodes and fragments?' (1998: 26). These
processes of flexibility or fragmentation effectively bring us to a situation
where 'no one can say what you must learn in order to be needed in the
future' (Beck 2000: 3).

Growing up in the risk society

In this book we describe some of the ways in which social changes occurring
over the last three decades or so have led to a heightened sense of risk and a
greater individualization of experiences among young people. Indeed, since
the first edition of this book was published in 1997, there is evidence that the
labour market has become increasingly casualized and precarious (Rifkin 1996;
Gorz 1999; Watson *et al.* 2003; Furlong and Kelly 2005). Under conditions
where work experiences are fragmented, it is often difficult to identify an end
point to 'transitions' (Dwyer and Wyn 2001). Despite the far-reaching and
ongoing implications of social change, we still hold to the view that there are
powerful sources of continuity: young people's experiences continue to be
shaped by class and gender. We also highlight the maintenance of inequalities
associated with 'race', while recognizing that experiences of different ethnic
groups can be quite distinct. In our view, 'race' is a socially constructed category but one which is central to the understanding of structured inequalities
within advanced capitalist societies. The analysis of the impact of 'race' on the
life experiences of young people is complex because many of the disadvantages faced by members of ethnic minorities are a consequence of their position within the class structure, rather than being a feature of racial exclusion.[3]
In this respect, we agree with Miles that 'racism and exclusionary practices is
[sic] always part of a wider structure of class disadvantage and exclusion'
(1989: 10).

Young people today are growing up in different circumstances to those
experienced by previous generations; changes which are significant enough

to merit a reconceptualization of youth transitions and processes of social reproduction. In other words, in the modern world young people face new risks and opportunities. The traditional links between the family, school and work seem to have weakened as young people embark on journeys into adulthood which involve a wide variety of routes, many of which appear to have uncertain outcomes. But the greater range of opportunities available helps to obscure the extent to which existing patterns of inequality are simply being reproduced in different ways. Moreover, because there is a much greater range of pathways to choose from, young people may develop the impression that their own route is unique and that the risks they face are to be overcome as individuals rather than as members of a collectivity.

In our view then, the risk society is not a classless society, but a society in which the old social cleavages associated with class and gender remain intact: on an objective level, changes in the distribution of risk have been minimal although they can be more difficult to identify as the social exclusivity of pathways begins to disintegrate. Subjective feelings of risk have also become a much more significant feature of young people's lives and this has implications for their experiences and lifestyles. With traditional social divisions having become obscure, subjective risks stem from the perceived lack of collective tradition and security. Whereas subjective understandings of the social world were once shaped by class, gender and neighbourhood relations, today everything is presented as a possibility. The maintenance of traditional opportunity structures combined with subjective 'disembedding' (Giddens 1991) is a constant source of frustration and stress for today's youth.

The idea that perceptions of risk are culturally constructed and that there is an inevitable mismatch between objective risks and subjective perceptions of risk is controversial and it is necessary to develop scientific methods which bridge the gap between objective and perceived risk. In this context Adams (1995) suggests that people's perceptions of the risks involved in different types of behaviour are socially constructed and affected by experiences and norms associated with their social groups. Applying for a place at university, for example, may be perceived as risky by a young person from a lower working class family, whereas a young person with similar qualifications from an advantaged family may take their acceptance for granted. Similarly, this mismatch between subjective and objective dimensions of risk is reflected in reactions to the use of illegal drugs by young people: socially accepted drugs like alcohol and tobacco pose far greater health risks.

Change in the economic order, the dismantling of Fordist social structures, the extension of education and the associated demand for credentials mean that in late modernity individuals are increasingly held accountable for their own fates. Individual accountability and achievement are values which are constantly reinforced by the school and the media, yet in reality individuals often remain powerless. The combined forces of individual responsibility and accountability, on the one hand, and vulnerability and lack of control on the other, lead to a heightened sense of risk and insecurity. Conditions of doubt penetrate all aspects of social life and self identity becomes fragile and subject to constant reinterpretation (Giddens 1991). For Beck and Giddens, this constant reinterpretation of identity signifies that life has become a 'reflexive project': individuals are constantly forced to reconstruct their biographies in the light of changing experiences.

In the space of one generation there have been some radical changes to the typical experiences of young people: patterns of schooling today are very different to those of the 1980s and the youth (and indeed, the adult) labour market has changed in such a way that it would be almost unrecognizable to members of previous generations. Young people from all social classes tend to remain in full-time education until a later age and higher education is becoming a mass experience rather than the preserve of a small elite. Education is increasingly packaged as a consumer product with costs to be borne by individual beneficiaries and people are encouraged to treat services as products. In Chapter 2 we provide an overview of changing educational experiences and argue that despite some convergence in experiences, many forms of differentiation still exist. Although we identify some sources of individualization which have an impact on young people's experiences, we argue that the traditional determinants of educational 'success' still have a powerful effect on educational pathways and outcomes.

Since the early 1980s labour market entry has become more casualized and precarious employment has become a typical part of labour market transitions for all young people, including university graduates. In Chapter 3 we describe the main changes in the youth labour market and highlight changes in the school to work transition. We suggest that collectivized transitions characteristic of a Fordist society have become much rarer as young people move into a highly differentiated market for skills and casual services. While school to work transitions have become more protracted, we argue that the essential predictability of transitions has been maintained. However, as a result of the diversity of routes, young people are faced with an increasing range of options which force them to engage with the likely consequences of their actions on a subjective level. While class and gender can still be considered as prime determinants of labour market experiences, there is evidence that less advantaged young people are becoming trapped in an enlarged and unstable labour market periphery while young people from all social classes, lacking fixed points of reference, experience a growing sense of unease and insecurity.

Along with the protraction of the school to work transition, there has been an extension to the period in which young people remain in a state of semi-dependency leading to calls to recognize a new phase in the lifecycle called 'young adulthood' (EGRIS 2001) or 'emerging adulthood' (Arnett 2004). Young people are remaining dependent on their families for longer periods of time and it has become more difficult for them to make successful domestic and housing transitions (Coles 1995; Jones 1995; Holdsworth 2000; Iacovou 2001; Heath and Cleaver 2003). While we argue that domestic and housing transitions are still strongly affected by class and gender (Chapter 4), it is suggested that changes in the sequencing of the three transitions (school to work transitions, domestic transitions and housing transitions) have led to changing family dynamics. For some, this new space is characterized by a freedom that is unencumbered by the responsibilities of adulthood while for others it is best seen as a frustrating limbo characterized by powerlessness and a lack of resources. These changes have implications for behaviour and experiences in other dimensions of life.

In the age of high modernity, as subjective class affiliations, family ties and 'traditional' expectations weaken, consumption and lifestyles have become central to the process of identity construction. Changing lifestyles and leisure experiences are discussed in Chapter 5. In this context we note that some commentators have argued that style and consumption have become more important than class in the shaping of young people's lives (Featherstone 1991; Abma 1992; Bennett 1999). We disagree with this position. Although the linkages between leisure lifestyles, youth cultures and social class may have weakened, consumption, which is central to the lived experience of young people, is not unrelated to class. Indeed, with leisure having become increasingly commercialized, some young people clearly lack the resources to participate regularly in a broad range of activities or to socialize with people from other class positions. Moreover, as Phoenix and Tizard (1996) have noted, patterns of consumption, fashion and lifestyles are symbolic of class position, with young people being adept at reading subtle indicators of class.

The increasing stresses and strains of modern life and their impact on young people's health are examined in Chapter 6. We suggest that as individuals are made to feel more responsible for life events, uncertainty and risk have taken their toll on young people's mental health. The incidence of mental illness, eating disorders, suicide and attempted suicide have increased as young people develop a sense of having 'no future' (West and Sweeting 1996). These trends are also affected by an increasing isolation from adult worlds. While risk taking has always been a feature of young lives, longer transitions have led to a greater vulnerability to risk, including those risks which stem from involvement in or vulnerability to criminal activities (Chapter 7). Domestic and work commitments have long been associated with a reduction in risk-taking activities and there is evidence that protracted transitions mean young people remain vulnerable for longer periods. Here young people are being denied the chance to become 'stake holders' in their society and in turn they may look for alternative sources of satisfaction, some of which carry health risks or make them more vulnerable to police surveillance and arrest.

The weakening of the traditional bonds of family and class, together with an individualization of experiences, personal risk and global insecurity can also be seen as leading to a weakening of traditional political affiliations (Chapter 8). In particular, changes in the subjective understanding of class have implications for young people's participation in the political process. The majority of young people feel that party politics have little relevance to their lives, yet at the same time they are politically active in a broader sense. Many of the issues young people regard as important cross the traditional lines of party politics and reflect concerns about global insecurity, injustice and environmental damage. Young people's engagement with politics can also be interpreted as reflecting a disintegration of older forms of collective identity as well as a scepticism about the extent to which meaningful processes of change are likely to emerge from within the traditional machinery of state.

Conclusion

In sum, this book aims to provide an assessment of conceptualizations of the new modernity through an empirical analysis of the social condition of contemporary youth. In doing so, a number of issues are raised which have important implications for sociological theory. Our central thesis is that while traditional sources of inequality continue to ensure the reproduction of advantage and disadvantage among the younger generation, various social changes have meant that these social cleavages have become obscure. Moreover, young people increasingly perceive themselves as living in a society characterized by risk and insecurity which they expect to have to negotiate on an individual level. While writers in the 'late-modernist' tradition – such as Beck (1992) and Giddens (1990, 1991) – are able to illuminate some of these processes, we suggest that there has been a tendency to exaggerate changes and to understate many significant sources of continuity. In particular, it is argued that social class and gender remain central to an understanding of the lives of young people in the age of high modernity.

2 Change *and* continuity *in* education

Education was to have been the means of overcoming the inheritance of social class. However, as presently constituted, the education system favours the already privileged and screens out the already disadvantaged. Rather than defeating stratification, formal education is a cause of persistent and increasingly rigid stratification.

(Forcese 1997, quoted in Wotherspoon 2004: 225)

Introduction

Many of the key characteristics of late modernity identified by Beck (1992) and Giddens (1991) are reflected in young people's changing experiences within educational settings. Young people today face new risks at school and in advanced educational institutions which they are increasingly expected to negotiate as individuals rather than as members of a collectivity. The demand for advanced educational credentials and flexible specializations associated with post-Fordist economies means that individuals are constantly held accountable for their performance and face increased risks should they fail. Collective identities, once manifest in class-based resistance to the school, have weakened as experiences have diversified and underlying class relationships have become obscure, although traditional sources of inequality remain intact.

Many of the changes we describe are a direct consequence of trends in education in the developed world that, in part, represent a policy response to economic change. In an attempt to establish a competitive edge in an advanced and increasingly global economy, governments have become aware of the need to develop a highly skilled workforce. Educational policies form the bedrock of a commitment to enhance the quality of the national human resource base. There has also been a desire, expressed particularly strongly in the Scandinavian countries, to use education as a platform for bringing about a more socially just society.

The development of socially inclusive systems that provide tertiary education for the masses, comes at a cost. In an era increasingly characterized by neo-liberalism, there has been a widespread reluctance to pass the costs of education in their entirety to the (individual or corporate) taxpayer. While recognizing the public benefits of a system of mass higher education, governments have increasingly taken the view that individual beneficiaries should bear a higher proportion of the costs. At the same time, the need to maintain affordability so as to encourage further expansion and promote wider access has been acknowledged (Huisman *et al.* 2003). In keeping with neo-liberal philosophy, many governments have been concerned to enable parents to exercise choice in what has become an educational marketplace, even when this has consequences for an equal opportunities agenda.

The result has been a tendency to try to portray education as a consumer product that individual participants are expected to finance in anticipation of personal economic advantage secured on the basis of advanced credentials. While in some countries, such as the USA, there has always been a strong market for private systems of higher education, in most other advanced countries the state has largely funded advanced tertiary education. This is changing rapidly: the UK and Australia, for example, now expect students and their parents to make substantial contributions to the cost of higher education through payment systems that are either partly deferred or linked to future taxation weightings, while in 2005 the German courts cleared the way for the introduction of tuition fees. The principled objection to fees on the grounds of social justice is no longer as evident as was the case twenty years ago.

The neo-liberal turn has effectively led to a situation where schools, colleges and universities are having to 'sell themselves' on the market with students and parents being invited to select the 'product' best suited to the needs of their child. In the UK and Australia, this process is highlighted by the use of television advertisements to promote particular universities and colleges (especially the least popular, which do not sell on the basis of reputation). At an extreme, one new university in the UK offers the inducement of entering applicants in a draw for £30,000 (€44,000) towards tuition costs. While these changes facilitate individualized consumer choices, the resources which social actors trade in the educational marketplace vary considerably. People stand in differential positions in relation to the means of consumption and have different amounts of social and cultural capital to trade in the educational marketplace. Consequently the rewards of the educational system remain unequally distributed. The illusion of choice created by the marketization of education masks the continued entrenchment of traditional forms of inequality.

Although we argue that educational changes have had little impact on patterns of social reproduction, new forms of educational provision and an increased demand for an educated and trained labour force have had far reaching effects on young people's experiences. In the Fordist era, the availability of relatively unskilled positions in large manufacturing units meant that employment opportunities existed for minimum-aged, unqualified school-leavers. In cities across the industrialized world in the 1950s, 1960s and 1970s, young males made mass transitions from the classroom to the factories and building sites, while young women followed pathways leading straight from school to shops, offices and factories. As academic credentials were unnecessary for many working class jobs, young people often had little incentive to strive for improved qualifications.

Prominent sociologists of the time frequently tried to explain differential performance and behaviour in schools in terms of the relative value of schooling for future careers. Paul Willis (1977), for example, tried to account for the experiences of lower working class boys in terms of their resistance to the middle class culture of the school, which was perceived as irrelevant to their futures as manual workers. In contrast to the ways in which working class youth often rejected the middle class definitions of success presented by their teachers, young people from privileged social backgrounds tended to develop an awareness that the maintenance of their economic and social advantages was partly dependent on their educational attainments. Their frames of reference, or what Bourdieu (1977) would refer to as their 'habitus', reinforced by experiences in the home and school, made these processes of social reproduction seem both natural and inevitable (Ashton and Field 1976; Brown 1987).

Strong and explicit lines of stratification in educational systems are a characteristic feature of industrial societies but take on a more covert form in post-industrial societies. In the UK, until the 1970s, the majority of working class youths were educated after the age of 11 in separate institutions from their middle class counterparts.[1] Even where comprehensive systems have been implemented, social class tended to affect the streams to which young people were allocated and the examinations for which they were entered (Ford 1969; Ball 1981; Kao and Thompson 2003). Young people from working class families tend to move through the lower streams of the school while those from middle class families tend to follow advantaged routes through the education system (Douglas 1967; Hargreaves 1967; Ball 1981; Kao and Thompson 2003).

While forms of delivery vary, most industrialized nations organize educational provision in ways that lead to a virtual social apartheid. In the post-war period all developed countries have made attempts to break down these social barriers, yet in some cases efforts have been somewhat superficial and in most cases ineffective. Germany, for example, has retained a tripartite system in which pupils are segregated from the age of 10; in Belgium and the Netherlands, selection takes place at the age of 12; in France some segregation still takes place after the first two years of secondary education; while in the USA, despite experimentation with a system of bussing in an attempt to engineer a greater social mix, patterns of residence and the existence of a strong private sector have helped maintain class-based differences in the quality of education received (Devine 2004). Such processes ensure the maintenance of socially differentiated systems of education. In Europe, the most socially differentiated schools are to be found in the UK, despite the widespread existence of comprehensive schools (Gorard and Smith 2004).

With the post-industrial era characterized by a dramatic decline in the demand for unskilled youth labour, levels of post-compulsory educational participation have increased quite rapidly. In the modern labour market, employment contexts are increasingly differentiated and with increased competition for jobs, individual academic performance has become a prerequisite for economic survival (Beck 1992). In this context, and despite the maintenance of fairly rigid forms of segregation, it has been argued that young people's relationships to the school have become individualized and that the class-based divisions which were once the key to understanding educational experiences have become diluted (Biggart and Furlong 1996). Caught in a situation where rejection of educational values or hostility towards school-based figures of authority almost guarantee a precarious future in the labour market, class-based resistance becomes covert and young people are pitted against each other in a bid to maximize their educational attainments so as to survive in an increasingly hostile world. One of the consequences of these changes is that the lives of young people have become busier and more intense as they are increasingly forced to chase credentials which are often necessary to smooth the entry into the world of work (Büchner 1990).

These changes in young people's experiences of schooling have been seen as involving a dual process of standardization and diversification (Olk 1988). On the one hand, the majority of young people are spending a greater number of years in educational institutions and building up a range of qualifications which are regarded as helping them make an effective transition to the world of work. On the other hand, routes through the educational system have become more diverse as young people experience a greater range of academic and vocational courses which are often available within the same educational institutional setting (Heinz 1987; Chitty 1989). Yet while educational experiences have become more diverse, or individualized, class and gender have remained important determinants of educational pathways and attainments. Jones and Wallace, for example, have argued that 'paths to adulthood, far from being individualized, can still be predicted from social class origins to a great extent in both Britain and West Germany' (1990: 137). Indeed, Bourdieu (1977) predicted that the social and cultural advantages possessed by middle class children would have a greater impact on levels of attainment as meritocratic educational policies became widespread: in fact the idea that 'cultural capital' has become increasingly central to the reproduction of social advantage is underlined by the development of ways of measuring different types of capital (Baron *et al.* 2000; Field 2003).

In this chapter we look at changing patterns of education and discuss the extent to which increasing levels of participation have been associated with a process of equalization. After reviewing the nature of these changes, we discuss some of the reasons why the enhancement of educational opportunities has had such a weak impact on the strength of the relationship between social background and educational attainment. In this context, we argue that in many advanced countries educational institutions remain divided with social class still representing a powerful determinant of 'success': indeed, the 'universalism' envisaged by Beck (1992) would be hard to identify in the educational systems found in most of the economically advanced nations.

Trends

Over the last few decades, education has come to play an increasingly prominent role in young people's lives. In the 1970s, in many advanced industrial nations, substantial numbers of young people (in many cases a majority) had left school by the age of 16 or 17. For many, this was effectively their last contact with formal education although some countries (most notably Germany) had developed systems under which the majority of early leavers embarked upon a period of structured training that involved both workplace and college-based learning.

From the age of 16 or 17, experiences were highly differentiated along lines that corresponded closely to social class divisions. Where those from working class families experienced further education (and many did not) it tended to be closely linked to occupational requirements – and was differentiated from middle class forms of tertiary education by the prominence of 'practical' application and by the use of the label 'vocational'. In virtually all advanced countries, 'academic' tertiary education, with its greater emphasis on the acquisition of theoretical knowledge, was largely the preserve of the middle classes.

Contemporary manifestations of this social apartheid within education are now much more subtle. Among all social classes the average length of schooling has risen substantially and although the academic-vocational divide still corresponds to a social class division, there has been a tendency to provide more uniform modes of delivery and curricula within the compulsory stages of education. One of the most significant trends, and one with the potential to force a rethink of assumptions about the rigidity of processes of social reproduction in educational settings, relates to the growth of higher education. Whereas higher education was once the almost exclusive preserve of the privileged classes, in most of the advanced nations a university education (albeit stratified) has been made available to the masses during the last 20 to 30 years (Smithers and Robinson 1989; McPherson and Schapiro 1991; Egerton and Halsey 1993; Forsyth and Furlong 2000; Huisman *et al.* 2003).

Changing patterns of participation and attainment

From the 1970s onwards, most advanced countries witnessed a fairly steady growth in levels of participation in post-compulsory education. While minimum-aged school-leaving was once the predominant pattern, especially among young people from working class families, far fewer young people now leave school at 16 and most early school-leavers continue to receive some kind of formal education or training on a part-time or block release basis (Roberts 1995; Surridge and Raffe 1995; Dobson 2003: Hayward *et al.* 2004; Aamodt and Kyvik 2005).

In the OECD countries in 2002, an average of 82 per cent of 15- to 19-year-olds and 38 per cent of 20- to 24-year-olds were participating in full-time education (Figure 2.1). Among the younger age group participation levels were significantly higher than the average in France, Germany[2] and Sweden and lower in the UK which is described (somewhat generously) by Hayward and colleagues (2004) as a 'medium participation system'.

In all of the OECD countries rates of educational participation among the 16-plus age group have increased sharply since the war, with particularly dramatic changes occurring in the 1980s. Although not all countries have followed the same trajectory, figures from England and Wales serve to

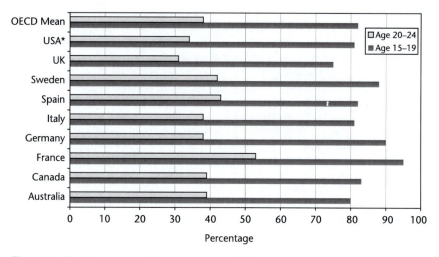

Figure 2.1 Participation in full-time education in 2002: selected countries
Note: * USA refers to 2003
Source: OECD 2004

highlight the magnitude of the changes that have occurred. In 1974, around a third of 16-year-old males (33 per cent) and less than four in ten females (37 per cent) participated in some form of full-time post-compulsory education. By 1989 male participation rates had risen to 43 per cent and female to 53 per cent and by 2004 around three in four 16-year-olds remained in full-time education (67 per cent of males and 77 per cent of females) although levels of participation appear to have reached a plateau in the early 1990s (Hayward *et al.* 2004; DfES 2005).

With a substantial growth in the proportion of young people who participate in post-compulsory education, there has been an overall increase in the qualification profiles of school-leavers and hence an expansion of the potential pool of applicants for university. Yet here there are important differences that relate to the ways in which education is organized and to the linkages between educational systems and occupational opportunity structures. From young people's perspectives, the incentive to invest in education appears to be greatest in systems that place an emphasis on general education and where, as a consequence, qualifications provide a signal of merit (such countries would include the USA, the UK and France) (Shavit and Müller 1998). These general systems are inherently inflational in that while young people are provided with an incentive to maximize qualifications, a general increase in the stock of qualifications devalues the currency. In countries such as Germany and Switzerland, a greater emphasis is placed on vocational education and on the development of job specific skills. With a strong relationship between vocational skills and occupational positions, it has been argued that such systems are less likely to lead to qualification inflation (Shavit and Müller 1998).

Both systems have advantages and disadvantages. The emphasis on skills and vocationalism may reduce the numbers of working class students entering unskilled jobs and lower the odds of unemployment (Arum and Shavit 1995; Shavit and Müller 2000), but the stratification of educational opportunities may deprive these young people of the opportunity to enter professional and managerial sectors of the labour market, thereby inhibiting long-range social mobility. Indeed, in the UK vocational courses have been promoted due to a belief that the academic curriculum could be somewhat irrelevant to those in the lower attainment bands. Vocational options are often popular with students, although they tend to have a lower status and fears have been expressed that vocational enhancement could lead to an increase in inequalities associated with class, gender and 'race'. In the UK vocational options in the school have largely been taken up by working class pupils in the lower attainment bands while leaving intact the traditional academic curriculum followed by middle class pupils (Brown 1987; Chitty 1987; Raffe *et al.* 2001).

A parallel process can be observed in Germany where academic routes are monopolized by those from the middle classes (Müller and Karle 1993). Similarly in the US, students from poorer families are over-represented in two-year community colleges (McDonough 1997). While it is very likely that vocational segregation of routes through secondary education will reduce the (already slim) chances of young people from working class families entering professional and managerial jobs, the compensation for this injustice is the reduced chances of unskilled work or unemployment for those who do follow vocational routes (Shavit and Müller 2000).

The link between educational attainment and patterns of participation is complex and involves a range of factors. Qualification inflation provides a partial explanation; qualifications, as a marker of educational 'success', encourage progression. Hence changes in the curriculum and in forms of examination can be implemented in ways that lead to an increase in participation, even when there is no underlying boost in performance. As post-compulsory educational participation becomes the norm, cultural contexts are adapted and groups that once expected to leave education at the earliest opportunity incorporate educational attainment and progression into their frames of reference. In the UK, the recent introduction of an educational maintenance allowance for young people from low wages families has acted as a financial incentive to continued educational involvement (Croxford *et al.* 2002). Changes in patterns of demand within the labour market, especially the increase in professional and technical positions and the decline in unskilled jobs in manufacturing, can also provide a strong incentive for young people to remain in education and to maximize credentials. A lack of opportunities in the local labour market can result in a 'discouraged worker' effect whereby young people remain in full-time education due to concerns about job availability (Raffe and Willms 1989).

Changes in the organization of education appear to have had provided young people with greater incentives to remain at school (Raffe 1992; Gorard and Smith 2004); consequently they have had an impact on patterns of participation and achievement. Yet other socio-economic changes have also had an impact on levels of attainment. With a relationship between the educational experiences of parents and children, we would expect that an increasingly educated parentage would result in improved educational out-comes among the new generation (Croxford *et al.* 2006). Any such changes, however, will take a couple of decades to filter through. A recent OECD report (OECD 2005a) drew attention to the strong relationship between parental education and completion of upper secondary education, while European researchers have shown that the link between parental education and young people's attainment is strongest in southern and eastern Europe, but relatively weak in the Nordic countries (Kogan and Jungblut 2004). It is also important to recognize the ways in which changing patterns of employment and the demands of employers for a better educated labour force have affected edu-cational attainments. Changing labour market structures have not simply provided positive incentives for young people to improve their qualifications; the sharp decline in opportunities for minimum-aged school-leavers in many places has produced an army of reluctant conscripts to post-compulsory education (see Chapter 3).

The growth of participation in post–16 education has, in turn, led to an increase in higher educational attendance in all of the advanced nations, although strong variations in levels of participation persist. With more than six in ten young people participating in tertiary education, Finland, Sweden and New Zealand are representative of the high participation countries (Figure 2.2). In contrast, participation has remained below 40 per cent in Germany, France and Japan.

These country specific differences in participation in higher education are not a straightforward reflection of patterns of attainment in schools or of the effectiveness of secondary education. International comparative work shows clearly that the size of the tertiary sector is linked more strongly to national policies and norms than to patterns of attainment. Skilbeck and Connell suggest that there are two main models upon which admission

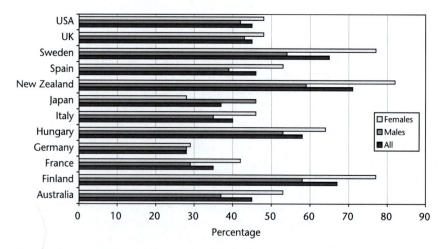

Figure 2.2 Entry to tertiary education in 2002: selected countries
Source: OECD 2004

procedures are based, a 'system-wide right of entry to all who are deemed qualified' (such as in the Netherlands and France) and 'institutional selection according to determinations made for particular programmes and courses' (such as in the UK; Skilbeck and Connell 2000: 15). The PISA study, which involves the use of standardized tests for 15-year-olds across a wide range of countries, has shown that at a national level the link between problem solving, reading and mathematics attainment (as measured through a series of stand-ardized tests) and educational progression is rather weak (Figure 2.3). In New Zealand and Sweden, for example, there was a close correspondence between the proportion of 15-year-olds with high scores for problem solving (3 plus) and the proportion who participated in tertiary education. In contrast, in France, Germany and Australia, the rate of participation in tertiary education was much lower than the proportion with high problem solving scores.

At the same time, PISA scores are strongly associated with social class. In most European countries, for example, average reading scores of young people from the poorest 10 per cent of families were significantly lower than among those from more affluent families. Differences associated with income were particularly large in Luxembourg, Portugal, Germany and France but relatively narrow in the Netherlands and Finland (Gorard and Smith 2004).

While throughout the industrialized world the numbers of young people entering higher education has been increasing since the war, in many coun-tries the pace of change increased quite significantly in the late 1980s/early 1990s. In the UK, for example, the number of full-time undergraduates

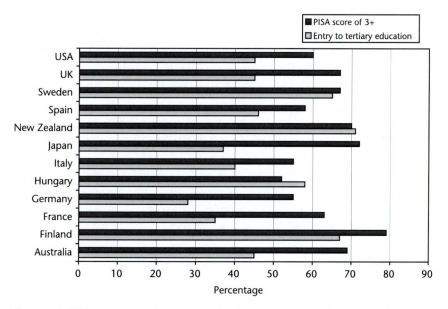

Figure 2.3 PISA problem solving scores and entry to tertiary education: selected countries 2002
Source: OECD 2002a

22 Young people *and* social change

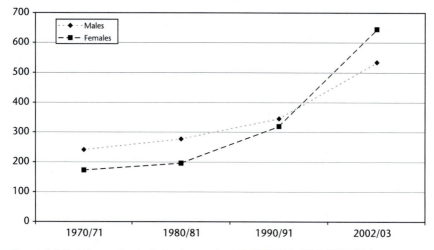

Figure 2.4 Full-time undergraduates by gender, UK 1970/71 to 2002/03 (000's)
Source: Summerfield and Gill 2005

increased almost threefold between 1970 and 2002 (Figure 2.4), while in Japan between 1970 and 2000 student numbers increased by around two and a half times. In both countries around two-thirds of this increase occurred between the late 1980s and 2000 (Frédéric 2005; Summerfield and Gill 2005). Similarly, in Australia between 1988 and 2000, student numbers increased by 65 per cent (Dobson 2003).

Since the 1990s these changes have led to a substantial increase in the proportion of the working age population who have tertiary level qualifications. Between 1991 and 2002, in the OECD as a whole, the number of 25- to 64-year-olds with higher educational qualifications increased from 18 to 23 per cent (Figure 2.5). In countries such as Canada, Spain and the UK the

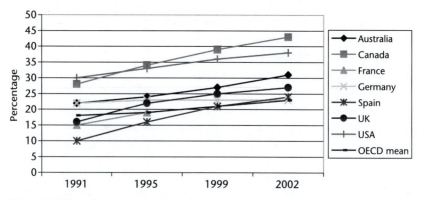

Figure 2.5 25- to 64-year-olds with tertiary qualifications: selected countries, 1991–2002
Source: OECD 2004

increase was over twice the OECD average, while in Germany the increase was negligible (1 per cent).

In a range of countries, (especially the UK, the Netherlands and Germany), the expansion of higher education was achieved by establishing a new sector that 'complemented' the old elite institutions. Through these means the elite were somewhat protected from the possibility of contamination by the masses (Huisman *et al.* 2003). In the UK, the recent increase in student numbers has been disproportionately located in the 'new universities' (the former polytechnics) and graduates of these institutions tend to face poorer employment prospects. Indeed, it has been argued that the employment prospects of graduates have become increasingly stratified with ex-students of the 'new universities' facing the greatest difficulties in the labour market (Furlong and Cartmel 2005). A degree from an established or 'Ivy League' university has greater capital value than one from a college or new university. In this respect, an increase in university places is unlikely to be associated with an equalization of employment opportunities, although across Europe graduates enjoy advantages in the labour market and, in general, believe that they have secured positive advantages (European Commission 2002).

Similar patterns can be identified in other countries. In the USA, for example, students from low income families are five times more likely than their peers from more affluent families to study at a (less costly and lower status) community college than a university (McPherson and Schapiro 1999) and it has been argued that increases in tuition fees have helped push low SES students into this sector (Skilbeck and Connell 2000).

While more young people now experience higher education, in many countries they do so under increasingly difficult economic circumstances. Most students, but particularly those from less advantaged families, are forced to juggle study with some form of employment, and new graduates tend to begin their careers with significant burdens of debt. In the European Union, most students now pay tuition fees, although study remains free in Denmark, Greece, Luxembourg, the Czech Republic, Hungary, Malta and Poland (European Commission 2002). In the UK in 2004 the average graduate left university with £13,500 (€20,000) of debt – which is estimated to triple by 2010 (Barclays Bank 2005) while in the USA the average annual fee charged by a private university is around £19,000 (€28,000). In a study of nine European countries, Vossensteyn (1999) calculated the relative affordability of higher education, taking into account factors such as study costs, fees and levels of support. He found that countries such as Finland and Denmark were the most affordable, while the least affordable countries included Austria, Belgium and the UK.

While changes in educational systems can be seen as leading to a greater standardization of the experiences of young people, it is clear that there are parallel processes of diversification (Chitty 1989). Vocational and academic divisions remain entrenched with the experience of higher education having become polarized between the 'old' elite universities and the 'new universities' with inferior resources and graduate employment rates (McDonough 1997; McPherson and Schapiro 1999; Forsyth and Furlong 2000).

In many respects, changes in the organization of education are a reflection of political ideologies which have resulted in an increased tendency to treat education as a consumer product within a neo-liberal framework. Describing trends in the new educational market place, Gewirtz suggests that 'schools (as producers) are now supposed to compete for the custom of children and their parents (as consumers)' (1996: 289), while the level of funding available to individual institutions is increasingly dependent on their success in the marketplace. The commodification of education, usually justified in terms of consumer choice, is a universal feature of western systems, but countries such as the UK, Belgium, Finland and Ireland all permit parents a degree of choice in state schools for their children (Gorard and Smith 2004). Yet there is strong evidence to suggest that processes of educational marketization result in greater levels of inequality (Ball 2003; Croxford and Raffe 2005; Harris and Ranson 2005).

In the context of the current discussion, it is important to note that the commodification of education is linked to the emergence of an epistemological fallacy: it may help to create an illusion of equality whilst masking the persistence of old inequalities. By giving families greater responsibility for the type of education received by their children, negative outcomes can be attributed to poor choices on the part of the parents as customers. As a consequence, the state is able to relinquish some of its traditional responsibilities as the provider of an educational system based on social justice and underpinned by meritocratic principles. In a market orientated system,

> it is acceptable for there to be winners and losers, access to resources which is differentiated but unrelated to need, hierarchy, exclusivity, selectivity, and for producers to utilise whatever tactics they can get away with to increase their market share and to maximise profits. In short, there is pressure on individuals (both producers and consumers) to be motivated first and foremost by self interest.
>
> (Gewirtz 1996: 293)

Moreover, as a result of processes of commodification, schools and universities are able to continue to reproduce social inequalities whilst maintaining a veneer of open access (Bourdieu and Passeron 1977). This process sustains the epistemological fallacy by helping to obscure the continued relevance of class to an understanding of differential outcomes in education.

Cultural dimensions of educational participation

Subjective orientations towards educational participation were once seen in relatively simplistic terms, essentially as class-based rejections or acceptances of middle class educational cultures and related expectations regarding future patterns of participation in the labour market. Essentially responses to education were seen as subjective reflections of objective structures of opportunity. Willis (1977), for example, explained the experiences of lower working class boys in terms of their resistance to middle class school cultures which were seen as largely irrelevant to their future lives in manual occupations. Today the cultural dimensions of decisions about educational participation are recognised as being more complex and as tending not to involve such strong, culturally-based, rejections of the value and benefits of extended education (Biggart and Furlong 1996; Ball *et al.* 2000; Furlong 2005). The increased emphasis placed on educational attainment in working class families stems, in part, from a growing awareness of the importance of credentials in the modern economy. It can also be linked to a breakdown of a visible dichotomy in the labour market between working class and middle class jobs that has accompanied the decline of manufacturing industry as well as a more educated parentage and a trend towards employment in smaller work units where social divisions are less visible. These factors can be linked to the 'epistemological fallacy' of late modernity in which linkages between objective structures of opportunity and subjective interpretations of social position become increasingly tenuous.

For young people to fulfill their potential educationally and to be well disposed towards continued learning, it is important that they develop positive, or at least instrumental, orientations towards the school during the compulsory years. As Ball and colleagues (2000) suggest, young people must establish a 'learner identity' and even identify a 'possible self' (Markus and Nurius 1986) that involves employment in an occupation requiring advanced education or training. Those who feel that their labours are not being recognized or rewarded, or fail to appreciate any future benefits that can be derived from school work, may reduce their efforts or seek to have their status acknowledged in non-school contexts such as the peer group.

It is clear though, that among the less academically successful young people (who are predominantly working class) many become seriously disillusioned with schooling at an early stage and either lose, or fail to develop, a motivation to engage with schooling. Sometimes disaffection seems to be entrenched within the culture of the schools; in some cases from an early age it is almost expected that young people from particular areas or families will leave at an early stage with few qualifications.

Some young people experience difficult transitions from primary to secondary schools and never manage to settle in their new environment. Noting the difficulties associated with the change from primary to secondary schooling, Ball and colleagues drew attention to one girl who had experienced primary school as an 'oasis of peace and quiet' for whom secondary schooling became 'yet another battleground that soon became intolerable' (2000: 206). Similarly, in a Scottish study (Furlong *et al.* 2003), many spoke of enjoying primary school but failing to engage with the secondary school. Young people could experience feelings of discontinuity and could feel lost or threatened in classes where there were no familiar faces. Whereas primary schools are often small, neighbourhood based and relatively homogenous in terms of their social composition, secondary schools tend to have wider catchments and are more heterogeneous socially. In the Scottish study, respondents thought that their social circumstances had had a detrimental impact on the ways they were treated by certain teachers. Some spoke of encountering negative teacher expectations more or less as soon as they entered the secondary school with teachers sometimes 'tarring' them with the same brush as older siblings or relatives. Others who struggled academically and who had been used to receiving extensive support from primary teachers sometimes felt that they were left to their own devices at secondary school.

Among those who do make a good start in the secondary school, some will lose interest as a result of poor performance. They lose confidence in their ability and the motivation to learn. Often there is a gradual loss of motivation which can be linked to patterns of attainment as well as the development of outside interests which begin to take up more of their time and energy. Among the middle and low attainment groups, attitudes to school are often ambivalent. They may appreciate a need for qualifications in order to get decent jobs, but are never stimulated academically and tend to regard school as a chore. These young people can often feel that teachers focus on the academic high-flyers and see themselves on the periphery of a system centred on the needs of an academic elite.

In schools in deprived areas there is often a culture of truancy to which young people must subscribe in order to be accepted as part of the peer group; the strong pull of the social and cultural environment can be hard to resist (Williamson 2004). In fact those who stand out as being bright or hardworking are frequently seen as 'different' by the peer group, resulting in a cycle of bullying ultimately leading to truancy as the victim attempts to avoid regular contact with the perpetrators (Furlong *et al.* 2003). As Williamson notes, in lower working class communities, it isn't 'cool to be clever' (2004: 26) and those who enjoy school have to keep quiet about it so as not to 'lose face' in their peer group (2004: 28).

To understand the ways in which social class impacts on young people's experiences of schooling, it is important to differentiate between the impact of class cultures on *orientations* to school and the, often rational, responses to *experiences* in an institutional setting that projects strongly held sets of assumptions on the part of teachers and fellow pupils. In hindsight young people frequently regard themselves as having been let down by the system. While they may admit that their own actions and behaviour at school have not been helpful, they tend to acknowledge the value of schooling, often regret not having worked harder, but rationalize this by highlighting a lack of support or even victimization. Although teacher expectations and curriculum content clearly contribute to the development of a culture of ambivalence towards, or even hatred of, schooling, such reactions tend to be comfortably accommodated and reinforced within community based peer groups.

While there are national variations in the ways in which class cultures impact on educational experiences, across the OECD countries almost one in four 15-year-olds have a poor sense of belonging to the culture of the school. In the PISA survey, respondents were asked about acceptance among their peers and about whether they felt like an outsider or out of place in the school. In Japan almost four in ten displayed a low sense of belonging, while in those countries with relatively high levels of belonging, such as Sweden and the UK, around 17 per cent had a poor sense of attachment (Figure 2.6). Low rates of participation (relating to frequent absences or skipping classes) were also evident among one in five 15-year-olds in the OECD countries. Young people in Japan, tended to participate even though they had a poor sense of

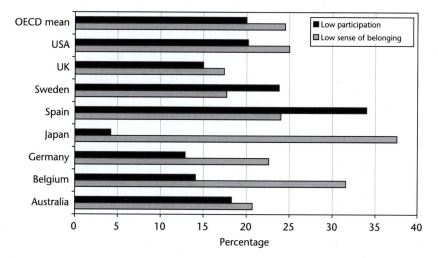

Figure 2.6 15-year-olds with a low sense of belonging and low participation: selected countries, 2000
Source: OECD 2004

belonging, suggesting a tendency to conform despite an uneasy relationship with the school.

Differentiated outcomes

As we move towards the establishment of a 'learning society' where people face a continual need to develop their skills and credentials, it is important to re-assess the extent to which old forms of inequality remain entrenched. Many of the reforms implemented in recent years (especially in Europe) have explicitly aimed to boost the performance of low attaining groups, thereby reducing inequalities in educational attainment and helping to prevent a wastage of talent which can be damaging economically. Other reforms have been introduced as a result of concern that the educational system was failing to deliver an adequate supply of suitably skilled personnel to meet the demands of employers operating in a technologically sophisticated global economy. Yet while it is true that some changes have had a measure of success (especially in terms of increased participation), it has proved difficult to overcome the deeply embedded inequalities associated with class. On the other hand, both gender differentiated patterns of attainment and levels of attainment of minority groups are becoming more equitable.

The persistence of class-based inequalities

Analyses of the effects of past periods of educational expansion have demonstrated that increasing levels of educational participation do not *necessarily* result in a process of equalization between social groups (Boudon 1973; Halsey *et al.* 1980; Shavit and Müller 1998; Croxford and Raffe 2005). Using comparative data from several countries, Raftery and Hout (1990) have suggested that educational inequalities associated with social class may remain entrenched until levels of middle class participation approach 'saturation point'. Due to the expansion of tertiary education and the increase in the number of young people leaving school with recognized qualifications, the odds of a young person securing a place in higher education have increased dramatically. However, the evidence suggests that young people from working class families remain less likely than their middle class peers either to remain at school beyond the minimum leaving age, to leave school with a recognized qualification or to secure a place in higher education (Shavit and Blossfeld 1993; Forsyth and Furlong 2000; Callender 2003).

In the UK between 1989 and 2000, levels of educational participation among 16-year-olds increased among all social classes (Figure 2.7). Among the manual classes, participation grew by around 30 percentage points, doubling the rate of participation among the unskilled class in the course of a decade. By contrast, expansion among the non-manual classes was much weaker – just 14 percentage points among the professional and managerial classes. The point though, is that while the gap between the classes has narrowed, a relatively large gulf still exists.

The maintenance of class stratification in education becomes even clearer if we look at higher educational participation. In the UK, between 1991 and 2001 the rate of expansion in the uptake of higher education among the non-manual classes was twice that of the lower working classes (Figure 2.8). In fact over the decade the gulf actually increased by seven percentage points (Summerfield and Gill 2005). Similar trends are apparent in other countries. As Green and colleagues argue in relation to EU countries, 'a constant factor in all

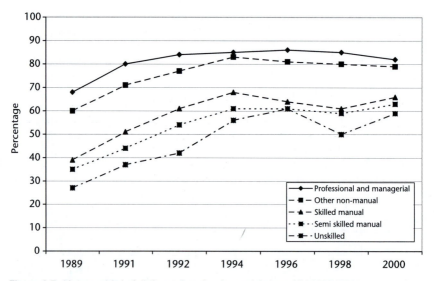

Figure 2.7 16-year-olds in full-time education by social class: UK 1989–2000
Source: Hayward *et al.* 2004

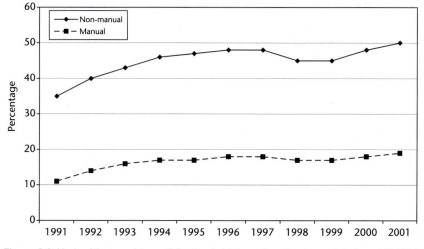

Figure 2.8 Under 21-year-olds participating in higher education by social class: UK 1991–2001
Source: Summerfield and Gill 2005

member states for which data are available, is that while absolute participation rates have increased for all socio-economic levels, the relative rates have barely changed' (1999: 204). In Germany, for example, only 8 per cent of young people from the lowest social class entered higher education, as compared to 72 per cent of the highest social class (Skilbeck and Connell 2000). In Denmark, despite high overall levels of participation, the relative chances of young people from working class families has not changed in forty years (Skillbeck and Connell 2000) while in Australia, during the 1990s, despite overall expansion, the share of higher education places taken by the lowest social class declined very slightly (Department of Education, Training and Youth Affairs 1999).

In exploring differential outcomes in higher education, it is important to bear in mind that systems of higher education have been transformed from elitist systems catering for a small minority of young people to mass systems which, in some countries (such as Finland), around two-thirds of young people will enter some form of higher education at some time in their lives. This transformation of higher education has entailed increased recruitment among groups that were previously under-represented, particularly young women, and has involved a shift from the old elite universities – various terminologies are used to differentiate the elite institutions, the *Grandes Ecoles* (France), the Ivy League (USA), the Russell Group (UK), the Gang of Eight (Australia) – that cater for the more privileged, to new 'parallel' institutions many of which developed out of vocational colleges.

Despite the far reaching changes which have occurred, class differentials in access to higher education have been maintained in most of the advanced nations and, during the 1990s, the affordability of higher education tended to decline in a number of European countries (Huisman *et al.* 2003). As Callender argues, costs and affordability are crucial to patterns of access. 'The decision to attend university and choice of educational institution are highly sensitive to tuition and financial aid levels for all students except those from the highest income families' (2003: 135). Affordability tends to result in a process of self selection (Forsyth and Furlong 2000), after which institutional or state selection plays an important role. According to Huisman and colleagues (2003) the most selective countries in western Europe are Finland, Sweden and the UK, while Belgium, the Netherlands and Austria are least selective (in the Netherlands, secondary school graduates have a constitutional right to enrol in higher education). The French system combines the elite and highly selective Grandes Ecoles (which reject 80 to 95 per cent of applicants) with a non-selective general university system (Huisman *et al.* 2003).

While most countries have seen extensive changes in systems of higher education, through various mechanisms, including stratification of provision and financial barriers, we tend to find clear evidence of class differentiated experiences. The older universities still tend to be the preserve of children from professional and managerial backgrounds, while students in the 'new universities' are more likely to come from working class families with many entering as mature students or after having followed 'non-traditional' academic pathways. In absolute terms, there has been a continuous growth in working class participation, but relative changes have been minimal (Burnhill *et al.* 1990; Halsey 1992; Blackburn and Jarman 1993; Dobson 2003; Aamodt and Kyvick 2005). Even in the Scandinavian countries which pride themselves on their subscription to equality of opportunities, recent university expansion has not been accompanied by increasing social equality. As Aamodt and Kyvick argue, 'the overall conclusion is that the expanding access to higher education over the last decades has led to surprisingly small changes in the enrollment patterns by socio-economic background in the Nordic countries' (2005: 133).

Changing gender differentials

Gender, like social class, remains an extremely strong predictor of educational attainment and progression with females tending to outperform males. These differences are evident in 15-year-olds' reading scores in a large number of countries (Gorard and Smith 2004) and are reflected in progression to higher education. Indeed, Skilbeck and Connell show that 'in ten out of thirteen OECD countries, women are the majority of first-time university level entrants' (2000: 32).

The superior performance and progression of females in advanced societies is a relatively recent occurrence. Up until the 1970s, males were clearly the educational winners and social scientists put substantial effort into explaining female disadvantage.

In the early 1970s, in the UK and many other western societies, girls tended to outperform boys in the early stages of the primary school, but their initial advantages were soon lost as boys began to overtake them in most areas of the curriculum (Douglas 1967). Young women tended to gain fewer school-leaving qualifications and were under-represented in the universities.

Moreover, females who entered higher education frequently accepted places in colleges rather than universities and were over-represented on vocational courses. Many explanations of the position of girls in the school made reference to differential patterns of socialization: it was argued that parents and teachers had lower expectations of females (which reflected disadvantages in the labour market; Delamont 1980) and even that girls faced pressure to limit their academic attainments for fear of frightening potential male suitors (Horner 1971).

By the early 1980s the situation had started to change and, from this point onwards, the gender gap increased in favour of girls. As Croxford and Raffe (2005) show, in the UK between the early 1980s and the late 1990s the attainment gap widened, with the greatest gains being made by middle class girls. By 2004, in England and Wales, 59 per cent of females as compared to 49 per cent of males achieved 5 or more GCSEs at age 16; a level of achievement signalling some merit (DfES 2005). Similar changes have been reported across much of Europe and North America.

With girls having become the educational high-flyers, attention has turned to focus on the reasons for male 'underachievement'. Undoubtedly, attitudes towards female education have changed and there is now a widespread expectation that women will spend the large part of their lives in the labour force, will regard paid work as a source of achievement and self-esteem and will rely on income from their employment to sustain a reasonable standard of living. Changes in the labour market are likely to have had a powerful impact: females today grow up in a world where work has become much more central to the lives of women. These changes in work patterns are likely to have affected the educational expectations of parents and teachers and to have had an impact on patterns of gender socialization.

The significant educational advances made by women, however, should not detract from the persistent inequalities of class that have a particularly strong impact on working class girls. Walkerdine and colleagues (2001) draw attention to a striking uniformity of performance of middle class girls that contrasts strongly with the, much more diversified, experiences of their working class peers. Among those from lower class families, underperformance, early exits from the educational system and lives often characterized by early motherhood and low paid insecure jobs remain common (Biggart 2002). As Walkerdine and colleagues argue, 'the notion that all boys are now failing and all girls succeeding has served to mask deep and enduring class differences between boys and girls' (2001: 111).

Despite the relative male underperformance in schools and universities, there is some evidence of a differential favouring males at the level of postgraduate study. In the UK, for example, men are still more likely than women to progress to a higher degree, with the differential being greatest in respect to research degrees (Wakeling 2005). Moreover, women are still underrepresented in certain subject areas (such as the sciences), are disadvantaged in the labour market (Biggart 2002) and remain heavily concentrated in a few occupations which offer inferior rewards and prospects (see Chapter 3).

'Race' and inequality

Inequalities associated with 'race' also continue to be a cause for concern to educationalists with young people from certain ethnic minorities still tending to underperform at school in comparison to majority populations. In the UK, at age 16 the performance of white and Asian young people tend to be similar, while African Carribeans (especially males) significantly underperform (DfES 2005). However, the average scores of Asians masks some very significant variations: those of Indian origin slightly outperform their white peers while Bangladeshis are far less likely to achieve a good standard of qualification. Reviewing trends in England between 1984 and 1999 and controlling for social class, (Croxford and Raffe 2005) show that, compared to the white population, those of Indian origin tend to have higher levels of attainment, Pakistanis were quite similar, while blacks and Bangladeshis perform significantly worse. According to Bradley and Taylor (2004), whites were twice as likely as African Carribeans to achieve five or more GCSEs.

In other countries similar disadvantages exist. In the USA, there is evidence that while the gap in attainment remains strong, the trend is positive. After reviewing a wide range of evidence, Kao and Thompson argue that 'racial and ethnic gaps in educational achievement and attainment have narrowed over the past three decades by every measure available to social scientists' (2003: 435). The gap in scores on reading tests between black and white youths, for example, shrank by about a half between 1971 and 1996 (Jencks and Phillips 1998). Yet children from minority groups are still more likely to be placed in low ability groups in schools, are more likely to drop out of high school and are less likely to enroll in higher education (Kao and Thompson 2003).

Young people from certain minorities groups are also more likely to be suspended from school for bad behaviour and even permanently excluded; in the UK, the Social Exclusion Unit has expressed concern about school exclusions. Some American states, such as Michigan, operate a tough permanent exclusion policy under which those who fall foul of the 'zero tolerance' policy are not usually provided with any form of alternative education. Those excluded are disproportionately African Americans (Holm *et al.* 2005). It is also important to be aware of the inter-relationship between class and 'race'. The relatively poor attainment of young blacks often has more to do with socio-economic disadvantage than ethnicity.

Conclusion

Despite far-reaching and radical changes in systems of education, experiences have tended to remain highly differentiated. On the surface, educational opportunities have increased for all social groups; participation has increased at all levels and many young people from working class families now enjoy access to higher education. At the same time, beneath the surface there is evidence suggesting a maintenance of differentiated educational experiences and, despite differences in the ways in which education is delivered, similar forms of inequalities exist across the industrialized world (Shavit and Blossfeld

1993). In terms of patterns of differentiation, continuity rather than change best describes educational outcomes over the last two decades.

Having reviewed the evidence, it may be tempting to suggest that few significant changes have occurred and that therefore Beck was somewhat premature in his argument that post-industrial society is characterized by a growing individualism: yet we suggest that the evidence does in fact lend some support to his ideas. On an objective level, traditional structures of social inequality remain intact, but our perception of these processes has certainly been obscured by changes which have taken place. The collectivist principles which underpinned many systems of education in the 1960s and early 1970s have gradually been replaced by the process of marketization. As Gewirtz argues, 'concern for social justice is being replaced by a concern for institutional survival, collectivism with individualism, cooperation with suspicion, and need with expediency' (1996: 308). The continuing process of marketization means that those who lack the cultural capital and information necessary to act as informed consumers will increasingly be marginalized as 'risks' accumulate in such a way as to strengthen existing patterns of inequality whilst those with adequate resources can 'purchase safety and freedom from risk' (Beck 1992: 35).

3 Social change *and* labour market 'transitions'

> Over the last couple of decades, youth transitions have become increasingly protracted and, seemingly, more complex. Routes between school and work which were once viewed as linear and predictable are seen as having been replaced by a set of movements which are less predictable and involve frequent breaks, backtracking and the blending of statuses.
>
> (Furlong *et al.* 2003: 24)

Introduction

In the previous chapter we suggested that changing patterns of educational participation could partly be explained in terms of the re-structuring of the youth labour market. With a sharp decline in demand for unqualified, minimum-aged school-leavers, in most of the advanced societies young people are remaining at school for longer periods of time and experience of university has become increasingly common. While a reduction in opportunities to engage in paid work helped spark these changes, the recent increase in levels of employment has not triggered a return to the patterns of labour market entry common prior to the 1980s recession. Indeed, as a result of the entrenchment of changes in educational participation, the transition from school to work tends to take longer to complete and, according to some commentators, has become much more complex: this has implications for domestic and housing transitions as well as for other life experiences which will be discussed in later chapters.

The transition from school to work is often regarded as an important phase in the life-cycle, one which holds the key to a greater understanding of the ways in which social advantages and inequalities are passed from one generation to the next. In the 1970s young people tended to make fairly direct transitions from school to full-time jobs: the situation today is very different. We suggest that short, stable and predictable transitions are characteristic of a 'Fordist' social structure in which the life experiences of the masses are relatively standardized and homogenous. Over the last three decades, transitions have changed in a number of ways. The transition from school to work has become much more protracted (Roberts *et al.* 1987; Roberts and Parsell 1992a;

Wyn and White 1997), increasingly fragmented and in some respects less predictable (Furlong *et al.* 2003). Indeed, questions are now beginning to be raised about the relevance of the term 'transition' in that the relatively stable employment biographies that once characterized adulthood are now proving elusive for large sections of the population (Dwyer and Wyn 2001; Furlong and Kelly 2005).

As Giddens suggests, social life in the modern world takes place in settings which are increasingly 'diverse and segmented' (1991: 83). Employment in manufacturing industry continues to decline, while the service sector has become increasingly significant. For some commentators these changes represent an important development in capitalist societies. Whereas the industrial revolution was accompanied by a sharp decline in agricultural employment, post-industrial society is characterized by a shrinking manufacturing sector and the dominance of the service sector (Bell 1973). Alongside these changes, there has been a growth in part-time working and non-standard employment (such as agency working), employment in smaller work units, an increased demand for technical skills and 'flexible specializations' which together have been taken as characteristic of post-Fordist economies (Kumar 1995; Furlong and Kelly 2005). In late modernity, individual skills and educational attainments are of crucial importance in smoothing labour market entry, while the collectivized transitions which were once central to an understanding of social reproduction have weakened. In these new contexts, labour market histories can sometimes be characterized by a constant, individualized, 'churn' between different forms of insecure employment (Furlong and Cartmel 2004; Macdonald and Marsh 2005).

For Beck (1992) these changes underpin the emergence of the risk society. Individuals are forced to assume greater responsibility for their, increasingly fragmented, experiences in the labour market and to assess constantly the implications of their actions and experiences. Life in the modern world involves a global insecurity of life (Jansen and Van der Veen 1992) and while successful labour market integration is achieved by some, others find themselves excluded or forced to eke out an existence on the margins of the labour market. Indeed, the increasing complexity of the skill market and the segmentation of labour means that some young people can become vulnerable to long-term exclusion at an early stage in their lives while others move from one temporary position to another without being provided with an opportunity to develop their skills or to move to the more secure sectors of the labour market.

In this chapter we describe the main changes in the youth labour market and in 'transitions' from school to work and consider their implications for our understanding of processes of economic integration and the reproduction of inequalities based on class and gender. While there is strong evidence that school to work transitions have become more protracted, differentiated, and perhaps complex, we are sceptical about the tendency to regard these changes as indicative of a new era in which social structures have become fragmented. The seemingly individualized 'churn' within the precarious sector of the labour market can perhaps be regarded as part of a new set of class-based experiences.

Here we argue that structures have become more obscure as individuals have been made more accountable for their labour market fates. It is argued that two, somewhat contradictory, processes can be observed within modern societies: on the one hand a trend towards differentiation and diversity which reflect the economic transformations which some interpret as leading to a 'post-industrial' society, and on the other, the maintenance of relatively stable, predictable transitions which help ensure that those occupying advantaged social positions retain the ability to transmit privileges to their offspring (Olk 1988). Finally, in the context of the risk society thesis, it is also important to examine the extent to which the greater protraction of transitions has led to growing unease and uncertainty as young people try to make sense of a world in which their future is perceived as risky and difficult to predict.

The changing youth labour market

Many of the key changes affecting the experiences of young people in the advanced societies stem from the collapse of the youth labour market that occurred in many countries during the early 1980s and the restructuring of employment opportunities within a policy framework which placed priority on increased training, 'flexibility' and securing a reduction in relative labour costs. With an increase in all-age unemployment caused by economic recession, in the 1980s minimum-aged school-leavers increasingly faced difficulties securing work and across Europe governments introduced a variety of schemes to aid labour force integration, maintain work commitment or compel claimants to work in return for benefits.

High levels of unemployment, together with the introduction of government interventions, and, in some countries, the development of new vocational initiatives, had a radical impact on transitions from school to work. As a consequence of the lack of 'proper jobs' educational options became more attractive and the number of young people leaving school to enter the labour market at the minimum age declined sharply. In England and Wales, for example, in 1988, around 52 per cent of the school year cohort entered the labour market at the minimum age, compared to just 34 per cent in 1991 and 28 per cent by 2004 (Payne 1995; DfES 2005). Similarly, in Australia, in 1981 around two-thirds (65 per cent) left school at the minimum age; by 2003 this was down to around one in four (25 per cent) (Williamson 2005).

In the early 1970s, in most OECD countries youth unemployment remained well below 10 per cent. In the late 1970s rates began to increase, with a peak in the mid-1980s, before falling back in the late 1980s (Figure 3.1). The recession of the early 1990s saw rates of youth unemployment rise again, with a reduction occurring from the mid- to late 1990s. By the early years of the new millennium, levels of youth unemployment tended to be lower than they had been since the early 1980s and long-term unemployment had fallen considerably (Office of National Statistics 2000).[1] Yet throughout the period, there were some notable country specific differences. Youth unemployment has tended to be much higher in the Mediterranean countries than in northern Europe (with the notable exception of Finland) and rises tended to be magnified in these countries. Patterns of youth unemployment in Japan were also very different. They did not rise significantly in the 1970s or 1980s, but have increased

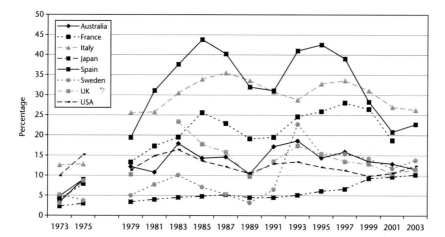

Figure 3.1 Trends in unemployment among 15- to 24-year-olds: selected countries, 1973–2003
Source: ILO 2003

fairly steadily from the 1990s leading to political concerns about young people's commitment to traditional forms of employment (Inui 2005).

Youth unemployment is much more sensitive to economic pressures than adult unemployment. It tends to increase more rapidly in times of recession and falls more quickly in times of recovery (Makeham 1980; O'Higgins 2001). Levels of youth unemployment in the advanced nations tends to be between two and three times higher than adult unemployment. In 2001, for example, in the UK and Sweden the ratio stood at 2.8 while in Canada it was 2.1 (ILO 2003). As a consequence, young people have to carry a particularly large share of a country's overall burden of unemployment. In 2001, in Australia 37 per cent of those who were unemployed were between the ages of 18 and 24, in the USA they accounted for 35 per cent and in the UK 33 per cent. In the 1990s, when all age unemployment rates were significantly higher, young people took an even greater share of total unemployment: 50 per cent in Spain, for example, and 43 per cent in Australia (ILO 2003).

Understandably, at the peak of recession, youth unemployment provoked great concern with some commentators suggesting that a high level of worklessness would be a central feature of post-Fordist societies. In particular social scientists were frequently pessimistic about future trends. Ashton and Maguire (1983), for example, were of the view that the increase in unemployment signalled the emergence of structural changes that would lead to a more or less permanent fall in the demand for labour in western economies as employers switched labour intensive production to developing countries that offered the possibility of reducing costs and increasing profits. While correct to predict an acceleration in outsourcing to non-western countries, it is now clear that commentators failed to appreciate the extent to which the service sector would come to absorb displaced manufacturing labour so as to facilitate a return to the sort of levels of unemployment that had been common in the 1960s and early 1970s.

In line with changes occurring throughout the industrialized world, the restructuring of the European economy has involved a continued decline in the manufacturing sector and the growth of employment in the service sector. Between 1975 and 2003, the proportion of employees working in manufacturing in the industrial countries of northern Europe fell from around 40 per cent to around 20 per cent (European Commission 1999; 2004a; Figure 3.2). In the UK, since the mid-1970s almost 1.6 million manufacturing jobs have been lost, with three quarters of a million being lost in three staple heavy industries: steel production, motor manufacture and shipbuilding (DfEE 2000). Indeed as Maguire noted (1991), during the 1980–83 recession alone, around a third of the jobs in the UK engineering industry were lost, a trend which affected the large number of young males who traditionally found employment in this sector.

Over the same period, employment in the European service sector increased from around 50 per cent of employees to around 75 per cent (European Commission, 1999, 2004a; Figure 3.3). Whereas school-leavers in many industrial centres once made mass transitions from school to manufacturing employment, today they tend to work in service environments that are usually of a relatively small scale and which tend to be fairly insecure (Kagan *et al.* 2005). Yet school-leavers with the highest qualifications are more likely to work in large firms, whilst the least qualified tend to be concentrated in small firms (Park 1994). In this respect the work situations of low attaining youth have become more individualized.

In the context of the growth of the service sector, it is important to note that young service workers tend to be concentrated in what Krahn and Lowe (1993) refer to as the 'lower tier services' such as the retail and hospitality industries. In Europe, 15- to 34-year-olds represent about half of the employees in hotels, restaurants and catering (Eurostat 2005). Here they frequently have little control over their working environment, often have poor job security and tend to earn minimum wages (Kagan *et al.* 2005). The poor working conditions of young service workers has been highlighted in the British press where attention was drawn to part-time employees at Burger King who were

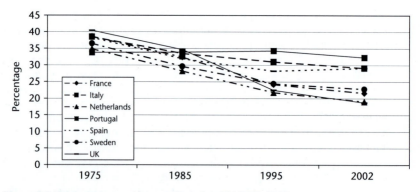

Figure 3.2 Total employment in manufacturing: EU 1975–2003
Source: European Commission 1999, 2004a

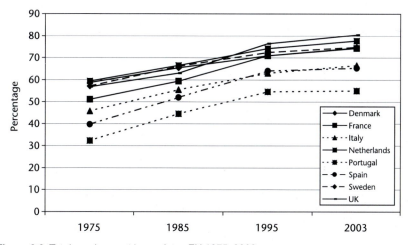

Figure 3.3 Total employment in services: EU 1975–2003
Source: European Commission 1999, 2004a

apparently forced to 'clock out' at those times during the day when customer demand was low. Similar stories illustrating the exploitative conditions experienced by young service workers have appeared in newspapers in many western societies.

Associated with these changing employment contexts, has been a weakening of collectivist traditions manifest in the decline of the trade unions which, in several countries, has been reinforced by legislation to curb their powers. Three out of four people currently employed in the countries of the European Union are not members of a trade union (Federation of European Employers 2005) with membership having declined significantly since the 1980s. In the UK, for example, union membership has fallen by a third since the 1980s (Bryson and Gomaz 2002) and currently stands at 29 per cent: Italy and Germany have similar levels of unionization (30 per cent and 27 per cent respectively) while in France just 9 per cent of employees are union members (Federation of European Employers 2005).

In part, the explanation for this trend lies in the shift in employment from (highly unionized) manufacturing to (weakly unionized) service industries. It has also been argued that a narrowing of the wage gap between unionized and non-unionized workers has been associated with a decline in union membership (Bryson and Gomaz 2002). Significantly, rates of union membership tend to be lowest in the sectors of economy in which young people are heavily represented (sales and personal and protective services). With many young workers in these sectors regarding their jobs as short-term, they have little incentive to engage in a struggle to improve pay and conditions. There is also evidence that some of the largest employers of young people in the service sector are vehemently anti-union. McDonald's, for example, who have been prosecuted in a number of countries for child labour law violations, have been noted for their refusal to negotiate with unions (Love 1995).

As trade unions once provided young people with an introduction to working class politics and collective action, the decline in union membership has implications for political socialization (see Chapter 8). While there have been few studies of young people and trade unions, Spilsbury and colleagues (1987) argued that levels of unionization among young people are primarily determined by overall patterns of union activity within an industry or firm. In this context, as a result of recent industrial changes, young people are increasingly finding employment in small firms and in areas where union activity has traditionally been weak. However, in a study of firms in the Swindon area, Rose noted that even in manufacturing industries, young employees displayed a 'sheer lack of interest' in trade unions (1996: 126). In the UK 78 per cent of young workers have never been members of a trade union and, between 1983 and 2001 the percentage of 18- to 24-year-olds who were union members fell from 38 per cent to 15 per cent (Bryson and Gomaz 2002).

Another particularly significant change in the youth labour market is that which stems from the development of 'flexible' employment practices. The recession of the 1980s provided employers with an incentive to seek ways of reducing labour costs and one of the ways in which this was achieved was through the increased use of part-time and temporary workers (Ashton *et al.* 1990). Indeed, during the 1980s, many firms reduced their core workforces and created a periphery of workers, many of whom were provided through labour hire agencies, working on time-limited contracts for sub-contractors, in non-standard forms of employment (such as zero hour contracts) or working fewer hours than desired. These strategies often relieved employers of a number of financial obligations, such as the provision of sick pay, holiday pay or superannuation (Atkinson 1984).

There is evidence showing a continued growth of insecure forms of employment, although the severity of the trend varies between countries, being particularly high in Spain and Australia, for example, but much lower in the UK (Furlong and Kelly 2005). It is also clear that young people – particularly young women and those with few skills – are most strongly affected by this trend. Indeed, in several European countries almost one in two temporary agency workers are under 25 (Arrowsmith 2006).

Drawing attention to the prevalence of 'fiddly' jobs, MacDonald and Marsh (2005) highlighted the ways in which less qualified young people frequently experience a succession of insecure, unpredictable and informally organized work within the service sector, usually paid at rates that were below the minimum wage and frequently used to supplement inadequate benefits. According to MacDonald and Marsh, young people become engaged in the marginal economy as a survival strategy; and they take up 'fiddly jobs' because of the shortage of mainstream job opportunities and because of the difficulties in surviving economically on benefits.

The growing insecurity of employment, the increase in non-standard work and the emergence of 'nomadic multi-activity' is something that has been highlighted by Beck (2000: 2) as characteristic of the risk society and is a theme that has been discussed extensively by Bauman (2001) and Sennett (1998). Beck refers to the process as the 'Brazilianization' of first world labour markets, predicting that future western societies will be strongly polarized with the majority forced to exist on the precarious margins of the labour market. While there may be some evidence to support the Brazilianization thesis, using data from the Australian and UK Labour Force Surveys, Furlong and Kelly (2005) argued that the process was structured rather than being all-pervasive with those most affected being groups who had traditionally occupied weak positions in the labour market.

Responding to labour market changes

Youth unemployment has long been a cause for concern among both academics and policy makers. When levels of unemployment rise (and overall increases in unemployment are magnified in the experiences of young people) there tends to be a growth of unemployment research and the development and implementation of new policies to prevent the marginalization that can stem from long-term unemployment. In many western societies, youth unemployment has been declining since the late 1990s and in some countries stands at a record low, yet the recessions of the 1980s and 1990s have led to a re-shaping of labour market experiences. In particular, the experience of dealing with youth unemployment and the political repercussions of high levels of worklessness among school-leavers has resulted in a new set of policy interventions that impact particularly strongly on the less qualified.

During the 1980s, in many countries, governments attempted to tackle increasing levels of youth unemployment by introducing a variety of training programmes aimed at minimum aged school-leavers (for whom levels of unemployment were particularly high). These programmes became a key part of transitional experiences for many young people during this period. While programmes adopted a variety of approaches, they tended to be based on deficit models whereby unemployment was linked to the supposed personal failings of those affected who were regarded as lacking in education or basic skills. The emphasis of the initiatives therefore tended to focus on the supply side of the labour market rather than on demand.

By the mid- to late 1980s, placement on training schemes had become increasingly common in a variety of countries, with national governments often providing work experience, vocational training or programmes of education in order to help smooth access to the labour market among those experiencing difficulties. With relatively high levels of unemployment prevailing among young adults until the late 1990s, a significant proportion of minimum age school-leavers were spending time on training schemes. Recognizing the ubiquity of programmes for the unemployed in the European Union, in 1997, an agreement was reached at the Luxembourg Summit on Employment which resulted in the establishment of a common set of principles to underpin provision for young people who had been unemployed for six months or more. Effectively it represented a 'guarantee'[2] of education, training or employment for those within a certain age group (although in some countries these were not introduced until levels of unemployment had begun to decline). Such provision tended not to be funded generously: despite the prevalence of youth unemployment, between the mid-1980s and 1999 OECD countries only spent an average of 0.1 per cent of their GDP on measures targeted at under 24-year-olds (OECD 2002b).

In the UK, the first national scheme specifically aimed at young people, (the Job Creation Programme), was introduced in 1975 in order to provide temporary work experience for school-leavers without jobs. At this stage, a small minority of young people experienced schemes, but with the introduction of the Youth Opportunities Programme (YOP) in 1978, providing six months of work experience for those who had been unemployed for six weeks, levels of participation grew. In 1981, YOP was succeeded by the year-long Youth Training Scheme (YTS) and in 1986 YTS became a two-year programme (subsequently renamed YT and, more recently, Skillseekers). The latest major overhaul of training programmes were implemented in 1998 with the introduction of the New Deal. The New Deal differed from earlier programmes in two important ways. First it targeted an older age group (18 plus) many of whom were experiencing recurrent problems in the labour market. Second, (in theory at least) it introduced a degree of choice and made an attempt to tailor interventions much more closely to individual needs and aspirations.

Both prior to and since the Luxembourg Summit, responses to unemployment in Europe have been extremely varied. Current measures include initiatives based on guarantees of employment, education or training (UK, Netherlands, Denmark and Sweden); programmes of 'socially useful' work and the extension of vocational education (France, Spain and Italy); the extended provision of apprenticeships and pre-vocational courses (Germany and Spain); and various placement initiatives (Germany and Italy) (Furlong and McNeish, 2000).

The development of activation programmes has also been underpinned by changing attitudes towards benefits for young people. As part of a process of retrenchment, the payment of unemployment and social security benefits to young people (once common in northern Europe), has, in many countries, either been abolished or eligibility criteria have been tightened up (Bonoli *et al.* 2000). Adopting 'Third Way' approaches resting on the principle of balancing rights and responsibilities, governments have increasingly made benefit payments conditional upon participation in activation measures. Based on a US style workfare approach linking eligibility to welfare payments with a willingness to work, European approaches now offer the unemployed a range of 'options' from 'workfare' to 'learnfare' to 'trainfare': approaches which share the objectives of 'reducing costs, preventing dependence, combating exclusion and linking rights and responsibilities' (Yeandle 2003: 53).

The introduction of 'guarantees' of work, education or training to young people has effectively changed the vocabulary used to describe the situation of young people who are not engaged in 'appropriate' activities. In the new vocabulary, youth unemployment has been removed from the dictionary and replaced with new terms that place responsibility for worklessness on young people. In the UK the term NEET (Not in Education, Employment or Training) is now used extensively to refer to those considered 'at risk' and statistics are collected on the prevalence of NEET. Similar processes can be observed in a range of countries such as Japan and Australia, although there are important differences in emphasis.

There are advantages in broadening definitions by focusing on NEET rather than unemployment. The adoption of the term NEET brings young mothers and those with disabilities into the frame rather than further marginalizing them by use of the traditional label 'inactive'. In other words, it promotes the recognition of forms of disadvantage that are not directly linked to unemployment in a traditional sense. On the negative side, it leads to confusion and makes comparisons difficult. It encourages commentators to make generalizations about the NEET group on the basis of the experiences or characteristics of one visible sub-group.

As used in the UK, NEET is a heterogeneous category that includes young people who are available for work and are actively seeking employment: a group that fits the ILO definition of unemployment. Also included are those who are not available or not seeking work. Groups such as the long-term sick or disabled or those with responsibilities for the care of children or relatives may not be available for work. Some of those who are not seeking work may be pursuing other interests, resting, developing skills in an unpaid capacity through voluntary work or taking time to travel. Effectively it combines those with little control over their situation with those exercising choice, thereby promoting a state of confusion about the factors associated with an apparent state of disadvantage. The sub-groups contained within the NEET category have very different experiences, characteristics and needs. Groups of vulnerable young people who require distinct forms of policy intervention in terms of welfare or training provision are grouped with the more privileged who may not require any assistance to move back into education or employment.

One of the key problems with the focus on NEET is that it encourages us to believe that young people who are employed no longer require assistance. However, with an increase in non-standard employment, underemployment and insecurity, there is a danger that those who occupy precarious positions are being ignored. Aware of the difficulties faced by young people in insecure forms of employment and of the dangers of marginalization, countries such as Japan and Australia now compile statistics on insecurity. Yet in both of these countries popular debate is tinged with deep suspicions that young people are choosing non-standard employment to help maintain leisure focused lifestyles and as part of a strategy to avoid long-term commitment. The evidence, though, suggests that most of those in non-standard forms of employment are disadvantaged rather than exercising life-style choices (Furlong and Kelly 2005; Inui 2005).

In modern labour markets, average job tenure has decreased for all workers, including the younger age groups who have always been more likely to switch jobs fairly frequently (Goodwin and O'Connor 2005). However, existing labour market statistics do not readily facilitate a distinction between movement representing voluntary flexibility and involuntary precarity. To what extent does the greater fluidity evident in the youth labour market represent a preference for control over employment biographies rather than signal a process of churn between a series of unsatisfying jobs? The answer is complicated by the new forms of labour stratification. Part-time and temporary jobs, for example, are frequently held by students supporting themselves through university as well as by young people who are unable to secure full-time or permanent employment. In these circumstances, young people from very different social classes may work alongside each other and their occupational positions may provide few clues as to future labour market prospects.

Irrespective of the generosity or source of financial support systems for students, there has been a long tradition of supplementing income through part-time working. In this respect, future graduates have tended to have some experience of part-time work in the lower-tier services. The expansion of higher education combined with a tendency to offer students less generous financial support packages has increased the number of young people who are combining part-time work with study and has changed the nature of education to work transitions for graduates. In particular, graduates are no longer such a privileged group and for many, graduate employment, at least in the traditional sense, will prove elusive.

With a close link between qualifications and employment outcomes and a belief in a connection between overall levels of education and economic performance, governments have tended to support the growth of higher education. At the same time, they have been reluctant to shoulder the financial costs of increasing participation. Although the evidence base is somewhat thin, research seems to show that, despite a much larger pool of graduates, labour market returns to graduates appear not to have been deflated (Futureskills Scotland 2006). Indeed, in the UK, recent estimates by the accountants PricewaterhouseCoopers (2005) show that compared to a qualified[3] 18-year-old school-leaver, a graduate will earn an additional 12 per cent over their working life.[4] While it will cost the state £21 000 (€30 000) to educate the average graduate, the working life benefit to the exchequer in the form of additional taxation will be around £93 000 (€134 000).

In many respects, the term 'graduate labour market' maybe something of an anachronism. The 'graduate labour market' has become segmented into secure and less secure zones as well as into segments that have a looser correspondence to graduate skills. Recognizing the ways in which the labour market has changed, Elias and Purcell (2004) have made a distinction between four types of graduate employment; traditional, modern, new and niche. Whereas traditional graduate jobs have long been the more or less exclusive preserve of those with university degrees (such as lawyers, doctors and scientists), the other three sectors of the graduate labour market refer to those areas that have gradually become (or are still becoming) dominated by workers with degrees; a process that can be linked to the growth of higher education and which may be interpreted as an indicator of qualification inflation. Modern graduate jobs relate to newer professions and to those areas of employment where graduate status started to become required in the 1980s (such as journalism and accountancy). New graduate jobs refer to those sectors of employment that have more recently begun to focus on graduate recruitment (such as marketing and physiotherapy) while niche occupations are those where a minority of incumbents are graduates but in which there are growing specialist niches where graduates are employed (hotel managers and buyers).

The maintenance of labour market inequalities

Changes occurring since the 1980s appear to have radically altered the nature of young people's labour market participation. Transitions to employment now tend to take longer to complete, while the diversification of routes means that experiences have become more individualized. Indeed, many researchers have highlighted the increasing complexity of the transition from school to work with young people finishing school at different stages and following a variety of overlapping routes into the labour market (Roberts 1995; Bynner *et al.* 1997; Wyn and White 1997). Between the ages of 16 and 18, young people build up a far greater range of experiences than previously: they embark on different courses of study, receive training in a number of contexts, and spend time both out of work and in employment. Yet few young people share identical sets of experiences and most encounter situations where they are able to select between competing sets of alternatives (Roberts 1995). In this context Roberts suggests that a process of individualization has occurred insofar as these changes have involved a reduction in the number of young people with closely matching transitional patterns.

However, the existence of individualized or diversified routes should not be taken as an indication that structural determinants of transitional outcomes have weakened. On a number of different levels, young people's transitional experiences can be seen as differentiated along the lines of class and gender.

Using data from a longitudinal study carried out in Scotland, Furlong and colleagues (2003) used cluster analysis based on monthly data on status changes between the ages of 16 and 23 to construct eight typologies of transition that reflected the preponderance of different experiences within the time frame (Figure 3.4).

The researchers also differentiated between those whose transitions could, in broad terms, be described as linear and those whose experiences were regarded as non-linear. The main criteria used to determine the linearity of transitions related to periods of unemployment and the number of status changes. The sample (between pp. xx and yy) was divided fairly evenly between linear and non-linear models. The experiences of each of the individuals between the ages of 16 and 23 are illustrated in the form of transitional maps in Figures 3.5 and 3.6. Noting that the maps underplay levels of complexity insofar as they show changes from one status to another, but not changes within the same status (such as directly from one job to another), it is clear that broken and complex transitions are not confined to those who leave education at an early stage, but extend to those who follow routes through higher education. Analysis of the characteristics of those described as following non-linear routes showed that, on a number of measures, they were less advantaged than those following more linear pathways. For both males and females, for example, a majority of those from the highest social classes made linear transitions while the majority of those from the lower social classes followed non-linear routes.

Indeed, despite an apparent increase in the possibilities to continue full-time education or embark on a course of training, young people from

Long higher education	Typically having completed a three- or four-year degree course
Short higher education	Typically having completed a two-year course in higher education or dropped out of a degree course
Enhanced education	Typically entered the labour market after having completed upper secondary education
Direct job	Typically moved directly into employment at age 16
Assisted transitions	Typically spent periods of time on youth training programmes
Unemployment	Typically encountered long periods of unemployment
Domestic transitions	Typically took time out of the labour market to care for children
Other	A small residual category that contains a number of people with health problems

Figure 3.4 Typologies of transitional experence
Source: Furlong *et al.* 2003

advantaged positions in the socio-economic hierarchy have been relatively successful in protecting privileged access to the most desirable routes. Although young people from working class families are increasingly experiencing post-compulsory education, in all advanced societies they continue to be over-represented among early labour market entrants. Moreover, there is no evidence to suggest that class-based differentials have declined over the period (Marshall and Swift 1993), although those from some ethnic minorities are becoming more likely than their white counterparts to avoid early labour market entry (Kao and Thompson 2003; DfES 2005).

The timing of entry to full-time jobs has also continued to be strongly affected by gender: in most OECD countries girls tend to remain in education for longer while boys are more likely to have entered the labour market by the age of 18 (OECD 2002b). This differential has increased since the mid-1980s, reflecting a growing tendency for young women to remain in full-time education which is partly explained by the demands of service sector employers for educated female workers. There is also evidence of raised occupational aspirations and expectations among young women. In virtually all OECD countries, young women are more likely than young men to expect to enter high-skilled white collar occupations (OECD 2004). The increased demand for female service workers has been reflected in narrowing wage differentials. In the UK, for example at age 18 women tend to earn slightly more than men (10 per cent more in 1999). However, among 18–20-year-olds males still earn about 2 per cent more than females, a gap which, by age 21–24, has increased to a 10 per cent advantage (DfES 2005).

Experiences of work-based training have also remained highly stratified by class, gender and 'race'. In the UK work-based training tends to be regarded as low status and those from working class families have always been more likely than middle class youths to join training schemes (Furlong 1992; Courtenay and McAleese 1993; DfES 2005): quality training tends to be reserved for those with strong academic credentials (who are often from more advantaged class positions). A number of writers have also noted the ways in which the most disadvantaged young people and those from ethnic minorities tend to be concentrated in certain programmes with low rates of post-training employment (Furlong and McNeish 2000). These second-rate training schemes, which often operate in contexts that are some way removed from the labour market, have been variously described as 'sink schemes' or 'warehousing' schemes (Roberts and Parsell 1992b): such programmes frequently fail to promote social integration or reduce marginalization (Schömann and O'Connell 2002) and may provide few opportunities for progression (Raffe and Shapira 2005).

The low status of work-based training in countries such as the UK and France partly reflects their historical origins as schemes for unemployed young people and their continued use in a variety of programmes available to those without jobs (Raffe and Shapira 2005). In the USA, work-based training is also regarded as a low status route (Ryan 2001) and even in countries such as Germany where work-based training has a different history and undoubtedly a higher status, in the main it is a route followed by young people heading towards working class occupations (Shavit and Müller 2000).

While short periods of unemployment are experienced by young people from a wide variety of social backgrounds, outside of the high unemployment Mediterranean countries, most of those who spend significant periods of time out of work come from working class families and are often located in ex-industrial areas that have been badly affected by the restructuring of labour markets (White and McRae 1989; Anisef *et al.* 2000; O'Higgins 2001; Iannelli 2003; White and Wyn 2004; MacDonald and Marsh 2005). Here it has been argued that most of those who encounter prolonged or repeated periods of worklessness suffer from the effects of multiple deprivation (OECD 1999; Franzén and Kassman 2005).

While in many countries statistics on unemployment and social class are not readily available, educational attainment represents a reasonable proxy. In a wide range of countries, it is clear that those with the most advanced qualifications are far less likely than their less qualified peers to avoid long-term unemployment. Focusing on unemployment three years after the completion of education (which allows time for young people to establish themselves in the labour market), those with university education were far less likely to be unemployed than those who had not completed upper secondary education (Figure 3.7) In the USA, for example, the unemployment rate among males who had not completed upper secondary education was 29 per cent, compared to 3 per cent among those with degree or tertiary level education. The figures also help illustrate the extent to which the German Dual System helps reduce

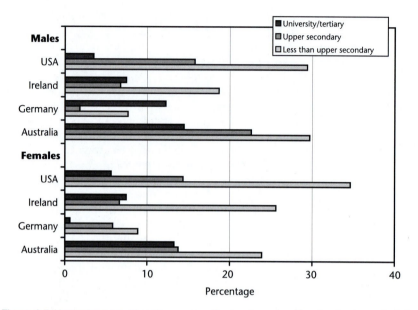

Figure 3.7 Unemployment rates three years after leaving education, by gender and attainment: selected countries
Source: OECD 1998

the risk of unemployment among lower qualified workers – although the Dual System also reduces the chances of young people from working class families accessing professional positions (Shavit and Müller 2000).

In many countries, differences in male and female rates of unemployment are linked to country-specific employment practices and traditions. In OECD countries in general, rates of unemployment among young females tend to be a little lower than for males, the exceptions being Spain and France where females have been more likely to experience unemployment. However, changes in the labour demand have led to a reduction in female vulnerability to unemployment (Figure 3.8).

In many countries males tend to be more likely to experience long-term unemployment, and extended periods of unemployment can result in withdrawal from the labour market or the abandonment of job-search activities. However, young women are much more likely to withdraw than males (Furlong 1992; Biggart 2002). Once a young person gives up hope of finding a job, labour market withdrawal may represent an option which provides positive psychological benefits. For young women, especially those who are married or have children, withdrawal may be a socially acceptable alternative to long-term unemployment, although in the UK and the USA attempts have been made to prevent the withdrawal of single mothers by restricting benefits.

Reconceptualizing social reproduction

The changes in the youth labour market described in this chapter have been reflected in the different ways in which sociologists have conceptualized the

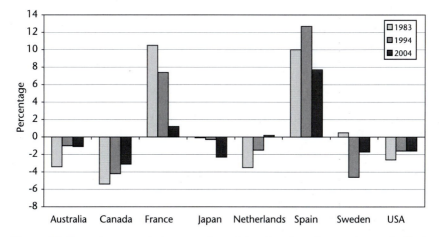

Figure 3.8 Percentage gap between male and female rates of unemployment: 15- to 24-year-olds: selected countries, 1983–2004
Source: OECD 1995, 2005b

transition from school to work. In the 1960s and 1970s, the predictability of transitional routes tended to be stressed (Carter 1962; Roberts 1968; Ashton and Field 1976; Willis 1977). Within these models, social class and gender were seen as powerful predictors of school experiences and educational attainment, which in turn helped determine the nature of the transition and the positions young people entered in the labour market. Ashton and Field (1976), for example, identified three main routes which young people followed from school to work: 'extended careers' involving higher education and access to the graduate labour market; 'short-term careers' involving short periods of training or post-compulsory education and leading to skilled manual or routine white collar employment and; 'careerless' routes which involved leaving school at the minimum age to take up semi-skilled or unskilled employment. In a context of collectivized transitions, young people were provided with clear messages about their destinations and the likely timing of their journeys and tended to develop an awareness of likely sequences of events.

With the transition from school to work tending to become much more complex during the 1980s, it became increasingly difficult for minimum-aged school leavers to secure jobs immediately after leaving school and routes into work tended to become more diverse. Yet despite this diversification of routes, sociologists tended to argue that transitional outcomes remained highly structured (Roberts *et al.* 1987; Bynner and Roberts 1991; Banks *et al.* 1992). This structural emphasis was underlined by the use of the term 'trajectory' implying that individuals had little control over their destinations (Evans and Furlong 1997).

Reflecting the theoretical influence of Beck and Giddens, transitional models introduced during the 1990s have tended to place a greater emphasis on the ways individuals actively negotiate risk and uncertainty: referred to by Evans and Furlong (1997) as a 'navigation' model. In the age of high modernity, the range of possibilities open to individuals mean that people are constantly forced to engage with the likely consequences of their actions on a subjective level. Indeed, Beck highlights the extent to which 'reflexive modernization' involves an ongoing 'self-confrontation with the effects of risk' (1994: 5).

The emphasis which is placed on subjective perceptions of risk and uncertainty represents an important break with earlier traditions. Prior to the 1990s, the predominant theme was that having followed well-trodden and predictable routes or trajectories from the family, through the school and into the labour market, the transition from school to work tended not to be associated with a subjective unease or discomfort (Carter 1962; Ashton and Field 1976).[5] Although we remain sceptical about the extent to which changes in the youth labour market have affected underlying patterns of social reproduction, we recognize that processes which appear stable and predictable on an objective level, may involve greater subjective risk and uncertainty.

During the 1960s and 1970s, as a consequence of following highly structured trajectories from school into the labour market, young people tended to develop sets of assumptions which helped make their experiences seem natural and normal. After spending their formative years in socially restricted networks, young people usually developed an awareness of the range of opportunities likely to be available to people like themselves and the nature of the associated lifestyles. Consequently Ashton and Field (1976) maintained that the transition from school to work, generally being a confirmation of earlier experiences and expectations, was a smooth and relatively untraumatic event in the lives of most young people.

In many ways, processes of social reproduction which are smooth and predictable on a subjective level can be regarded as characteristic of a traditional social order in which children, who often followed in the footsteps of their parents, may not have given very much consideration to a wider range of jobs or careers. In communities with a limited range of job opportunities young people may tailor their expectations to the main types of jobs which are available. In the mining communities of the North East and in the Welsh valleys, boys often grew up expecting to follow their fathers down the pits (Dennis *et al.* 1956). In the West Midlands, Willis (1977) highlighted subjective continuities among working class males who celebrated the masculine culture represented on building sites and the factory floor. Similar patterns have been identified among females. Westwood (1984), for example, argued that working class girls expected to enter the textile factories of the East Midlands before withdrawing to become involved in full-time domestic labour.

The restructuring of the adult labour market and the decline of the youth labour market have important implications for the way young people experience the transition to work on a subjective level. These changes, which stem from the continued decline in demand for low-skill labour, have led to a demand for a better educated, more skilled labour force in advanced industrial societies. But the speed of change has meant that the current generation of young people are making their transitions to work in a period of turmoil (which is perhaps a characteristic of modern labour markets) and, as a consequence, may lack the clear frames of reference which can help smooth

transitions. In this respect, entry to the world of work today can be characterized by a heightened sense of risk.

Having parents who experienced very different transitions, young
people often perceive the process as filled with risk and uncertainty. Many,
fearing the consequences, shelter from the labour market as long as possible by
remaining in education (Biggart and Furlong 1996). Yet it is important to stress
that subjective perceptions of risk can be present even among those whose
routes appear relatively safe to the outside observer: even young people from
privileged social backgrounds and with excellent academic credentials frequently worry about failure and about the uncertainty surrounding future
events and experiences (Lucey 1996; Walkerdine *et al.* 2001).

The weakening of social class as a subjective frame of reference has also
had an impact on processes of social reproduction. Whereas employment contexts were once closely tied to class position both objectively and subjectively,
in modern contexts, and promoted by management strategy, many young
people who occupy working class positions regard themselves as part of a
transient middle class. In *No Logo*, Naomi Klein (2000) describes the ways in
which some employers encourage perceptions of transience among service
workers. When workers regard their positions as short term, they are less likely
to fight to improve pay and conditions. One of her respondents, a shop assist-
ant at the Borders book chain, suggested that his colleagues regarded themselves as middle class even through they were only earning $13 000 a year.
Klein also highlights a television advertising campaign in which McDonalds'
employees were shown at work serving food with captions such as 'future
lawyer' and 'future engineer'. On an objective level, the turbulence of non-
linear transitions makes it much easier for young people to hold on to aspirations regarding careers and class positions that are unlikely to materialize. In
a recent study of young working class males in the UK, for example, despite
being employed in a range of 'Mcjobs', it was not uncommon to find them
holding onto a belief that they were on their way to something better
(McDowell 2003).

Conclusion

In this chapter we have highlighted the extent to which labour market experiences of young people have changed. The types of jobs which young people
enter and their experiences of the transition from school to work have
changed quite significantly, largely as a result of global economic changes in
the demand for labour but also as consequence of policies developed in
periods of recession. Although greater opportunities for advanced education
and training are available to all young people, existing social disadvantages
seem to have been maintained. Indeed, young people from less advantaged
families face a new set of disadvantages which stem from the development of a
labour market periphery. New forms of 'flexible' working have reduced job
security and many of the least qualified young people have become trapped on
the labour market periphery where they are vulnerable to periodic
unemployment and to a process of churn between one poor job and another.
Moreover, the creation of opportunities in small service environments has

been associated with a decline in collective traditions and union membership for working class youth, while the professional and technical middle classes have become more organized and increasingly unionized (Lash and Urry 1987). In this respect, we agree with Jessop and colleagues who argue that post-Fordism is characterized by a 'division between a skill-flexible core and a time-flexible periphery, which is now replacing the old manual/non-manual division' (1987: 109).

While the demand for flexible, skilled workers in the new 'information society' creates advantages for some young people, the continued segmentation of labour markets helps ensure that traditional privileges are protected. Yet despite the maintenance of traditional lines of inequality, subjectively young people are forced to reflexively negotiate a complex set of routes into the labour market and in doing so, develop a sense that they alone are responsible for their labour market outcomes. Young people are forced to negotiate a complex maze of potential routes and tend to perceive outcomes as dependent upon their individual skills, even when the objective risks of failure are slim. In turn, the perception of risk can lead to subjective discomfort.

The evidence we have presented in this chapter provides some support for Beck and Giddens. Transitions have become more individualized and young people from all social backgrounds perceive their situations as filled with risk and uncertainty. At the same time, there is strong evidence that, on an objective level, risks are distributed in an unequal fashion and correspond closely to traditional lines of disadvantage. For many young workers there is a lack of clarity about the ways in which occupational experiences link to social class and gender and this increased obscurity can be linked not just to the speed of change but also to the fragmentation of labour market experiences.

4 Changing patterns *of* dependency

Family formation, then, is no longer a once and for all event, the end product of a linear movement towards clearly defined notions of adult-hood. Instead, today's young adults are increasingly likely to find themselves moving back and forth into a variety of living arrangements over the life course, invariably linked to the creation and dissolution of household forms based on intimate relationships with parents, friends and partners.

(Heath and Cleaver 2003: 2)

Introduction

The changing patterns of schooling and the protraction of the school to work transition which have been discussed in the previous two chapters have led to an extension of the period during which young people remain dependent on their families and, in some countries, on the state. As financial independence through employment provides young people with the resources to leave the parental home and establish more autonomous patterns of residence, extended school to work transitions and fragmented patterns of involvement in the labour market will have an impact on patterns of dependency. Yet in modern societies adult status tends not to be conferred solely on the basis of successful completion of the school to work transition, but can be linked to the completion of a series of linked transitions. Coles (1995) suggests that there are three inter-related transitions made by young people, some of which must be achieved before being accepted into adult society. Aside from the transition from school to work, young people may make a 'domestic transi-tion', involving a move from the family of origin to the family of destination, and a 'housing transition' involving a move to residence away from the par-ental (or surrogate parental) home. These three transitions are inter-related in so far as experiences in one dimension of life will have an impact on other life events: a school to work transition which is interrupted by unemployment, for example, is likely to affect the stage at which young people make domestic and housing transitions. Arnett (2004) takes a different approach, but one that has similar implications: here adulthood involves taking responsibility for yourself, making independent decisions and being financially independent.

The extension of transitions, together with changes in typical sequences of events has implications for the establishment of identity and for processes of individualization and risk. While it can be argued that all three transitions identified by Coles have become more protracted and difficult to complete (Coles 1995; Heath and Cleaver 2003), our interest in this chapter is to explore some of the implications of the extension of youth dependency and to assess the extent to which new patterns of individualization and risk can be linked to changes in domestic and housing transitions. We argue that recent social changes, which have led to an enforced increase in the period of youth dependency, have resulted in a situation in which the future is often seen as filled with risk and uncertainty: in such circumstances it can be difficult to maintain a stable identity. Changes in family structures in some countries together with the introduction of social policies that reduce young people's access to housing support, represent a new set of hazards to be negotiated by today's youth. Those with access to the appropriate social and economic resources remain less vulnerable to the consequences of failure while others who lack family support can face extreme difficulty. In this context we suggest that the ability to make successful transitions to adulthood is still powerfully conditioned by 'traditional' inequalities such as class and gender.

The extension of semi-dependency

In the modern world, youth is an intermediary stage in the life cycle. In law, children are regarded as dependent and in need of protection while adults are regarded as full citizens and expected to take responsibility for their own lives (Coles 1995: Arnett 2004). Young people are treated differently from children, granted certain rights and responsibilities, but denied the full range of entitlements accorded to adults (Jones and Wallace 1992; Coles 1995; Arnett 2004). Full citizenship is not automatically conferred on reaching a certain age and, as Coles suggests, 'there is no clear end to the status of childhood and no clear age at which young people are given full adult rights and responsibilities' (1995: 7). Moreover, the legal rights and responsibilities which signify adulthood are granted in stages, some of which are based on chronological age, others being dependent on the completion of stages in the transitional process (such as the completion of full-time education).

In England, young people are able to engage in some part-time employment at the age of 13, can leave school and enter full-time employment at 16 but cannot marry without parental consent or vote in elections until 18 and are not entitled to full 'adult' social security benefits until the age of 25 (Harris 1990; Craig 1991; Coles 1995). The stages at which rights are granted varies from country to country but legislative fragmentation of adult status and seemingly illogical phasing of adult rights is fairly typical. In the USA, for example, young people can leave home, marry and drive motor vehicles several years before they are allowed to drink alcohol. In contrast, in Portugal young people are able to drink alcohol several years before they can marry, vote or drive.

Youth is therefore a period of social semi-dependency, framed by legislation and cultural norms, which forms a bridge between the total dependence of childhood and the independence of adulthood. Consequently it is largely defined in the negative: by what it is not, rather than by what it is. A youth is no longer a child, but is not quite a mature adult living an independent life. As a stage in the life cycle which lacks clearly defined boundaries, the period we refer to as youth is historically and socially variable. Just as childhood became recognized as a distinct part of the life course during a specific period of industrial development (Aries 1962), the terms 'youth' and 'adolescence' are social constructs which emerged at a particular stage of socio-economic development.

The term adolescence was first used by Stanley Hall (1904) to describe a physiological process linked to the onset of puberty and sexuality in young people, with psychologists tending to regard adolescence as a period of physical, sexual and emotional development occurring between the ages of about 12 and 18. However, the onset of puberty, being affected by nutritional standards, occurs earlier now than in the past (Donovan 1990). Psychologists also developed an interest in the ways in which individuals came to terms with these physiological changes and established adult identities (e.g. Erikson 1968). Since the 1920s, psychologists have tended to make a distinction between the physiological process of maturation and the social processes through which young people come to terms with their new statuses and develop adult identities. Bühler (1921), for example, referred to the process of social and psychological maturation as *Kulturpubertät* or 'cultural puberty'. Despite this refinement in psychological approaches, it is important to make the distinction between the term 'adolescence', which still tends to be used primarily in a psychological context, and 'youth' which has traditionally been the focus of sociological investigations. Whereas adolescence is seen as covering a limited time span, the term youth covers a much broader period of time; extending today from the mid-teens to the mid-20s (Springhall 1986). Unlike adolescence, youth is a social concept which lacks a physiological base.

Although defined differently, youth and adolescence once covered broadly similar periods of the lifespan and, as a consequence, are sometimes erroneously used interchangeably. With youth now covering a much longer period of the lifespan than adolescence, some social scientists have begun to question the usefulness of youth as a concept that can cover people whose experiences are very different: from young teenagers with little independence to those in their mid- to late 20s who may remain financially dependent on their parents or the state but may otherwise have considerable autonomy over their lives and even have responsibility for others (EGRIS 2001; Bynner 2005; Arnett 2004, 2006). As Arnett suggests,

> 'youth' is too vague and elastic a term to be useful in describing the new and unprecedented period that now lies after adolescence but before full adulthood. . . . Any word that is intended to be applied to people in the entire age range from 10 or 12 until at least 25 cannot possibly work,

because the typical 10 or 12 or 15 or 17 year-old in simply too different from the typical 25 year-old.

(2006: 119)

This uneasy balance between dependency and autonomy which has become characteristic of the lives of increasing numbers of people experiencing protracted transitions has led to the suggestion that youth and adulthood are now separated by a new phase that can best be referred to as 'young adulthood' (EGRIS 2001), 'emerging adulthood' (Arnett 2004), 'post-adolescence' or 'psychological adulthood' (Côté 2000). While terms like young adult, or emerging adult can help capture some of the contradictions that surface in late modernity, to date we have not been provided with a convincing definition through which we can make a conceptual break between youth and young adulthood or young adulthood and full adulthood. In other words, researchers seem unable to say what it is, other than chronological age, that separates youth from young adulthood. As Côté makes clear, adulthood is now 'based more on individual preference than on social norms' (2000: 32).

Being defined as a period of semi-dependency which young people pass through prior to the granting of adult status, youth is historically and socially variable because the attainment of independent adulthood is conditioned by social norms, economic circumstances and social policies. Illustrating the historical variability of the life stage referred to as youth, Springhall (1986) argues that in the early modern period, young people frequently entered service or took up apprenticeships which involved living away from home some time prior to reaching puberty. At the same time, males often delayed marriage and the establishment of an independent household until their mid- to late 20s. These practices, at a time when the average life-span was somewhat shorter, meant that the semi-dependence of youth often covered a substantial proportion of the life cycle. In contrast, in the 1950s and 1960s, youth was often seen as synonymous with the teenage years: beginning at puberty and, for many, ending soon after they secured their first full-time jobs in their mid- to late teens. Viewed in this way, it could be argued that the relatively speedy transitions that were characteristic of the mid-twentieth century were an historical aberration.

During the 1960s and 1970s, as a result of economic conditions and social policies, young people in many countries were able to make fairly direct school to work transitions and it was possible for them to gain a degree of economic independence from the age of 15 or 16. Parents tended to expect young people to assume a degree of self-responsibility on leaving full-time education and expected a contribution to household expenses: families frequently expected young people to undertake part-time work while at school. Leaving education and collecting the first wage packet was symbolic for both young people and their parents and tended to be accompanied by the granting of greater freedoms and responsibilities (Kiernan 1992; Coles 1995). This is not to argue that young people automatically assumed adult roles on entering the labour market; as Goodwin and O'Connor (2005) demonstrate, many young workers in the 1960s continued to be treated as little more than children by parents who expected to receive their wage packets and handed over some pocket money in return.

In late modernity, however, the sequencing of transitions and of key events in the life cycle of young people has changed. Whereas transitions in the 1950s and 1960s involved a sequence of events in which young people typically first left school, then had their first sexual encounter, left home and married sometime later, today, young people often become sexually active prior to leaving school and marry or cohabit and have children later.

Due to different patterns of educational participation, in the 1960s and 1970s working class youth tended to become economically independent much earlier than those from the middle classes who often remained dependent on their parents until their early 20s (Roberts 1985; Goodwin and O'Connor 2005). Although most teenagers continued to live in the family home, school-leavers were expected to make a contribution towards household expenses. At this time, in northern Europe and Australia, even those who failed to find jobs were able to assume some financial independence through the ability to claim state benefits within a few weeks of leaving school. Although the level of financial aid was based on the assumption of some continued parental support, there was a recognition on the part of the state that school-leavers, as young adults, had a right to some economic autonomy at this stage in their lives. This principle started to be abandoned during the 1980s as several governments began to relinquish economic responsibility for young people and forced parents to underwrite their offspring financially until their mid-20s. Today the types of economic support for young people that were fairly common in the 1970s are confined to parts of Scandinavia and even there eligibility has been restricted. Although strong class- and gender-based differentials continue to exist in respect of routes followed from the age of 16, there are now few opportunities for young people to establish a relatively autonomous adult existence in their teenage years. For some this is seen as a blessing, for others it is a source of regret.

In the UK, a number of pieces of legislation were introduced during the 1980s which formalized this lengthening period of semi-dependency and, according to Jones (1995), effectively extended dependency to the age of 18 and semi-dependency to the age of 25. During this period, young people's relationship with the state is mediated by their parents and full citizenship is not conferred until they are able to assume a direct relationship to the state as independent adults (Jones and Wallace 1992). These legislative changes reflect the Government's view that young people should be in full-time education or training and should not have the option of living off state benefits (see Chapter 3). It has also been argued that the changes were based on the view that families ought to assume financial responsibility for their offspring until they were able to stand on their own feet (Finch 1989) and were triggered by the impact of rising unemployment on state expenditure. Similar processes can be found in many of the countries where the state previously accepted a financial responsibility for older teenagers.

In effect these changes have led to new inequalities both in the ability to leave the parental home as well as in the experiences of those who continue to live with their parents. At this stage, the transfer of economic resources from parent to offspring helps facilitate domestic and housing transitions, yet the most significant resource transfers occur in wealthier and more educated households (de Vaus and Qu 1998; White and Wyn 2004). The experience of living in the parental home as a young adult is also qualitatively different in affluent families. As White and Wyn suggest, 'more affluent households also provide more physical and monetary space for individuals to "do their thing", and greater privacy in what household members may wish to do' (2004: 110).

This enforced lengthening of dependence in youth through the introduction of new legislation is a feature of many advanced societies and can be linked to economic change and the wish to establish mass systems of higher education without a significant increase in the tax burden. However, the changes do not simply relate to the provision of state benefit; in several countries, for example, there have been changes in criminal justice systems that restrict the movement of young people (see Chapter 7). Such changes highlight the extent to which structural changes have been reinforced by social policies so as to formalize the extension in the period of youth dependence in late modernity.

While highlighting the external circumstances that helped shape modern 'youth', it is important to recognize that, for some, these changes have opened up new possibilities. Despite the uncertainty and anxiety that characterizes the modern youth phase, it has created space where those with resources to draw on are able explore possibilities and enjoy freedoms that were closed to most members of previous generations. A good example here would be the 'gap year' that has become common in many countries. As people like du Bois Reymond (1998a) and Arnett (2004) have noted, long emerging adulthoods are partly a reflection of choices: young adults are entering live-in relationships and having children later partly because they want to be able to enjoy the freedoms contained in the space between conventional childhood or youth and full adulthood. At the same time, Bynner (2005) is right to remind us that access to the 'freedoms' of young adulthood are strongly dependent on access to economic and cultural resources.

Identity

The extension of dependency which we have described has important implications for the establishment of identity. The social construction of youth in the modern period and the extension of dependency which has occurred over the last few decades is seen by some as providing a space in which young people can develop as individuals and experiment with different lifestyles in a context where the influence of the family is less prominent (Ainley 1991; Miles 1998). However, others argue that these changes have had a negative impact on identity formation. For young people, the lengthening of the period between physical maturity and the attainment of adult status can be seen as problematic due to difficulties involved in constructing a stable identity in a period characterized by economic and social marginality. While psychologists such as Erikson (1968) regard the establishment of identity as one of the central tasks of adolescence, the youth phase is a period of uncertainty and, where young people have no clear picture of what the future holds, this confusion can play a central role in the construction of identity. In this context, Côté and Allahar see adolescence in late modernity as characterized by an 'identity moratorium' which can have negative psychological consequences. Adolescence is a time of confusion in which some young people get lost or become sidetracked: as such youth can be the 'most destructive or wasted period of their lives' (1996: 74). For Côté, many adolescents 'wallow in forms of immaturity characterized by partially formed ideals, identities and skills' (2000: 31).

For much of the twentieth century, the establishment of adult identities was much more straightforward because of the speed with which transitions were completed, their relative simplicity, and because of the fairly stable nature of the occupational world. As we noted in the previous chapter, young people tended to follow clearly defined routes through the school and into the labour market, frequently following in the footsteps of their parents and older siblings (the so-called 'normal biography'). In these circumstances, identities tended to be developed in socially restricted networks and young people developed assumptive worlds which reflected established class and gender-based relationships. In late modernity, young people frequently lack these clear frames of reference and attempt to establish adult identities in a world which they perceive as filled with risk and uncertainty.

In an uncertain and rapidly changing social world, young people can find it difficult to construct stable social identities and changes in education and the labour market mean that they are subject to an increasing range of social and cultural influences (Melucci 1992). Côté and Allahar (1996) also suggest that the identity crisis of youth in late modernity is socially produced with young people being particularly vulnerable to manipulation by adult profiteers. The mass media, for example, attempt to sell identity scripts which frequently involve stereotyped gender images. Leisure and youth cultures are also seen as having become much more central to an understanding of changing social identities among young people (see Chapter 5) and have implications for processes of individualization and risk.

This is a theme that has been developed by du Bois Reymond (1998a) in relation to a group she refers to as 'trendsetters'. These young people, who are overwhelmingly middle class, are seen as striving to blend contexts of work and play, as trying to achieve congruent identities and as attempting to avoid the situation in which work identities and lifestyles are compartmentalized in traditional ways. For these young people, traditional adulthood, with its associations of conformity, routine and separation of work and life are to be avoided at all costs. Similarly, Japanese researchers describe the experiences of 'freeters' – derived from the terms 'freelance' and 'arbeiter' and meaning 'free worker' – who are regarded (incorrectly) by the media and government as having a preference for part-time or casual work rather than the full-time, stable, employment that characterized a more staid generation (Inui 2005). Here the term 'choice biography' may be seen as an acknowledgment of the interconnectedness of spheres of life that were once thought of as distinct and a recognition that, for the most privileged young people at least, agency plays a prominent role in the establishment of identity.

On a more theoretical level, some of the implications of social change for young people's identities have been explored by Rattansi and Phoenix (1997).

Their position is based, first, on an acknowledgement that one of the consequences of the changes associated with late modernity is the disembedding of identities – a process that we would argue creates the preconditions for an epistemological fallacy through the decoupling of subjectivity from its traditional grounding in economic life. Second, to understand late modernity we have to appreciate that there are multiple sites of identity construction and that they may contradict as well as overlap. The de-centring of identities in late modernity mean that young people, especially those from less advantaged socio-economic positions, must find ways of managing or rationalizing fragmented and incongruent identities. In this context, youth is about learning to live with uncertainty.

Housing and domestic transitions

The protraction of the school to work transition, together with legislative changes affecting patterns of dependency, have had an impact on young people's ability to make the housing and domestic transitions which are central to the attainment of adult status. As Coles (1995) notes, the three main transitions made by young people are closely inter-related and delays in the completion of one transition can have 'knock-on' effects on other transitions. Since the early 1980s, along with changes in school to work transitions, there have been important changes in the ways in which young people make their transitions from the parental home to independent living and the stage at which they establish their own families. Jones (1995) has argued that during the 1950s and 1960s domestic and housing transitions tended to occur very soon after completion of the school to work transition. This was particularly true for young people from working class families who tended to leave the parental home, marry and have children relatively soon after entering the full-time labour market. From the 1970s, the spacing of the three transitions tended to widen, returning to a form which was common during the eighteenth and nineteenth centuries (Springhall 1986; Jones 1995; Heath and Cleaver 2003).

It is clear that there have been significant changes in housing and domestic transitions in recent years with many experiencing a wide variety of living arrangements: alone, with friends, with partners, with fellow students or workers, with relatives, homeless or in sheltered accommodation. There is no set sequence that can be said to describe normal movements between different forms of living and transitions can appear disorganized or even chaotic. Indeed, for some commentators, these changes have been interpreted as reflecting a disordered transition (Rindfuss *et al.* 1987), although others regard changes in residence as indicative of role transformation (such as that involved in completing a course of education) rather than of a failed transition (DaVanzo and Goldscheider 1990) and of processes of adaptation to the realities of modern economic life. However the trends are interpreted, they represent more than a simple extension of dependency. Young people, especially those from more affluent families, have actively negotiated new living arrangements that fit with the complexity of their lives. The result has been a change in the power structures, with the modern family containing young adults having been 'turned from an authority-orientated family to a negotiating one' (du Bois Reymond 1998b: 59).

Leaving home

Since the 1980s there have been changes in the stage at which young people tend to leave the family home. These changes have had a differential effect on members of different social classes and, in general, have led to an increase in the numbers of young people who live with their parents. Members of the working classes in particular have tended to remain in the parental home for longer partly due to delays in marriage and cohabitation which are linked to the time taken to establish the stable employment careers that provide the means for independent living. While changes in employment conditions have made it increasingly difficult for young people from working class families to leave home at an early stage, another route to independent living has been opened up as a result of the growth of mass higher education and the opportunities that this affords, in some countries, for moving away.

In any discussion about young people's housing transitions, it is important to make the distinction between 'living away' and 'leaving home' (Jones 1987; Young 1987). A substantial number of those who move away from home subsequently return (Kerckhoff and McRae 1992; Iacovou 2001). Many students return to the family home after their college courses, and it is common for them to spend the long vacation in the family home. In the USA, more than four in ten (46 per cent) young people who moved away to attend college subsequently returned home (Mulder and Clark 2002). On the other hand, while young people from working class families tend to leave home at an older age, their departure is more likely to be permanent (Young 1984; Goldscheider and DaVanzo 1986; Jones 1987). In this context it is important to stress that although in some countries young people are tending to 'live away' at a younger age than previously, it has become more common for them to return to the family home, especially within a year or two of first leaving (Young 1989; White 1994).

There are very significant differences between countries in the reasons why young people leave the family home. In southern European countries like Portugal, Spain and Italy, more than two-thirds of males leave home to move in with a partner (nearly nine in ten in the case of Portugal), the others tend to leave unattached with virtually none leaving for educational purposes. In northern European countries such as Denmark and the Netherlands, between four and five in ten males leave to live alone, around three in ten leave with a partner and between one in four and one in five leave for educational purposes. For females, the pattern is broadly similar: in the north and the south slightly fewer leave to set up home as unattached, slightly more leave with a partner and similar numbers leave for educational reasons (Iacovou 2001).

For young people from middle class families, in many countries, patterns of leaving home have been strongly affected by their increased participation in higher education which, for those with the resources, frequently means moving away to study (Kiernan 1986: Jones 1987; Mulder and Clark 2002). To add to the complexity and counter this trend, there has been a greater tendency for students to return home after completing university as ex-students require access to financial support for transitions to graduate employment. In southern Europe in particular, it has been noted that parents are happy to provide extended support to ex-students as they seek graduate careers (sometimes over several years) rather than allow them to work in the non-graduate sector (Furlong and McNeish 2000).

A range of factors impact on the age at which young people first move away from home. Gender has a powerful effect with females tending to leave home sooner than males (Iacavou and Berthoud 2001; Aassve *et al.* 2002; Jones 2004). This is partly because females are more likely to move away to study, but is also affected by their younger average age of marriage and first cohabitation (Young 1984; Jones 1987; Furlong and Cooney 1990; Ferri and Smith 2003). The younger age at which females tend to leave home has also been linked to the different ways in which parents treat daughters and sons: the behaviour of young women may be subject to closer scrutiny (Ward and Spitze; 1992; White 1994) and they may be expected to provide a greater contribution to the household labour (White 1994). Although there has been little work on the domestic and housing transitions of members of ethnic minorities living in Europe, evidence from the USA suggests that due to the significance of extended families, irrespective of marital status, black youths are more likely to live with their parents (Hogan *et al.* 1990; White 1994).

Another factor associated with early departures from the parental home is family affluence and there is evidence of an increase in inter-generational resource transfers among middle class families (White and Wyn 2004). As Ermisch (1997) has argued, where parents are able to subsidize their children financially, early moves tend to be common. Rural youth (especially women) tend to leave at a relatively early stage, as do members of ethnic minorities, those who are highly motivated and those with a large number of siblings (Garasky *et al.* 2001; Garasky 2002). Young people who live with a step-parent, those whose parents are divorced and those whose family life is characterized by a high degree of conflict are also over-represented among early leavers (Bernhardt and Gähler 2001; Bernhardt *et al.* 2005).

According to White (1994), changes in patterns of residence among young people can be explained by economic, political and demographic factors. On an economic level, the availability of jobs and relative wages of young people are of crucial importance. In terms of recent trends, it can be argued that the shift from an industrial economy to one increasingly dominated by service industries (with a corresponding rise in the demand for educated workers on the one hand and increased supply of part-time and insecure jobs on the other) reduces young people's chances of establishing their independence at an early age. On a political level, the changes in entitlements to social security benefits which are evident in several countries can also be seen as having an impact on housing and domestic transitions. Demographic factors, such as patterns of fertility, marriage and divorce also affect patterns of residence. An increase in the average age of marriage, cohabitation and childbearing may lead to delayed housing and family transitions, while the increased tendency for young people to experience the divorce of their parents may provide greater incentives to establish independent forms of residence.

   With young people's ability to leave home being affected by factors such as the supply of jobs, the availability of economic support and prevalent patterns of marriage and cohabitation, there are very strong variations by country. In particular, in southern Europe the lack of state support combined with a strong tradition of family support and, until the mid- to late 1990s, extremely high levels of youth unemployment and a lack of well-paid jobs made it extremely difficult for young people to leave home at an early stage. Indeed, it is still not uncommon for young adults to live with their parents until their early 30s, even when they are married or have a regular partner. In this context, Holdsworth has noted that in Spain, 'early leaving, especially prior to marriage, is not supported by the wider opportunity structures (including the housing market and welfare regimes) nor is it a culturally established pattern' (2000: 219).

   In describing patterns of home leaving across Europe, Iacovou and Berthoud (2001) show that in Italy just 7 per cent of males and 19 per cent of females between the ages of 21 and 25 had either left home or were living with their partner in the family home (Figure 4.1). This contrasts strongly with Denmark (which retains a system of youth benefits) where the majority had left by this stage (73 per cent of males and 90 per cent of females). In most countries, due to a tendency to marry or cohabit earlier than males, females were more likely to have left home by age 25 with gender gaps being particularly wide in Finland, Germany and Greece.

   A crucial factor to examine in any discussion of patterns of leaving home relates to the increased importance of 'intermediary households' (Penhale 1990; Jones 1995; Heath and Cleaver 2003). In many advanced countries, since the 1970s, it has become common for young people to spend time living alone or with peers prior to making a domestic transition to marriage or cohabitation (Harris 1983; Young 1984; Jones 1995; Heath and Cleaver 2003). Indeed Heath and Cleaver (2003) argue that in Europe, Australia and North

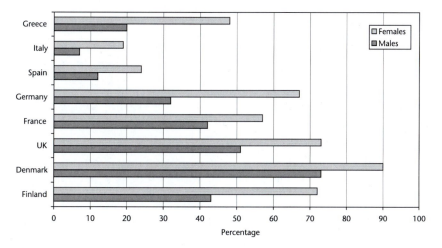

Figure 4.1 21- to 25-year-olds who have left home: selected countries
Source: Iacovou and Berthoud 2001

America most young people will experience some form of communal living arrangement. Experience of living in intermediary households has affected young people from both middle class and working class families, although there are important differences: among the middle classes the transition to intermediary households tends to coincide with entry into higher education and involves living in student accommodation or sharing flats with peers. On the other hand, young people from working class families are more likely to move into hostels, board with relatives or live in accommodation supplied by an employer (those joining the forces, for example, will live in military quarters, while those going into nursing may live in hospital accommodation) (Jones and Wallace 1992; Iacovou 2001).

Young people move away from the family home for a variety of reasons: some leave to study or take up the offer of a job away from home, others leave to marry or to set up home with a partner. Others leave because of an uneasy co-existence with their parents, perhaps as a result of difficult relationships with parents or step-parents or due to domestic violence or abuse. Some are asked to leave or are 'kicked out', and those leaving local authority care are required to set up independent households at a relatively young age (Coles 1995). With employment prospects being greater in some areas than others, young people may also leave home for work-related reasons.

Although the proportion of young people leaving home due to various 'problems' is small, Jones (1995) has argued that the numbers leaving home due to family problems is increasing. In particular, the increase in divorce, 'reconstituted families' and single parent families affects the stage at which young people make housing transitions and the level of support which they can expect. Those growing up in reconstituted and single parent families tend to leave home earlier than those living with both natural parents (Kiernan 1992; Jones 1995). However, the association between reconstituted families (which are often regarded as less cohesive than natural families) and an early departure of young people from the family home tends to be stronger for females than males and more significant among whites and Asians than among African Carribeans (Goldscheider and Goldscheider 1993). It has become more common for children to experience changes in family circumstances, spending time living as part of a single parent family or with step-parents: in the UK between 1981 and 2002 the number of children in lone parent families doubled so that one in five dependent children reside with just one parent (ONS 2003). Within deprived areas the rise has been more dramatic: in the London Borough of Lambeth, for example, one in three young people live with a lone parent (ONS 2003).

Although many children spend their entire childhoods in stable single-parent families, young people who have experienced the breakdown of their parents' marriages tend to make school to work transitions at an earlier stage. They also tend to have lower academic qualifications and an increased risk of unemployment (Wadsworth and Maclean 1986; Kiernan 1992; Jones 2000); this has implications for domestic and housing transitions. Jones (1995) reports that 40 per cent of males and 23 per cent of females who had previously lived with a step-parent gave 'family problems' as their main reason for leaving home. Indeed, there is evidence to suggest that there has been an increase in the numbers of young people who become homeless because their families are unable or unwilling to support them (Bynner *et al.* 2004). While current policies often require families to assume extended financial support, increasingly young people come from family situations where such support is unlikely to be forthcoming. These young people may be under pressure to make rapid housing transitions, and they do so under increasingly risky circumstances. Indeed, young people who leave home for work related reasons, to make domestic transitions or because of difficulties at home have tended to report economic problems such as difficulties managing money or finding accommodation. Ainley suggests that moving away from home 'put virtually all young movers at an immediate material disadvantage' (1991: 108). Recent legislative trends are likely to have exacerbated these problems.

Attention has also been drawn to the relationship between accelerated housing careers and homelessness (Coles 1995; Fitzpatrick 2000). In particular, it is argued that those who spend time in care often find it difficult to successfully accomplish a housing transition and as a consequence they frequently become homeless and are over-represented among the prison population. Although relatively few young people spend time in care, in the UK around one in four of the homeless population and nearly four out of ten prisoners have spent time in local authority care (Anderson *et al.* 1993; Coles 1995). Members of ethnic minorities are over-represented among the homeless, as are those with mental health problems (Bynner *et al.* 2004). Similarly, in the USA, homeless young people have often led chaotic lives, many have been in care and a substantial minority have been abused physically or sexually (Polman and Vitone 2004).

There are few reliable statistics on changing patterns of homelessness among young people because those who are single tend not to register with local authorities for re-housing. The official trend in homelessness certainly underestimates the proportion of young people without a home, yet in the UK Pleace and Fitzpatrick (2004) estimate that a fifth of 16- to 24-year-olds will experience at least one period of homelessness. In the USA there is also evidence that the number of homeless people is increasing in the majority of cities, as is the average duration of a period of homelessness (United States Conference of Mayors 2005). There is evidence of a similar trend in Australia (Mackenzie and Chamberlain 2003).

Cohabitation, marriage and parenthood

Although marriage and parenthood has traditionally been regarded as the 'definitive step to adulthood' (Kiernan 1986: 11), in recent years there has been a greater separation of housing and domestic transitions. At the same time Ainley (1991) argues that domestic transitions remain a particularly significant step in the attainment of full adult status due to an underlying shift in responsibilities: the young adult is no longer the responsibility of their parents and comes to assume responsibility for others. It has also been suggested that the idea of a clear shift from dependence to independence is an oversimplification. A pattern of reciprocity is often established before young adults leave home and is continued after the marriage (Millward 1998; White and Wyn 2004).

During the 1960s and 1970s, marriage was often the principal reason for leaving home and in many working class communities it was 'almost unheard of for young people to leave home prior to marriage' (Leonard 1980: 61). However, in recent years, there has been a rise in cohabitation in many countries, the age of marriage has increased in most and the link between leaving the parental home and marriage, as well as between parenthood and marriage, has weakened (Jones 2000; Heath and Cleaver 2003).

In fact there is evidence of more people in stable relationships choosing to live apart: sometimes referred to as living apart together, 'LATs', or by the French as *cohabitation intermittente* (Caradec 1996; Trost 1999; Haskey 2005). In the UK, Haskey (2005) argues that around three in ten 16- to 59-year-olds (about 4 million people) can be described as LATs, with about half of these being in the 16 to 24 age group. Moreover, around six in ten LAT couples say that they are happy to maintain these arrangements permanently (Ermisch 2000; Heath and Cleaver 2003).

Another key change over the last few decades has been the increase in cohabitation (Heath and Cleaver 2003), especially in northern Europe, North America and Australia. Heath and Cleaver show that in the UK, rates of cohabitation doubled between 1980 and 2000 so that the majority of young people experience cohabitation during their 20s. In the European Union,[1] 14 per cent of 20- to 24-year-old women and 9 per cent of males cohabit, with figures ranging from 45 per cent of females and 43 per cent of males in Denmark to 1 per cent of females in Greece and 1 per cent of males in Spain and Portugal (Kiernan 1999). In southern Europe, cohabitation is not common and marriage still tends to mark the beginning of a partnership (Wasoff and Morrison 2005).

Cohabitation can be temporary, experimental relationships, or may be the first stage in a long-term relationship leading to marriage or may signal a rejection of marriage as an institution (One plus One 2004). To take the case of Britain (which is fairly typical of the northern European countries), of those living with partners for the first time, around seven in ten will be co-habiting with such relationships largely being experimental and lasting an average of two years (Ermisch and Francesconi 2000; One plus One 2004). But cohabitation (often a second or third cohabitation) is often a prelude to marriage: in the late 1990s around 80 per cent of married women had cohabited with their spouse prior to marriage (Haskey 2001).

Protracted transitions and the increased popularity of cohabitation has resulted in a delay in the age of marriage and has led to a reduction in rates of marriage. In the European Union between 1971 and 2002 the average age of first marriage rose from 26 to 30 for men and from 23 to 28 for females. While females have tended to marry at an earlier age than males, those whose parents have divorced and those who live with step-parents tend to marry early (Kiernan 1992) and class-based differences in the average age of marriage have been observed in a wide range of countries, partly due to the tendency of the middle classes to remain in education for longer periods of time.

Similar differentials exist in respect of childbearing with the longer transitions to work, which are more characteristic of the middle classes, tend-ing to result in delays in family formation. On average, in Europe there is a gap of three to seven years between a female entering their first full-time job and having their first child (Nicoletti and Tanturri 2005), although overall fertility rates have fallen and significant variations still exist between countries. In Italy and Greece, for example, late labour market entry significantly delays family formation while in the UK, Denmark and Finland the impact is rela-tively small (Iacovou and Berthoud 2001), partly due to a greater tendency for childbirth to precede marriage (Wasoff and Morrison 2005).

Across all social classes, the average period of time between marriage and birth of the first child has increased. Among women in Europe, just 5 per cent of 20-year-olds have children, rising to 28 per cent of 25-year-olds (Iacovou and Berthoud 2001). There are strong variations between countries with around one in four 21- to 25-year-olds having children in the UK, Sweden, Greece and Austria, compared to little more than one in ten in Italy, Nether-lands and Spain (Iacovou and Berthoud 2001). As with all-age fertility rates, the numbers of teenage mothers has declined in all advanced societies, although the USA, some Eastern European countries and the UK still have levels of teenage pregnancy that are far higher than counties that are similar in other respects (Selman 2003; ONS 2005) (Figure 4.2). In all countries, those from lower social classes and those without advanced educational qualifica-tions are more likely to have children at an early age (Nicoletti and Tanturri 2005). In the UK, for example, the average age at birth of the first child was

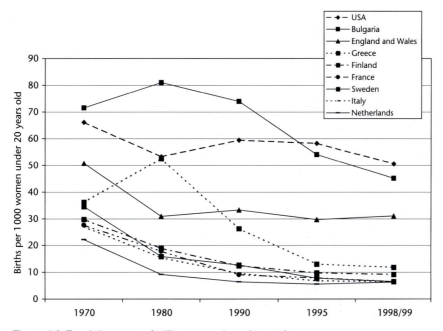

Figure 4.2 Trends in teenage fertility rates: selected countries
Source: Selman 2003

23.7 among those from semi- and unskilled backgrounds, compared to 27.9 among those from professional and managerial families (ONS 2005). Rates of teenage pregnancy were ten times higher in the lowest social class as compared to the highest (Social Exclusion Unit 1999).

Single parenthood, young mothers and welfare dependency

In the European Union, births outside marriage tripled between 1980 and 2004 with young women from working class families being twice as likely to have a child outside marriage as those from the middle classes (Babb and Bethare 1995; ONS 2006). However, many 'illegitimate' children are born to parents in stable relationships and the birth is jointly registered by two parents living at the one address who frequently marry soon after the birth of their babies (Hess 1995; One plus One 2004).

The increase in the numbers of young women having children outside of marriage has been the focus of media attention and political debate. In the UK one of the reasons for the removal of housing benefits from the under 25 age group was a concern that young people were abusing the benefit system to make transitions from the parental home at an earlier stage than their personal finances permitted. While high levels of youth unemployment between the 1970s and 1990s reduced young people's access to the independent resources which would permit early housing and domestic transitions, the UK government felt that young people were able to continue to make these transitions due to the availability of social security and housing benefits.

Media attention was also focused on teenage mothers who were seen using early motherhood as a strategy to 'jump the queue' for local authority housing and benefits. In response, the UK government imposed further benefit restrictions. Similar political responses are to be found in a range of other countries. In the USA, for example, Clinton stopped benefit payments to mothers under the age of 18 who were not living with their parents or in an approved, adult-supervized, setting.

National differences in teenage pregnancy rates are often explained by reference to sex education and access to contraception, as well as the availability of opportunities for employment or educational advancement (SEU 1999; Chase *et al.* 2003; Bernstein 2004). Here Chase and colleagues (2003) argue that countries with relatively low rates of teenage pregnancy typically provide a strong programme of sex and relationship education in schools and ensure access to contraception and sexual health services. In the UK, for example, 66 per cent of 16- to 19-year-olds used contraception the first time they had penetrative sex as compared to 85 per cent of young people in the Netherlands (Chase *et al.* 2003). On top of this, countries with low rates of teenage pregnancy tend to have 'good quality family and societal communication about sex and a positive attitude towards young people's sexuality' (2003: 2). Such positive attitudes are notable by their absence in the USA where funding has increasingly been diverted into abstinence programmes rather than contraception and sexual health programmes (Singh *et al.* 2001).

There is evidence of a strong association between high levels of unemployment and a high teenage birth rate (Ainley 1991; Tomal 1999;

Kirkby *et al.* 2001), with young people who are unemployed being more likely to have children than those in full-time jobs or education (Coffield *et al.* 1986; Harris 1990; Tomal 1999; Kirkby *et al.* 2001). This tendency has been explained in terms of the desire for status and independence among a group of young people who have been denied access to other sources of fulfilment in the form of opportunities for jobs or education (Coffield *et al.* 1986; Wallace 1987; Banks and Ullah 1988). In other words, parenthood can provide a source of identity for young people who are marginalized in other life contexts. It has also been argued that young women from poor neighbourhoods tend not to see early motherhood in negative terms and are more likely than their middle class peers to disapprove of abortion (MacDonald and Marsh 2005).

Rather than being seen as a consequence of rapid labour market change and of a decline in demand for unskilled young workers, an increase in births outside of marriage and subsequent labour market withdrawal has sometimes been presented as indicative of a culture of welfare dependency and weak labour market commitment (Murray 1990). In this context, the increase in the numbers of single mothers existing on welfare benefits has also been linked to concerns that children are being socialized into a dependency culture. As Bagguley and Mann argue,

> the focus on single mothers emphasizes their marital status and long-term dependence on public welfare. It is then assumed that they inculcate their offspring with the idea that welfare dependency carries no stigma or material disadvantage. From this it is claimed that the next generation are less willing or able to escape.
>
> (1992: 122)

Bagguley and Mann argue that with many children from welfare dependent homes managing to make successful labour market transitions, the empirical evidence does not lend support to the idea that there is a self-perpetuating underclass characterized by a cultural commitment to continued welfare dependency. Indeed, the increase in young single parents who are dependent on welfare benefits is more likely to reflect the economic difficulties faced by young mothers in a period characterized by low youth wages and a declining demand for unskilled youth labour. Craine argues that young single parenthood cannot be explained by irresponsibility, but is 'the result of a fatalistic ethos generated within a context of economic and social insecurity' (1997: 143). Indeed, as Tomal puts it, 'teen birth rates are not about abstinence or contraception . . . [they] are about the underlying socioeconomic fabric of the teenager's environment and act as both a symptom and cause of unfavorable socioeconomic statistics' (1999: 5). In this context it is hard to avoid the conclusion that we can best learn about why young women from less advantaged families tend to have children early by understanding why middle class young women don't – a difference that relates to resources and opportunities.

Conclusion

In some respects, it can be argued that recent changes in domestic and housing transitions reflect an increase in the range of possibilities open to young people. The extension and desequencing of transitions has been seen by some as helping to create the space in which young people can experiment with different forms of living and establish a self identity in a context where they are free from some of the constraints which shaped the experiences of the previous generation. The evidence for this is powerful and some young people clearly relish the lack of responsibilities and the freedom of young adulthood. Others find themselves unable to establish the adult lifestyles they long for and are frustrated by a lack of resources which would help them establish independent lives. Indeed, we have suggested that in late modernity many young people face difficulties in constructing stable social identities and that these problems will be reflected in different dimensions of their lives. These differences will be explored in subsequent chapters.

Two to three decades ago, young people from working class families tended to leave home in order to establish a marital household and parental responsibilities were assumed at a relatively early age. Housing and domestic transitions were frequently made simultaneously and residence with peers, co-habitation and independent living were patterns largely reserved for middle class youth. With the protraction of domestic and housing transitions and with increasing levels of post-compulsory educational participation, today there are more similarities between the experiences of working class and middle class youths and between young men and women. By the 1990s, outside of the Mediterranean countries, most young people first left home for reasons other than marriage and the desire to establish the basis for independent lifestyles had become particularly significant (Poole 1989).

Yet while these changes can be seen as reflecting a process of individualization through which young people are presented with a greater range of choices, domestic and housing transitions remain highly structured. The timing of transitions and the ease with which they are made are largely determined by the individual's social location and the risks associated with unsuccessful transitions are not distributed in an equal fashion. Indeed, we suggest that recent trends in social policy have resulted in an increased dependence of young people on their families in a period when the family as an institution is undergoing some fundamental changes. The extension of dependency, which has been reinforced by legislation, runs counter to the demands for greater autonomy which come from both young people and their parents (Harris 1990). Many contemporary policies rest on the assumption that families are able and willing to support their offspring up until their mid-20s or later and that young people are willing to submit to the authority of their parents during this period. Clearly family dynamics tend to evolve in ways that ensure greater space and freedoms for young adults and many parents take steps to ensure that resources are made available to their offspring (White and Wyn 2004). Yet many parents simply do not have an excess of resources that makes such transfers possible, and some retain the belief that, as in their day, young people should become independent whilst in their teens. As a consequence, we suggest that many of the most vulnerable young people lack support from family and state and are subject to new risks and uncertainties.

5 Leisure *and* lifestyles

For marginalized working class youth, 'leisure' is shaped by a lack of money, a strong sense of neighbourhood boundaries, and the stigma attached to geographical and class location. . . . Being able to marshal resources leads to very different social experiences and opportunities in the world of leisure, as well as in other spheres of activity. For middle-class youth, the transformed night-time economies of late capitalism present myriad leisure choices.

(White and Wyn 2004: 16–18)

Introduction

During the last few decades, changes in patterns of educational participation, protracted labour market transitions and an extension in the period of dependency have all had implications for the lifestyles which young people adopt and for the ways in which they spend their free time. Although leisure and lifestyles continue to reflect gender and class locations, there is evidence that these divisions have blurred as a consequence of the influence of leisure industries and the common experience of delayed transitions (Roberts and Parsell 1994).[1] Males and females from all social classes tend to have more free time than previously and engage in a greater range of leisure pursuits which, on the surface, appear to display greater similarities than differences. Young people tend to marry and have children at a later age, and this may increase the period of their lives in which they have a relatively high discretionary element to their spending (Stewart 1992). While the expansion of higher education and changes in student support regimes can cause hardship, for the middle classes intergenerational resource transfers can facilitate the maintenance of leisure lifestyles that involve varied and costly pursuits.

The changes that have occurred have resulted in new freedoms as well as constraints. In late modernity, people are faced with a greater range of choices in many different aspects of their lives, yet at the same time they remain subject to a powerful set of constraints and influences. This contradiction is particularly evident in the closely linked spheres of leisure and consumption.[2] Young people are now able to select from a wide range of leisure pursuits and through the development of specific modes of consumption are encouraged to adopt styles which highlight their individuality. At the same time, the media, leisure and consumption industries play a central role in the post-industrial economy and, through the use of advanced marketing strategies, large corporations are able to shape the preferences of consumers (Clarke and Critcher 1985; Klein 2000; Chatterton and Hollands 2003) and exploit cultural trends. Indeed, Clarke and Critcher (1985) argue that rather than being shaped through individual choice or fashion, leisure is a product of the class struggle and tends to be shaped by the dominant class. As Klein (2000) suggests, similarities in young people's fashion and musical preferences illustrate the successful strategies used by multi-national corporations. Patterns of diversification and individualization of style, leisure and consumption, which are often evident can reflect advanced marketing techniques and attempts to promote niche products.

Rojek (1985) has argued that within modern capitalism four trends can be identified: privatization, individuation, commercialization and pacification. Leisure has become increasingly privatized insofar as the widespread ownership of home-based entertainment systems such as satellite and cable television, DVDs, Playstations, home-based internet access and third generation mobile phones have helped transform leisure from a public to a private form of activity. This trend is particularly acute in Japan where there are concerns about young people referred to as 'hikikomori' whose lives are so embedded in privatized leisure that they become virtual hermits, refusing to leave their rooms and connecting with others only by electronic means (Saito 1998; Shiokura 2002). The individuation of leisure is linked to its commercial development as a commodity which helps to define individual lifestyles. The commercialization of leisure is reflected in the dominance of large corporations who organize their highly profitable businesses in ways which shape demand and manipulate patterns of use. The process of pacification highlights the ways in which leisure can be portrayed as a process of social control, providing a mechanism through which social integration can be maintained in a society characterized by an increasing division of labour and diverse life experiences.

It is in the context of these debates about leisure and lifestyles in the age of late modernity that we will assess Beck's claim that people are now constrained to assert their individuality and creativity through modes of consumption and associated lifestyles. In our view, trends in leisure highlight the ways in which the epistemological fallacy of high modernity is sustained. The blurring of class and gender divisions in leisure, which largely arise from processes of commercialization, help create an illusion of individuality and classlessness. Social identities are partly shaped through lived experiences in the related spheres of leisure and consumption and any apparent weakening of class divisions in these fields will therefore be manifest in the ways in which people subjectively locate themselves in the social world. In this respect our views come close to those members of the Frankfurt school, (Horkheimer and Adorno 1972), who suggested that the culture industry can be regarded as a source of ideological manipulation.

We begin this chapter by describing some of the ways in which young people's leisure and lifestyles have changed and later return to examine the extent to which we can regard these changes as representing an individualization of leisure and lifestyle. Through an analysis of changing youth cultures we also look at the influence of peer groups and at the way in which fashions are subject to constraints of the market. We argue that while there are now great similarities in the portfolio of leisure pursuits enjoyed by different groups of young people, significant differences exist in the framing of activities and in patterns of participation. Moreover, despite an outward appearance of diversity and choice young people can increasingly be seen as constrained within a 'neon cage' (Langman 1992) of consumerism which blinds them to the underlying realities which condition their social existence.

Leisure

Young people spend their free time in many different ways. While some spend much of their leisure time in informal pursuits or solitary activities, others regularly participate in a range of organized and group activities. The difference is often one of emphasis: the vast majority spend some time engaged with core activities such as watching television, socializing with friends, shopping, playing computer games and so on, while certain groups place a strong emphasis on particular activities within the broad portfolio. An exclusive focus on the types of activity in which young people are involved can conceal differences and may exaggerate the uniformity of patterns of engagement that are in fact heavily stratified. More affluent young people may join sports clubs with top of the range facilities while others may use public facilities. Some might visit exclusive night clubs while others use clubs that cater for the masses. In other words, we should not assume that common leisure interests lead to socially heterogeneous forms of engagement as access will always be restricted by resources as well as by preferences.

Older studies of young people's leisure activities tended to highlight the strong gender divisions which were often seen as more significant than class or differences associated with 'race' (Roberts *et al.* 1989). It was noted that girls were less leisure-active than boys, were expected to spend more of their 'freetime' helping out in the home and were often required to return home earlier on an evening. Moreover, they tended to have fewer resources to help enrich their leisure time; they received lower wages and less pocket money and had higher 'self-maintenance costs' (Roberts 1983). Gender divisions are still significant, but appear to be weakening – a trend that has often been a source of concern and even outrage rather than a cause for celebration. In the UK, for example, the media has focused on 'ladettes': young women who adopt 'laddish' behaviours such as heavy drinking and violent or yobbish behaviour.

The leisure preferences of young people are affected by local and national cultures and conventions. In northern Europe, climatic conditions lead to an emphasis being placed on indoor pursuits for much of the year while in countries like Australia, South Africa and the southern American states, more activities take place outdoors.

The European Time Use Survey (European Commission 2003a) highlights the ways in which young people use their time and shows reasonably

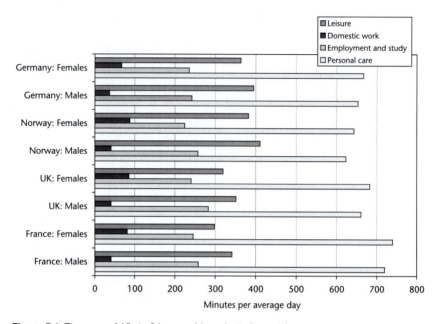

Figure 5.1 Time use of 15- to 24-year-olds: selected countries
Note: Shopping has been classified here as a leisure activity rather than as domestic work.
Source: European Commission 2003a

strong similarities in the time use of 15- to 24-year-olds (Figure 5.1). Personal care, which includes time spent eating and sleeping, accounts for the largest block of time, followed by leisure, employment and study and domestic work. In countries where young people have slightly less leisure time, such as in France, this tends to be a consequence of greater time being spent on personal care rather than being due to more time being spent on work or study. In all European countries males spend less time than females on domestic activities and males tend to have more free time.

Looking specifically at the ways in which leisure time is used, in Europe watching television is by far the most popular way of filling free time among males and females. Indeed, research has shown that in the UK about half of all leisure time is spent watching television (ONS 2005) while in a study of six European countries, the main leisure activities of 12- to 15-year-olds were found to be watching television and listening to music (Brettschneider and Naul 2004). Comparing the leisure activities of 15- to 24-year-olds in Norway and the UK (Figure 5.2), Norwegians spent more time socializing which, in both countries, was more common among young women than young men. The British, especially the males, spent more time watching TV. Females in both countries spent more time reading books than males and also used more of their time to shop. In contrast, males in both countries spent much more time on computer-based activities.

From a policy perspective, governments tend to have clear ideas about those activities that they regard as desirable youthful pursuits and those

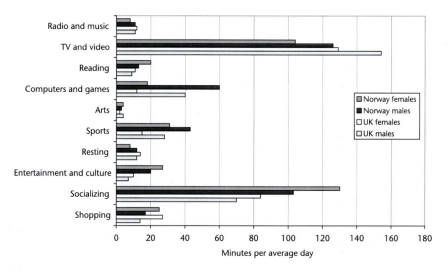

Figure 5.2 Leisure activities of 15- to 24-year-olds: Norway and UK
Source: European Commission 2003a

activities that arouse concerns or suspicions. Inevitably there is often a huge gulf between youth and adult perspectives on 'healthy' leisure and use of free time can become a generational battleground. From its heyday in the inter-war years (and despite associations with totalitarian philosophies), organized, and often competitive, sport has long been central to adult constructions of whole-some, character building, leisure. Yet levels of participation in sports falls with age (European Commission 2004b; Green *et al.* 2005) and, in some countries, appears to be falling over time (MORI 2005). In Brettschneider and Naul's (2004) study of six European countries, recreational sport was the sixth most popular activity while organized sport was ninth. The association with age reflects a preference for commercial and less organized forms of activity among older age groups, but is also explained by coerced participation among younger age groups who may be offered few choices, especially while at school.

Hendry and colleagues (1993) have argued that the non-home-based leisure patterns of both boys and girls move through three age-related stages: 'organized leisure', 'casual leisure' and 'commercial leisure' with boys making transitions from one phase to the next at a later age than girls. Organized leisure includes sports participation which tends to decline from the ages of 13 to 14. Casual leisure includes 'hanging around' with friends, and this tends to be less common after the age of 16. Commercial leisure becomes the pre-dominant form after the age of 16 and includes cinema attendance as well as visiting discos and pubs. Within the commercial leisure stage, young people start to spend greater amounts of time in mixed gender environments.

Young women tend to abandon sports participation earlier than males and as teenagers are less likely to be participants. However, the evidence suggests that the gap between men's and women's sports participation has narrowed (Roberts 1999; Farrell and Shields 2002) and that there has been a growth in the number of females taking part in activities once associated with males such as football and kickboxing. The lower levels of sports participation among young women partly reflects a tendency to dislike collective team activities as well as concerns relating to the compatibility of sports with their perceptions of womanhood (Flintoff and Scraton 2005). Coakley and White (1992) argue that boys regard sporting activity as congruent with the masculine role and gain kudos from engaging in competitive and aggressive leisure activities. On the other hand, girls tend not to connect sports activity with the process of becoming a woman and may avoid participating in leisure activities which may be perceived as threatening to their femininity. Hendry and colleagues (1993) suggest that female cultures tend to emphasize 'best friends' and close relationships with small groupings and that this results in a general discomfort with collective team situations.

In a variety of ways, at all stages, women's leisure participation is constrained by gender relations (Deem 1986; Green *et al.* 1990; Roberts 1999; Flintoff and Scraton 2005). In particular, leisure opportunities are restricted through conventions governing the use of space. There are a number of restrictions regarding the use of space which inhibit women's freedom of access. Restrictions also apply to members of ethnic minorities, may be enforced more strongly in Muslim cultures (Benn 2005) and are reflected in lower levels of sports participation among young people of Asian origin (Sport England 2000). It has been argued, for example, that when girls want to participate in a sport, they often need to involve a friend or relative before it is considered safe or appropriate. Coakley and White (1992) cite conventions which tend to prevent young women entering snooker halls alone, while accepting women who accompany a boyfriend or brother as a spectator. There are fewer conventions which restrict the activities of young males.

A number of writers have highlighted the ways in which women's fear of public spaces, especially after dark, represent an important constraint on their leisure activities outside the home (Deem 1986; Green *et al.* 1990). In this respect, women's perception of particular spaces as risky results in a process of self-surveillance and curtailment of leisure activities (Massey 1994; Seabrook and Green 2004). At the same time, there is evidence of change which is partly driven by leisure industries' eagerness to capitalize on the spending potential of independent and sometimes affluent young women. Bars and public houses, which were once only concerned with their core clientele comprised of male industrial workers, once made little attempt to attract young women. Indeed, during the 1990s there were concerns within the industry that the 'rave generation' did not regard alcohol as central to their leisure lifestyles, but 'regarded beer and spirits as they would ecstasy and cannabis, as another option in the polydrug pharmacopeia, one buzz among many' (Collins 1998: 279). The industry challenge, according to the development director of a major UK brewer, was 'to make alcohol part of that choice' (quoted in Brain 2000).

With a decline in the core client group and with fears that the industry was failing to attract the younger generation, theme bars and 'female friendly' venues were developed and new products were introduced (Chatterton and

Hollands 2003; Measham 2004). Yet the industry's success in attracting more females and younger customers has provoked the concerns of the public health lobby and, on occasions, led to media-driven moral panics about 'binge drinking'.

Changes in the night-time economy have also had an impact on the ways in which access to leisure is restricted by social class. For Chatterton and Hollands changes in the urban landscape have led to a 'displacement of lower-order activities and working-class communities by higher-order activities aimed at cash-rich groups' (2003: 10). Loader also highlighted the ways in which unemployed young people were 'confined to their communities' (1996). In these circumstances less privileged groups, who may be excluded from the new night-time economy due to lack of resources, may be forced to socialize on the streets where they are subject to intense police surveillance and harassment (White and Wyn 2004; MacDonald and Marsh 2005; Shildrick and MacDonald 2006). Restrictions in access to leisure are also evident in the experiences of young people from ethnic minorities who, finding themselves excluded from certain venues, develop a range of collective strategies to maintain night life options (Bóse 2003).

While leisure lifestyles which involve 'excessive' alcohol consumption or the use of illegal drugs draw vocal disapproval from adults (many of whom indulged or continue to indulge in such activities themselves), young people who spend a lot of their time engaged in more privatized pursuits also provoke adult indignation. In particular, computer games which have increased significantly in popularity as games have become more complex, now account for a relatively large proportion of young people's time and income. Games now rival music with some new computer games outselling bestselling albums. In 2002, the computer game 'Grand Theft Auto' sold eight million copies in the UK in the eight weeks leading up to Christmas while by 2005 the all-time best selling game, 'Super Mario', had sold 181 million copies worldwide (Gillett 2005). The USA retains the lead for sales of computer games, with sales forecasts of over 250 million units between 1995 and 2009. While some way behind the USA, Japan and the UK, followed by Germany, France and Italy are also large consumers of computer games.

Concerns about computer games relate to the time being spent on what are sometimes solitary pursuits, fears about 'addiction' and anxiety about the impact of extensive use of games involving violence or illegal activities. In the UK, young people who play computer games spend an average of 11 hours a week behind their consoles with males spending more time playing than females and with those in the younger age groups playing more than those who are older (Figure 5.3). In Japan, it is estimated that the 'hikikomori' (who are defined as those who have spent at least six months largely confined to their rooms playing games) represent up to one in five young males and, in the extreme, there are reports of young adults who have spent more than ten years as hikikamori, being fed and tended to by indulgent parents (Saito 1998; Shiokura 2002).

To an extent, these discussions lend support to Putnam's (2000) thesis about disengagement from social and community life as a consequence of people spending more and more time on solitary pursuits. Using American

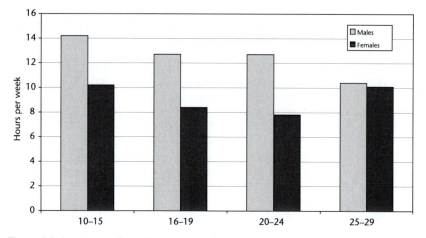

Figure 5.3 Average number of hours per week spent playing computer games: UK
Source: Gillett 2005

statistics, Putnam shows that patterns of civic disengagement are strongest among the youngest generation and much more pronounced when compared with the activities of similar aged people twenty years ago. On the other hand it can be shown that young people spend a relatively high proportion of their time socializing. In the UK the pub remains an important social hub with concerns being expressed about the social drinking patterns of the young. In the UK in 2004, cinema attendance, which tends to be a social rather than a lone activity, stood at its second highest level for over three decades (ONS 2005). Whereas in 1984 less than one in five 15- to 24-year-olds attended the cinema at least once a month, in 2004 more than one in two were regular cinema goers.

While it may be true that there has been a reduction in patterns of civic engagement as patterns of sociability have changed, it is misleading to rely on static indicators (Putnam uses indicators like union membership, church attendance and signing petitions). For young people, email, participation in internet chat rooms, mobile phones and on-line gaming can be regarded as new, sometimes virtual, forms of social engagement that are more suited to the modern age. In the UK, more than one in two regular internet users in the 12 to 19 age range had visited civic or political websites (Livingstone *et al.* 2004). In this context it is interesting to note that parents can regard their child's internet use as a solitary activity through misconceptions about patterns of use. Here Livingstone and colleagues reported that 72 per cent of regular 9- to 15-year-old internet users visited chat rooms while only 30 per cent of their parents thought that they did so. Among the same group, 47 per cent viewed pornography on-line while just 15 per cent of their parents thought that they did so.

Use of mobile phones, for talking, texting, exchanging photos, down-loading ringtones and screensavers represents a popular new form of communication and sociability as well as a lucrative opportunity for the industry to profit from young people's leisure expenditure. In Europe and Japan, mobile phone penetration has almost reached saturation point. In the UK, nine out of ten young people with mobile phones send texts daily, with more than half sending more than five texts a day (Haste 2005a). Phones allow parents to track the movements of teenagers, but also facilitate greater privacy for young people who can make calls without fear of eavesdropping. In Japan, for example, where small apartments are common, young people seem to value the mobile phone as a means of keeping communications private (Oksman and Rautiainen 2002).

While leisure commentators frequently draw attention to the ways in which patterns of engagement are affected by gender and age, with the exception of a few sociologists, class divisions are often neglected or misinterpreted. As Roberts (1999) notes, the fact that young people from all social classes engage in a similar range of activities, does not provide evidence of a 'leisure democracy'. Differences are primarily qualitative and linked to inequalities of income and wealth. Roberts, for example, argues that

> economic capital (in the form of disposable income) continues to lie at the root of the main differences between social class groupings' uses of leisure: differences that are basically and blatantly inequalities rather than alternative ways of life.
>
> (1999: 87)

With leisure representing an important source of informal learning, it has been noted that the most privileged young people have the greatest opportunity to acquire 'leisure capital' through the breadth of their leisure pursuits (Zeijl *et al.* 2001: 395). In Australia, Garton and Pratt (1991) concluded that the recreational leisure activities of school students were at least partly determined by the availability of resources. While those from working class families tend to lack resources to participate in certain activities, they can also be reluctant to participate in activities they associate with the middle classes due to a fear of ridicule. Indeed, Coakley and White suggest that decisions relating to participation were 'integrally tied to the way young people viewed themselves and their connection in the social world' (1992: 32).

The association between social class and income though, is not simply a function of financial resources but also relates to cultural practices. In a classic American study, Cheek and Burch (1976) discovered that once education and occupational prestige had been accounted for, income level did not help explain variations in leisure activities. Lottery winners, for example, will not necessarily emulate upper class leisure pursuits. Recognizing that people often engage in a wide portfolio of leisure pursuits, Chan and Goldthorpe (2005) argue that in the UK there is little evidence of a cultural elite who exclusively consume 'high' culture with individuals from across the social spectrum tending to combine cultural forms in different ways. To describe different forms of consumption, they use the terms 'cultural omnivore' and 'cultural univore' to refer to the extent to which groups have broad or narrow tastes and practices. They conclude that the chances of being an omnivore increase with status.

Although there is still a significant association between social class and young people's leisure lifestyles, it is possible that ongoing changes in young people's experiences will lead to a process of homogenization. Roberts and Parsell, for example, have argued that one of the consequences of extended transitions will be 'the blurring of class-related leisure patterns' as young people from across the social spectrum increasingly share leisure tastes and milieux (1994: 47). Yet while trends such as the increase in post-compulsory education may broaden the leisure horizons of working class youth, other trends (such as the concentration of unemployment, precarious working patterns and low income among the working classes) may counteract the impact of educational changes. As noted in Chapter 3, young people with low educational attainments, (who are predominantly from working class families), are particularly vulnerable to unemployment (O'Higgins 2001) and, in some countries, those who spend time out of work tend to lead narrow and unfulfilling leisure lifestyles. Unemployed youths often lack the resources to participate in commercial leisure activities (at a time when these are becoming much more central to the lives of their peers in employment and education) and tend to spend greater amounts of time hanging around (Hendry and Raymond, 1983; MacDonald and Marsh 2005). Indeed, as Hendry and colleagues suggest, 'a major consequence of unemployment is to deny young people entry to the "package" of work and leisure which is integral to "adult" lifestyle' (1993: 54). Here there is evidence that benefit levels have an impact on levels of sociability (Furlong and Cartmel 2001). In a number of Scandinavian countries, for example, the relative generosity of unemployment levels has resulted in a somewhat weak association between unemployment and social isolation (Heikkinen 2001).

Youth cultures

As well as having an impact on the use of leisure time, changing transitional experiences, together with more aggressive and sophisticated marketing techniques, have also affected young people's lifestyles and the patterns of consumption which tend to symbolize cultural identification. Young people now spend longer periods of time in a state of semi-dependency and in the company of their peers and this has had an impact on the styles they adopt and the groups and products with which they identify. While there was once a close correspondence between lifestyles, fashions and class membership, there is evidence that this relationship has either weakened (Roberts and Parsell 1994; Bennett 2000; Miles 2000) or become more obscure. In the fields of fashion and popular music, the early dominance of working class youth has declined and the middle classes have become increasingly influential leading to a process of convergence (Frith 1978; Roberts and Parsell 1994; Forsyth 1997; Chatterton and Hollands 2003). These changes, which reflect both changes in class-related income differentials stemming from the collapse of the youth labour market and the search for new markets by the leisure industries, are regarded as significant.

The relationship between social class and contemporary youth cultures is complex and under-researched. Given the vast literature on youth cultures, this may seem somewhat surprising but stems from a preponderance of work written within a post-structuralist perspective. Here Greener and Hollands have suggested that post-structuralist approaches to youth cultures often 'focus on particular groups of young people, analysing them according to the tenants of their theory, and then projecting their approach onto youth as a whole social group' (2006: 23). Social class is not a fashionable concept and the idea that the lens of class might cast new light on cultural formations is rarely entertained.

The idea that the relationship between class and youth culture is weak or non-existent contrasts strongly with ideas being advanced by members of the Centre for Contemporary Cultural Studies in the 1970s (Cohen 1972; Hall and Jefferson 1976; Hebdige 1979). Hebdige (1979), for example, argued that through visual style, young people expressed their resistance to authority. Youth cultures were seen as class based and as providing an arena in which young people sought generational solutions to political questions (Hollands 1990). Sidestepping this tradition, contemporary researchers frequently make explicit attempts to 'distance themselves from the class-based analysis of CCCS' (Chatterton and Hollands 2003: 76).

During the 1950s and 1960s, youth cultures were seen as having their roots in the working class (Roberts and Parsell, 1994; Osgerby 1998). The predominate styles of the time, Teddy Boys, Mods and Rockers, were seen as adaptations of working class cultures and middle class youth were largely excluded. Working class youth, for example, were responsible for the growing popularity of rock and roll in the 1950s. In this context, Murdock and McCron (1976) argued that there was a strong connection between musical tastes and class. During the 1960s the situation began to change: middle class youths, who once had little involvement in youth cultures (which were effectively working class sub-cultures), started to develop their own styles revolving around 'progressive rock' music and radical politics. By the late 1960s, musical tastes and youth styles had begun to cross class boundaries. Douvan and Adelson (1966) argued that popular music had been responsible for a homogenization of youth cultures in America, while in Britain the popularity of the Beatles and the 1960s British pop scene was also seen as helping to dilute the significance of class divisions among young people (Murdock and McCron 1976).

From this stage onwards, the association between class and youth styles started to weaken: changes which were resented by Skinheads who attempted to re-establish a traditional working class youth culture in a period characterized by a decline in working class communities and manual employment. Despite resistance by some groups, by the 1990s, Roberts and Parsell were arguing that 'virtually all leisure activities and types of sociability linked rather than separated young people in different class locations' (1994: 33).

The blurring of the boundaries between classes in the sphere of leisure has been interpreted in a variety of ways. Some commentators, including Roberts and ourselves, take the view that the greater obscurity of class cannot be interpreted as a weakening of the objective relationships of class which continue to be reflected in inequalities of access to leisure and in (sometimes subtle) cultural differences in the areas of fashion and musical taste. At the other extreme, post-modernists like Bennett (1999; 2000) regard musical preferences and stylistic taste as 'fluid' rather than being linked to social class.

rowing Maffesoli's (1996) concept of tribe, and substituting it for the term sub-culture, which is seen as retaining out-dated connotations of class, Bennett argues that

> tribal identities serve to illustrate the temporal nature of collective identities in modern consumer society as individuals continually move between different sites of collective expression and 'reconstruct' themselves accordingly.

> (1999: 606)

Tribes, or, as Bennett prefers, 'neo-tribes', are seen as 'temporal gatherings characterized by fluid boundaries and floating memberships' (1999: 600).

The post-modern position applied by Bennett is rejected by many youth researchers who feel the need to highlight the link between social class and leisure lifestyles (Hodkinson 2002; Blackman 2005). The term sub-culture is frequently used as a way of drawing attention to the association between class cultures and their expression by younger class members in their leisure activities and in fashion and musical taste. Post-modernists signal their rejection of the link between class and lifestyles by the use of the somewhat clumsy and confusing term 'post-subculture'.

Since the emergence of distinct youth sub-cultures during the 1950s, young people's lifestyles have frequently been portrayed as threatening and as posing a 'challenge to the symbolic order which guarantees their subordination' (Hebdige 1988: 18). Groups as diverse as Teddy Boys, Mods, Rockers, Hippies, Rastas, Punks, Skinheads and Rappers have all been used by the press to generate 'moral panics' over youth cultures and their threat to 'civilized' society. Widdicombe and Woffitt see Teddy Boys as particularly significant as reactions to them 'set the scene for public, media and academic concern with subsequent youth cultures' (1995: 8). In the 1960s, Mods and Rockers were portrayed as violent hooligans, while left wing and anarchist philosophies of hippies and student activists were seen as representing a more direct threat to the political order. The latest threats to the symbolic order include the rave scene, with its links to drug culture, and 'gangsta' rap with its associations with violence and gun culture.

The emergence of youth cultures in the post-war period and their development up to the present day can be linked to economic changes and to interventions by the leisure industries in an attempt to capture the spending power of an increasingly important consumer group: developments which are closely linked to the relative affluence of youth. From the mid-1950s, in the affluent post-war years, teenagers started to be regarded as forming a specific market niche with distinctive purchasing styles and patterns of consumption (Abrams 1961; Davis, 1990) and became the prime focus of the music and fashion industries. Davis (1990) argued that by the late 1950s the average teenage earnings had increased by more than 50 per cent in real terms compared to the pre-war levels. The post-war boom meant that young workers had relatively high wages compared to their pre-war counterparts and in real terms their contribution to the household economy fell (Stewart 1992). Young people's spending tended to be concentrated in 'non-essential' sectors and this made them a target for the growing leisure industry (Abrams 1961) and led to the formation of a specialized youth market, supplying goods and services ranging from fashion and entertainment to food and drink.

In a variety of ways, changing styles and preferences have been manipulated by the marketing strategies of an industry that targets the spending power of contemporary youth and attempts to identify trends in what it regards as a fast-moving market place. Here Ferchoff (1990) has argued that in Germany youth cultures and styles are not so much related to specific class cultures, but should be regarded as commercialized and incorporated forms with cultural styles being packaged and marketed to a wider section of the young population. 'Acid House', for example, began as a small sub-culture but elements were rapidly absorbed by mainstream youth culture. Similarly, Punk originated as the antithesis of commercial youth fashion, but the style was eventually marketed to a wider population. While some young consumers succumb to the marketing strategies of the leisure industries, others offer some resistance – although resistance can provide an opportunity to develop and exploit a niche market. Among a group of young adults in Birmingham, for example, there were some who liked to avoid chain or brewery owned pubs, preferring to seek out independent pubs which had character and authenticity (Holt and Griffin 2005). As one young man put it,

> y'know when you go into the Bank's pub, an Ansells pub, a Firkin pub, y'know or an O'Neills, you know what it's going to be like because they *control* the atmosphere in there so precisely, basically it kills it.
>
> (Holt and Griffin 2005: 261)

In late modernity, the visual styles adopted by young people through the consumption of clothing are regarded as having become increasingly central to the establishment of identity and to peer relations (Miles 1996). While traditional sources of social differentiation based on social class and communities are thought to have weakened, young people are seen as attempting to find self-fulfilment and ways of identifying with other young people through their consumption of goods, especially fashion (Willis 1990; Miles 1995; Phoenix and Tizard 1996; Holt and Griffin 2005; Croghan *et al.* 2006). In this context, Kellner argues that whereas identity was previously shaped in occupational settings, in late modernity 'identity revolves around leisure, centred on looks, images and consumption' (1992: 153). Indeed, for Beck (1992) individual consumer choices and styles are something which have been created through marketing strategies and the media. In turn, 'consumer styles and artefacts come to be perceived as an integral part of [young people's] identity' (Jones and Wallace 1992: 119).

For Miles (1995; 1996), patterns of youth consumption are seen as central to the social construction of identity and he argues that it is necessary to focus on the meanings young people attach to the goods they purchase and the ways in which they communicate and establish shared values through tastes in fashion. With changes in the youth labour market, young people have increasing turned to the market place to purchase 'props' for their identity which can make them more confident in their relationships with their peers. In late modernity, patterns of consumption and leisure lifestyles have also been regarded as central to the establishment of masculine and feminine identities (Hollands 1995). Yet youth styles can often be seen as highlighting similarity rather than difference: 'street cred' comes from conforming to dominant fashions rather than being an expression of individuality. In this context, Croghan and colleagues (2006) highlight the contradiction between conformity and individuality and argue young people must simultaneously establish themselves as members of specific groups while at the same time demonstrating that they have a certain style that will allow them to stand apart from the mass.

These themes of confidence and conformity also come across strongly in the work of Miles (1995), although class-based divisions should not be over-looked. In one of the few pieces of research to analyze the relationship between consumption and class, Phoenix and Tizard (1996) provided an important insight on the ways in which young Londoners constructed class through consumption. Croghan and colleagues (2006) also note that there are strong links between money, style and social worth.

For Phoenix and Tizard (1996), the consumption of fashion and other lifestyle indicators are used to give signals to others about social position and therefore have a powerful 'symbolic significance'. While certain fashions may transcend class, if a style becomes too closely associated with lower social classes, it becomes devalued and even subject to ridicule by members of other classes. The Burberry brand, for example, was widely perceived as an upper class designer label until it was adopted by young people from the lower social classes. Known in England as 'Chavs', this lower working class sub-culture is distinguished by gaudy gold jewellery ('bling'), white trainers and tracksuits and Burberry baseball caps and other items of clothing made from the distinctive Burberry tartan (often illegal copies). Female members are further distinguished by fake tan and often wear their hair pulled back in a very tight bun or ponytail (sometimes referred to as a council house facelift).

The UK Chav phenomenon has clear links to social class and provokes a level of snobbery that would not usually be regarded as acceptable. A form of dress is linked here to delinquency, low intellect, promiscuity and teenage pregnancy. In the popular website *www.chavscum.co.uk*, people are encouraged to download pictures of Chavs and the 'Chavesque' phenomenon while visitors leave sets of derogatory comments. Holt and Griffin (2005) refer to this process of deriving class position from consumption-based signifiers as 'Othering' and argue that it is a process through which 'dominant group members distain and exclude less powerful groups in specific social, historical, and political contexts in order to support their own identities'.

> Othering enables the middle classes to focus on aspects of their identities which they wish to uphold as defining their group's characteristics (e.g. middle-class taste, intelligence and refinement), while denying these characteristics to the working-class Other.
>
> (Holt and Griffin 2005: 248)

For young people growing up in the contemporary world, especially those excluded from full-time paid employment, their relationship to the means of consumption is sometimes more significant than traditional class differences in explaining cultural identification. Those who have access to the necessary resources are able to participate in youth cultures which cross-cut class boundaries and can enjoy varied and fulfilling leisure lifestyles. At the same time, it is important to recognize that the obscurity of class boundaries and the illusion of choice masks the powerful commercial interests which shape both lifestyles and identity. Indeed, Côté and Allahar argue that young people have been manipulated by commercial concerns and sold identities which are 'illusory and fleeting': processes which have led to 'an epidemic of socially produced identity crises in advanced industrial societies' (1996: xvii). The centrality of consumption in shaping the identities of young people has also been interpreted by Seabrook as 'a subtle and less readily discernible bondage' for the working classes. Young people are seen as 'trapped, functionless and without purpose', locked into an acquisitive culture of yearning for material possessions. The 'primary determinant' in their lives being a 'lop-sided insistence on buying, getting, having' representing 'an even greater subjection than has been known before' (Seabrook 1983: 8–11).

Although there is evidence that class has weakened as a predictor of youth styles and social identities, there are still important differences in access to lifestyles which can only be explained on a material level. While some young people have access to resources which will allow them to participate fully in the predominant patterns of youth consumption, others find themselves marginalized and excluded. In addition to financial exclusion, the unemployed may become culturally excluded as they lack the means to sustain 'appropriate' cultural identities. Jones and Wallace (1992), for example, argue that even those on low incomes are under pressure to purchase clothes which emphasize a particular style, while those who are excluded from the process of consumption are portrayed as 'weak-willed and unable to exploit their freedom' (Tomlinson 1990: 13). Difficulties in securing legitimate access to culturally valued fashion accessories may lead young people to seek alternative, (illegal), means of satisfying their desires (see Chapter 7).

Conclusion

With the extension of youth as a stage in the life cycle and with a growing range of possible activities in which young people can engage, the lives of the younger generation in Britain have changed significantly. Of the changes that have taken place, the one which perhaps casts most light on the characteristics of life in high modernity concerns the apparent weakening of social class as a predictor of leisure and lifestyles among young people. Few young people now make rapid transitions from school to full-time employment, and differences in the spending power of those following educational routes and those leaving school at an early stage to enter training have become narrower. Although gender differences remain powerful, there is evidence that they have weakened with the narrowest gender differences being observed in those following the increasingly popular educational routes.

While youth cultures frequently cross-cut traditional class divisions and with patterns of leisure having become less differentiated, it is apparent that some young people have been marginalized and are being excluded from various forms of commercially organized leisure. Indeed, the most significant differences in leisure and lifestyles become apparent when we look at the situation faced by the unemployed and by those located on peripheral housing estates. Those without jobs are often denied access to the rich leisure lifestyles enjoyed by the majority of today's youth. Moreover, in settings which have become increasingly commercialized, the unemployed are excluded from the consumer culture which is central to the shaping of young people's identity in the modern world. Exclusion from consumer cultures can reduce young people's confidence and prevent their acceptance within youth cultures that cross-cut class divisions.

These changes in young people's leisure and lifestyles highlight the implications of the process of individualization identified by Beck (1992). Young people are often able to choose between a wide range of activities and construct their identities in an arena where the impact of traditional social divisions appears weak. Yet the obscurity of class in these crucial life contexts has powerful implications for social life in general. Indeed, the lived and mediated experiences of young people in the fields of leisure and consumption is an important mechanism via which the epistemological fallacy of late modernity is maintained and reproduced.

6 Health risks *in* late modernity

One of the human prices paid for the current economic condition is the widespread loss of confidence in the future felt by working class youth. ... drug dependency, mental illness, even suicide; these are all symptoms of the changes experienced by youth.

(Cashmore 1984: vii)

Introduction

The protraction of the school to work transition, changes in domestic and housing transitions, as well as the commercialization of leisure and lifestyles which have been described in previous chapters, have all led to new forms of risk and vulnerability. In this chapter we highlight some of the main health risks faced by young people growing up in modern societies and examine the extent to which the distribution of these risks reflects what Beck would regard as 'traditional' inequalities. While many of the health risks encountered by young people are still differentially distributed along the lines of class and gender, we suggest that processes of individualization, coupled with the stress which develops out of uncertain transitional outcomes, have implications for the health of young people. In particular, it is argued that the protraction and de-sequencing of youth transitions have had a negative impact on young people's mental health. In this respect, Beck and Giddens are correct to suggest that reflexive individualization, together with the need to establish adult identities and sustain coherent narratives in a rapidly changing social world, can lead to new risks.

Youth has traditionally been portrayed as a period of exploration and experimentation and youth styles sometimes involve risks which can adversely affect the health of young people and even lead to premature death. While some of the physical risks associated with youthful activities may not have changed much over the last twenty or thirty years, we suggest that the changing transitional experiences of young people have led to a generalized increase in stress which is reflected in a rise in suicide, attempted suicide (parasuicide), and eating disorders such as anorexia and bulimia. In addition, there are many health risks faced by young people which are related to their everyday experiences: smoking, social drinking and sexual discovery, as well as new activities such as driving, for example, are central experiences in the lives of young people which can have harmful consequences. In this chapter we attempt to put some of these risks into perspective and show the ways in which the vulnerability of youth may have changed and the extent to which these risks accrue to particular social groups.

Health inequalities in youth

Youth and early adulthood are frequently portrayed as periods in which young people reach a peak in terms of general health and physical fitness. Compared to earlier and later stages in the life cycle, few young people suffer from acute or life threatening conditions. The risks posed by congenital and infectious diseases during childhood (such as respiratory conditions) are reduced, while degenerative diseases (such as heart conditions and cancer) tend to pose minimal threats (Hurrelmann 1990; Kutcher 1994). In the late teenage years, injuries and poisoning are the main causes of death in all developed regions with road accidents accounting for the largest proportion of deaths from injuries (Woodroffe *et al.* 1993; Blum and Nelson-Mmari 2004). Suicide and self-inflicted injuries cause the second highest number of deaths among 15- to 29-year-olds, while homicide represents the third highest cause (Blum and Nelson-Mmari 2004). As Hurrelmann (1990) argues, it is misleading to portray adolescence as a period characterized by an absence of health risks: accidental death, suicide and violent crime are central to an understanding of health risks in adolescence, together with sexual disease, mental disorders, the consequences of early pregnancy and drug abuse. Moreover, many aspects of young people's lifestyles and behaviours have longer-term consequences for their health, such as smoking, poor diet, alcohol abuse and lack of exercise.

The myth of a healthy adolescence is reflected in the lack of research specifically addressing the epidemiology of youth. Indeed, some of the most comprehensive and influential studies of health, such as the UK Black Report (Townsend and Davidson 1982), have used such wide age bands that youth has been rendered invisible (West 1988, 1997). It is clear, however, that whilst in childhood girls are healthier than boys, in adolescence this pattern is reversed and females are more likely than males to suffer from chronic (but not life threatening) illnesses and psychological disturbances (Sweeting 1995). However, while females are more likely to become ill during adolescence, males are more likely to die (Sweeting 1995).

One of the implications of the lack of sociological research into the health of young people has been a tendency to assume that factors which are strongly associated with the distribution of health risks in childhood and adulthood (such as social class) have an equally powerful affect in youth. In fact one of the few sociologists who has focused specifically on the health of young people, Patrick West, has challenged this view.

Rather than representing a continuity of patterns evident among younger and older age groups, the 'West hypothesis' maintains that early youth is a period of relative equality (West 1988, 1997). Drawing on UK national statistics such as the Census, the General Household Surveys as well as the longitudinal 'West of Scotland Twenty-07 Study', West has analyzed the distribution of a number of illnesses and symptoms among young people from different social backgrounds. The conclusion he draws is that although there is a significant correlation between social class and a range of measures of ill-health in childhood and adulthood, in the UK early youth is a period of relative equity. After reviewing evidence relating to the social distribution of seven aspects of health (mortality, chronic illness, self-related health, symptoms of acute illness, accidents and injuries, mental health and specific conditions[1]) West argues that severe chronic illness (which is class differentiated from infancy) is the only dimension on which social class can be seen as significantly related to health.

West can be criticized on the grounds that while health inequalities in early adolescence appear to be absent, physical variations and differences in health-related behaviours which have implications for health in later life can still be identified among this age group (Bennett and Williams 1994). Macintyre (1988), for example, has argued that the well established correlation between social class and height reflects underlying variations in standards of nutrition and health status which will be reflected in the distribution of degenerative diseases in adult life. It can also be argued that important sources of health variation stem from occupational experiences in adult life which will serve to reinforce class and gender differences in later life. Young people continue to make in-roads to an occupational world characterized by marked differences in health risks, although susceptibility to such risks may not be immediately apparent.

A significant challenge to West has also been made by Torsheim and colleagues (2004) in a study of self-rated health of adolescents in 22 European and North American countries. Torsheim and colleagues reject the idea of a process of 'equalisation' in youth, while accepting that there is some evidence to suggest a 'reduction in inequalities' (2004: 9). Noting evidence showing a link between material deprivation and self-reported poor health in all of the countries they studied (including the relatively wealthy and egalitarian Nordic countries) they suggested that the equalization thesis may be linked to inadequate methodologies that rest on young people's (poor) knowledge of their parents' occupations which is then used as a basis for allocation to social classes. 'In studies that have used *parental* reports of occupations, education or income, relatively robust social inequalities in adolescents have been reported' (2004:2, original emphasis). Using multilevel logistic regression, Torsheim and colleagues showed that the most deprived young people were three times more likely than the least deprived to assess their health as poor.

Aside from noting that females are more likely than males to suffer ill-health in adolescence and that a pronounced class differential in the health of young people appears to be relatively weak, it is not within the scope of this chapter to engage in a detailed discussion of the epidemiology of youth. Indeed, as a consequence of the invisibility of youth in the eyes of many medical researchers, there is a lack of trend data which can be drawn on to comment on changes in the distribution of health risks. In the remainder of this chapter we intend to focus first on some specific aspects of young people's health which have been seen as symptomatic of the increased sources of stress which stem from the unpredictable nature of life in high modernity: poor mental health and related increases in suicide, suicidal behaviour and eating disorders. Second, we focus on the social distribution of health related behaviours (such as smoking, use of alcohol and sex) which may have implications for health either now or in the future.

Mental health

Evidence from a number of sources suggests that changing experiences may have resulted in increased levels of stress which are subsequently manifest in psychological ill-health (Smith and Rutter 1995; West and Sweeting 1996, 2003). Although youth transitions have always involved some psychological adjustment as young people attempt to establish adult identities, levels of depression and stress related problems among the younger generation appear to have increased. Indeed, it has been argued that since 1945, 'psycho-social disorders' (including depression, eating disorders and suicidal behaviours) among adolescents have become 'substantially more prevalent' (Smith and Rutter 1995; Fombonne 1998), and since the 1980s the numbers of young people diagnosed as mentally ill or admitted to mental hospitals has increased (Fombonne 1998). The World Health Organization predicts a 50 per cent increase in adolescent psychiatric disorders over the next 15 years (Blum and Nelson-Mmari 2004). Yet while the trend evidence is convincing, it is important to bear in mind that people have become more likely to seek professional help for psychological problems and doctors may have become more predisposed to diagnosing psychological malaise (Hill 1995).

The risk of depression does increase substantially during the teenage years, especially among young women (Meeus 1994; Smith and Rutter 1995; West and Sweeting 1996, 2003). In this context, adolescence has been referred to as a 'window of risk' (Burke *et al.* 1990). In a comparison of young people in three European countries, Offer and colleagues (1988) reported that nearly three in ten young people suffer from depression. The World Health Organization estimates that, globally, one in five children and adolescents suffer from disabling mental illness (Blum and Nelson-Mmari 2004). In the USA, in the region of one in ten young people have an impairment linked to a severe mental disorder, although a small minority obtain treatment (Blum and Nelson-Mmari 2004), while between 10 and 15 per cent of adolescents have serious emotional or behavioural problems (Kutcher 1994). There is also evidence suggesting that the situation has worsened. In a comparison of two Scottish cohorts, the first carried out in the late 1980s, the second in the late 1990s, West and Sweeting (2003) found evidence showing an increase in levels of psychological distress among females.

The reduction in psychological well-being among young people can be seen as reflected in an increase in suicide and eating disorders. Since the 1950s, the suicide rate among young people has increased in many regions including Europe, North America and Australasia, while suicides have declined among older people (Smith and Rutter 1995; Eckersley and Dear 2002). Worldwide, up to 200,000 young people per year take their own lives (Blum and Nelson-Mmari 2004). In North America, Europe and the Western Pacific, suicide is the second biggest cause of death among 15- to 29-year-olds (in all of these countries unintentional injuries, particularly as those resulting from road traffic accidents, are the most common causes of death; Blum and Nelson-Mmari 2004). In part, differences between youth and adult suicide rates reflect the greater acceptability of suicide among the younger generation: according to Hill, 'parents are more likely to judge suicide in religious and moral terms, while their children regard it in terms of individual rights' (1995: 89). It has also been suggested that the media has made young people more familiar with suicide: it has been argued, for example, that in America the average young person will have seen around 800 screen suicides prior to leaving school (Hill 1995). Celebrity suicides (real or fictional) have also been linked to fluctuations in the suicide rate (Hill 1995).

Since the 1960s, in western countries such as the USA, Australia and New Zealand, suicides among young people have quadrupled (Ryland and Kruesi 1992) with particularly sharp rises evident among males in the 15 to 19 age group (increasing in the UK by 72 per cent between 1970 and 1998), although during this period there was slight fall in the female suicide rate (McClure 2001). As a result of these trends, in both the UK and the USA male 15- to 19-year-olds are almost four times as likely as females to take their own lives (Woodroffe *et al.* 1993; Blum and Nelson-Mmari 2004). Yet while the sharp increase in male suicides is a cause for concern, it is important to stress that relatively few young people take their own lives. In England the annual suicide rate among 15- to 24-year-olds is currently around 8 per 100 000 for males and around 2 per 100 000 for females. However, in some countries, such as New Zealand and Finland, male suicide rates are much higher at around 30 per 100,000[2] (Eckersley and Dear 2002).

While suicide among young people remains relatively rare, parasuicide and suicidal thoughts are more common.[3] In Australia it has been shown that for every successful male suicide there are 15 attempts while for each female suicide there are more than a hundred attempts (Mission Australia 2001). In France, around 800 teenagers commit suicide each year, although around 40 000 have suicidal thoughts. While French females are around three times more likely than males to attempt suicide, they are also three times more likely to make a second attempt should they fail first time around (Henley 2005a). Recent evidence from the UK has suggested that one in four 15-year-old females have either considered killing themselves or made serious attempts to self-harm (Priory 2005). In a survey of 15 000 Dutch students, Diekstra and colleagues (1991) found that almost one in five (19 per cent) had entertained suicidal thoughts during the past year, although obviously many of those who contemplate suicide subsequently fail to take any action. Statistics on parasuicide vary considerably depending on the source of information and it is argued that only around a quarter of cases are brought to the attention of the medical authorities (Diekstra *et al.* 1995). In a review of literature on parasuicides, Diekstra and colleagues (1995) argue that in any year, according to the source of statistics used, between 2 and 20 per cent of young people attempt to end their lives.

Throughout the 12 to 17 age range, (and especially in mid-adolescence), young people become increasingly likely to consider suicide, with females being most likely to consider taking their own lives (Diekstra *et al.* 1995; Smith and Rutter 1995). Males, however, are most successful in taking the act through to conclusion, partly because they tend to choose more aggressive methods (Diekstra *et al.* 1995; Eckersley and Dear 2002); in the USA male suicides usually use a gun. As Eckersley and Dear suggest, 'young women continue to attempt suicide more often than young men, but die less often because they tend to use less fatal means' (2002: 1894).

Suicide and parasuicide have been linked to a range of factors: a history of mental illness is particularly important, while factors like poverty, unemployment, poor school performance and low social class have all been viewed as significant (Hawton *et al.* 1998, 1999; Agerbo *et al.* 2002; Smith and Blackwood 2004). Researchers have also highlighted excessive use of drugs and alcohol, homelessness and judicial involvement (McClure 2001).

Another symptom of increased stress in adolescence relates to eating disorders. Eating disorders such as anorexia nervosa and bulimia nervosa are most common in adolescence and early adulthood (Mennell *et al.* 1992; Fombonne 1995; Rutter and Smith 1995; Gard and Wright 2005). The distribution of anorexia is bi-modal with peaks at around the ages of 14 and 18 (Hsu 1990; Mennell *et al.* 1992; Fombonne 1995) while the average age for the onset of bulimia is between 19 and 20. Both anorexia and bulimia are disorders which tend to be concentrated among white, middle class, female teenagers. Young women are more likely than young men to develop both of these disorders by a ratio of around ten to one (Fombonne 1995; Smith and Rutter 1995). Peer groups are important in this context and eating disorders are seen as rife in educational institutions. Although members of ethnic minorities are less likely to suffer from eating disorders, among black women the highest rates tend to be found among those from upwardly mobile families (Garfinkel and Garner 1982).

A number of writers have suggested that the age distribution of eating disorders reflect the impact of key transitions. The first peak in the age distribution of anorexia, for example, coincides with the development of sexual maturity and it is argued that the weight changes associated with the onset of puberty lead to bodily dissatisfaction among young women which can 'trigger' eating disorders. Conversely, males tend to regard an increase in body weight as something which enhances their masculinity (Fombonne 1995). The second peak in anorexia coincides with the transition from adolescence to adulthood and may reflect increased pressure to succeed in education and the labour market and to be accepted socially outside of family-based circles (Fombonne 1995).

Although there has been some debate about the extent to which the rising number of recorded cases of anorexia and bulimia represents a real underlying trend rather than a medically fashionable diagnosis, Mennell and colleagues (1992) suggest that the balance of evidence seems to rest in favour of the former argument. Anorexia nervosa was first recognized during the twentieth century, although it has only received serious attention since the 1970s (Mennell *et al.* 1992; Fombonne 1995). In the modern world, it is fashionable to be thin and slimness is associated with positive attributes such as success and sexual attractiveness. Conversely, plumpness is associated with negative traits, such as laziness, and fat people are often portrayed as unhealthy and as sexually repulsive (Mennell *et al.* 1992). Various studies have highlighted the role of the media in promoting the association between positive social attributes and low body weight (Kaufman 1980; Garfinkel and Garner 1982; Gowers and Shore 2001). Kaufman (1980) studied the portrayal of female characters in American television commercials and argued that slim women tended to be portrayed as intelligent, popular and attractive. Highlighting the promotion of unrealistically thin body images, Garfinkel and Garner (1982) argued that although the average weight of women has been increasing, successful models and beauty contest participants have been getting thinner. Black females appear to be more accepting of fuller figures and, as a result, less prone to eating disorders (Thompson *et al.* 1997).

In contrast to anorexia and bulimia which are largely middle class disorders, the prevalence of obesity among the working classes clearly illustrates the existence of class-based inequalities that have long-term implications for health (Gard and Wright 2005; Viner and Cole 2006). Alarming increases in obesity, which is often blamed on the fast food industry, have serious implications for public health and one of the consequences is likely to be a reduction in average life-spans among the current generation of young people. In the USA, levels of obesity among adolescents have tripled since 1980 and almost two-thirds of Americans are overweight or obese (Trust for America's Health 2004). In the UK it has been estimated that between 20 and 30 per cent of adolescents are obese (Parry-Jones 1988; *Guardian* 2006) while comparisons between cohorts born in 1958 and 1970 show significant increases in obesity (CLS 2006).

The corporate promotion of 'junk' food and the health implications of diets based on fast food were illustrated in Morgan Spurlock's film *Super Size Me* while a range of surveys have charted the rise of obesity. In recent UK report, for example, it was argued that rates of obesity among 11- to 15-year-olds doubled between 1995 and 2005 (*Guardian* 2006). Obesity, which tends to be concentrated among the less advantaged and can be linked to poverty and to restricted food choices, may carry less of a social stigma among the lower working classes (Fombonne 1995; Trust for America's Health 2004; Gard and Wright 2005; Viner and Cole 2006), but will almost certainly be reflected in patterns of later life ill-health and mortality.

While most young women neither suffer from medically diagnosable forms of anorexia and bulimia or are clinically obese, the desire to control weight is central to the lives of many. Concern about weight is common among the female population. Button and Whitehouse (1981), for example, suggest that between 80 and 90 per cent of women in the industrialized world monitor their calorie intake and frequently fail to eat enough to satisfy their appetites. Among 16- to 19-year-olds, it has been shown that around one in three have dieted to lose weight (Rudat *et al.* 1992) with diets often initiated following comments from male family members (Gowers and Shore 2001). As Fombonne suggests, ' "normative discontent" with weight is now part of the day to day psychological life of most young women, accompanied, at least temporarily, by some alteration in their behaviour' (1995: 647). Indeed, Mennell and colleagues (1992) argue that many of the symptoms of medically diagnosable disorders exist among a sizeable minority of the female population.

In Giddens' (1991) view, eating disorders are significant as he regards them as a modern phenomenon, linked to the desire to establish a distinct self-identity. As he expresses it, 'anorexia can be understood as a pathology of reflexive self-control, operating around an axis of self-identity and bodily appearance, in which shame anxiety plays a preponderant role' (1991: 104). In this interpretation, eating disorders are seen as a determined attempt to control body image and identity during a period in which young people are increasingly denied autonomy in many other aspects of their lives.

The increased health risks posed by eating disorders, suicidal behaviours and other mental health problems have common causes. To an extent each of these changes arise out of the protraction and desequencing of transitions and from the increased uncertainty with which young people move into the labour market and assume domestic and housing responsibilities. Young people seems to have been affected by changes in post-16 experiences, they face greater uncertainties and it is more common for them to enter situations where their expectations conflict with their subsequent experiences (Furlong 1992). The link between unemployment and mental health has been highlighted by a number of writers (Fryer and Payne 1986; Warr 1987; West and Sweeting 1996; Julkunen and Malmberg-Heimonen 1998; Hammarström 2000) and it is likely that the uncertainty associated with fragmented early labour market experiences have implications for mental health. Indeed, Smith and Rutter (1995) suggest that the rise in expectations associated with lengthening educational experience can have an adverse effect on mental health if they ultimately lead to disappointment.

Expressing concern over the impact of economic re-structuring on young people, West and Sweeting argue that the 'economic recession, unemployment, low paid jobs and the sense of having no future are all potentially components of a social malaise that may affect the health of us all, but especially the young' (1996: 50). Psychologists also provide evidence that the incidence of a highly stressful life event, or especially the *accumulation* of stressful events, and a sense of hopelessness are linked to suicidal behaviours (Jacobs 1971; D'Attilio *et al.* 1992; de Wilde *et al.* 1992).

Although there is a large body of literature highlighting a connection between unemployment and mental health problems (Banks and Jackson 1982; Hammer 1992; West and Sweeting 1996), Smith and Rutter (1995) remain sceptical about the extent to which changing levels of aggregate unemployment can be used as predictors of general trends in mental health. Despite low rates of unemployment, psycho-social disorders rose sharply during the 1950s and 1960s. Moreover, they argue that the rapid rise in unemployment during the 1930s and in the recession of the late 1970s and early 1980s was not matched by a corresponding rise in disorders.

While general trends in psychological malaise may be weakly correlated with unemployment rates, there is plenty of evidence suggesting that personal experience of unemployment leads to an increase in mental health problems. Using longitudinal evidence, West and Sweeting (1996) found that among males and females the experience of unemployment was associated with a significant increase in psychological morbidity (GHQ 'caseness') compared to members of their sample who did not experience unemployment. They also report that rates of attempted suicide among unemployed youth were much higher than among those in jobs or on training schemes. However, Diekstra and colleagues (1995) cast doubt on the causal significance attributed to unemployment and argued that during the 1970s there was an overall increase in attempted suicide by employed men and a decrease in parasuicide among the unemployed.

Even when young people do not spend time unemployed, the greater protraction of the youth transitions, changes in the sequence of key transitions and the prolongation of semi-dependency can be associated with psycho-social problems. Smith and Rutter (1995), for example, suggest that longer transitions can lead to conflict with parents. They suggest that smooth transitions are best accomplished one step at a time with young people gaining confidence through the successful completion of one transition before the next is negotiated. Smith and Rutter (1995) argue that the increasing malaise among young people is the consequence of a de-sequencing of transitions rather than protraction *per se*. Indeed, trend data shows that the increase in psycho-social disorders among young people began sometime before transitions began to lengthen.

Furthermore, both Smith and Rutter (1995) and West and Sweeting (1996) suggest that one of the keys to understanding the increasing malaise among young people is the increasing importance of youth cultures. Young people today spend longer periods in the company of their peers and youth cultures have become more isolated from the adult world. Perhaps surprisingly, social class does not seem to be associated with psycho-social problems among young people (Mann *et al.* 1983; Glendinning *et al.* 1992; West 1997). Although there are clear class-related gradients associated with the mental health of children and adults, among adolescents social class is not significant (West 1997). West argues that these findings can be explained by the cross-cutting effects of the school, peer group and youth culture which serve to reduce the strength of factors associated with social background. During adolescence friendship networks have been shown to increase in significance relative to the influence of parents (Meeus 1994). Changing family structures have also been seen as related to increasing psycho-social problems of young people. Although the evidence linking family breakdown with mental health problems is inconclusive (Shafii 1989), the lack of parental support or involvement which may accompany family breakdown appears to have a significant effect (Smith and Rutter, 1995). Indeed, it has been suggested that 'between 1960 and 1985 the divorce rates of European countries were among the most accurate predictors of changes in youth suicide' (Hill 1995: 73).

Health related behaviours

While there is some evidence of an increased risk of psycho-social disorders among young people, it is important to stress that the majority move through adolescence and into adulthood with their physical and mental health intact.

Although most young people remain healthy, many forms of behaviour which are common among young people do have consequences for long-term health. In this section we focus specifically on the risks which stem from smoking, alcohol consumption, drug use and from sexual encounters and examine the extent to which these risks are unevenly distributed throughout the youth population.

Smoking and drinking

Despite a reduction in smoking among the general population which in most countries can be traced back several decades, the decline in the use of tobacco by young people has been less sharp than among the adult population and a significant number of young people will use tobacco during their teenage years (Lader and Matheson 1991; Woodroffe *et al.* 1993; Currie *et al.* 2004; Naidoo *et al.* 2004). The use of tobacco by young people tends to be associated with social class and educational attainment. Young people from working class families are marginally more likely to smoke than those from middle class families, (mainly because of a link between smoking in parents and their children) as are those who leave school at an early stage, those from less advantaged families (especially those living in poverty) and black and minority ethnic groups (Green *et al.*, 1991; Plant and Plant 1992; Naidoo *et al.* 2004; Department of Health 2005). Prior to the 1980s, males were more likely to smoke than females. However, in many countries the decline in smoking has been sharpest among the male population and today in many western societies females are more likely to smoke than males. The prevalence of smoking increases sharply with age so, in the UK, just 1 per cent of 11-year-olds are regular smokers but 21 per cent of 15-year-olds (Department of Health 2005). Despite different taxation policies and restrictions of purchases for young people, between country differences are not particularly large: in general somewhere between one in four and one in five 15-year-olds in western societies are regular smokers (Figure 6.1).

Given the serious risks associated with smoking, the reduction in the proportion of young people who smoke has long-term health consequences. As Plant and Plant note, significantly more young people are likely to die through diseases linked to tobacco than from any other causes and therefore a decline in smoking is likely to lead to a significant fall in premature death: 'among 1000 young adult males in England and Wales who smoke cigarettes on average about 1 will be murdered, 6 will be killed on the roads and 250 will be killed before their time by tobacco' (1992: 62).

Like smoking, under-aged drinking is common. Young people in many western societies are brought up within a 'wet culture' (Plant and Plant 1992) in which the introduction to social drinking is an important rite of passage on the road to adulthood. While there are strong differences between countries in the restrictions placed on the sale and availability of alcohol, legislation appears to have relatively little impact on practice. In much of Europe and in Australia, legal consumption status begins between the ages of 14 and 18. Despite legal restrictions, among 15-year-olds, weekly consumption of alcohol is particularly common among males in England, Italy and Germany (Figure

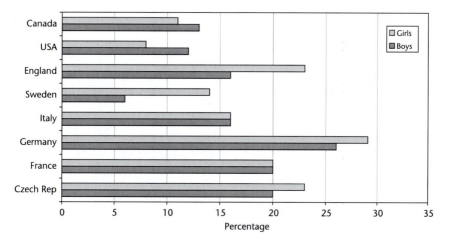

Figure 6.1 15-year-olds who smoke daily: selected countries
Source: Currie *et al.* 2004

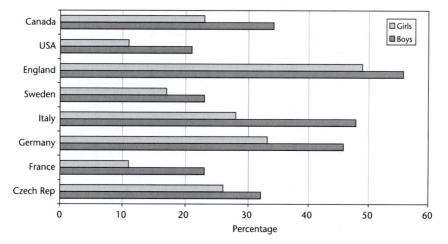

Figure 6.2 15-year-olds who drink alcohol weekly: selected countries
Source: Currie *et al.* 2004

6.2). Yet even in the USA, where drinking is not permitted until the age of 21, more than one in five 15-year-old males claim to drink alcohol weekly.

In the UK, it is estimated that almost one in two 13-year-olds, nearly three in four 14-year-olds and more than nine in ten 15-year-olds will have tried alcohol (Priory 2005), while Fossey and colleagues (1996) suggest that around a third of boys and girls are consuming alcohol regularly by the age of 16. Parental drinking habits have a significant impact on young people's use of alcohol, with middle class youth tending to drink more than those from working class families (Green *et al.* 1991). There are also cultural differences that can be linked to 'race': among young people between the ages of 9 and 15, slightly more African-Carribeans than whites will have tried alcohol, while relatively few Asian youths will have tasted alcohol (HEA 1992).

Between 1970 and 2001 per capita consumption of alcohol in the UK increased from 8.5 to 10.4 litres per year. In Europe there were also significant increases in Ireland and the Netherlands, but a fall in Europe as a whole, mainly due to a sharp reduction in consumption in France and Italy (British Heart Foundation 2005). However, for young people the main risks from alcohol do not relate to any long-term damage to health but are linked to the ways in which excessive alcohol consumption many increase the likelihood of involvement in violence or participation in other risky activities. Here the evidence suggests that for young people the short-term health risks associated with drinking have decreased, partly as a result of drink-driving campaigns. Plant and Plant (1992), for example, show that in the UK between 1979 and 1989 there was a sharp reduction (by over 50 per cent) in fatalities among 16- to 19-year-old drivers associated with high alcohol consumption. Although drink-related road deaths have declined, the use of alcohol is still frequently associated with car accidents and violent crime and is a significant factor in many early deaths (Woodroffe *et al.* 1993; Blum and Nelson-Mmari 2004). In Europe, it has been estimated that one in four deaths of men in the 15–29 age group is associated with alcohol (Blum and Nelson-Mmari 2004).

Despite the normality of alcohol use among young people, their drinking patterns frequently cause concern among the adult population and have been the focus of numerous 'moral panics'. In the UK, media attention on the so-called 'lager louts' led to legislation which enabled local authorities to prohibit outdoor drinking in specified public areas. There have also been concerns about drinking fashions that have been driven by the alcohol industries attempts to capture the young adult market that was once seen as declining. Up until the early 1990s, there was little age-related differentiation in the market in alcohol; standard beers, wines and spirits were consumed by all age groups. With sales falling among sections of the youth population who were more interested in the drug and club scene, the UK industry began to market niche products. The first phase involved the development of high strength bottled beers, cider and alcoholic lemonades – 'alcopops' ('Hooch' and 'Diamond White', for example). The second phase revolved around high strength bottled spirit mixers, ('Smirnoff Ice' and 'Bacardi Breezer'). The third phase involved the introduction of cheap shots of cocktails of spirits (Measham 2004). These marketing strategies appear to have been successful in boosting young people's alcohol consumption.

Media driven panics about young people's alcohol consumption tend to draw on extremes in behaviour and infer general trends. While most young people do consume alcoholic beverages, the majority drink relatively small amounts and alcohol dependence and chronic heavy drinking is unusual in under-21-year-olds (Fossey *et al.* 1996). Among young people, drinking is associated with sociability and there may be considerable social pressure to drink heavily on occasions. Indeed, a 'substantial minority' (Fossey *et al.* 1996: 58) of young males and females drink heavily, although there are strong differences between countries. In Ireland, the UK and Sweden, for example, more than one in four 15- and 16-year-olds report 'binge drinking'[4] three or more

	Boys		Girls	
31		Ireland		33
26		UK		29
27		Sweden		25
20		Portugal		10
19		Italy		8
15		France		7
10		USA		10

Figure 6.3 Percentage of 15- to 16-year-olds reporting 'binge drinking' three or more times in the last 30 days: selected countries, 2003.
Source: Institute of Alcohol Studies Fact Sheet 2005

times a month. In contrast, levels of 'binge drinking' tends to be much lower in France, Italy and the USA, especially among females (Figure 6.3).

Many of the risks associated with alcohol stem from the links with 'anti-social' behaviour, such as vandalism, fighting and petty crime (Marsh *et al.* 1986) (see Chapter 7) as well as through the greater risk of road accidents (as pedestrians as well as drivers) and suicide (Hill 1995). These risks are not new. At the same time, the introduction to alcohol forms an important part of normal transitions to adulthood and learning to use alcohol sensibly in social contexts is a necessary skill in most western societies.

Use of drugs and solvents

Since the 1950s associations have been made between youth and drug cultures. In the 1960s drugs like cannabis and LSD were an important part of hippie culture, in the 1990s use of ecstasy became common among ravers, while over the last decade a fall in the price of cocaine has led to an increase in demand. Like alcohol, drug use is a normal part of the adolescent experience and there is evidence that young people who use drugs most frequently are the same as those who drink or smoke excessively (Plant 1989). There is also strong evidence to suggest that young people today are more likely to experiment with drugs than they were a decade ago (Measham *et al.* 1994). While many recreational drugs carry no greater risk to the health of the user than alcohol or tobacco, the illegality of many of these substances, combined with frequent media-generated 'moral panics' over usage (especially over fashion drugs such as ecstasy and ketamine), mean that users risk police attention and legal sanctions (see Chapter 7).

In much of Europe, between one in four and four in ten 16-year-olds have used cannabis (Hibell *et al.* 2004) (Figure 6.4) Among young adolescents, solvents remain fairly popular and there has been a rise in the number of deaths attributed to them (Plant and Plant 1992; Rutter and Smith 1995). However, while drug use may have become more common, changes in use often involve shifts from one type of substance to another reflecting current fashions. Among 16-year-olds in Europe, leaving aside cannabis (while there are fears about the link between cannabis use and impaired mental health, most developed countries regard cannabis use as on a par with alcohol), few

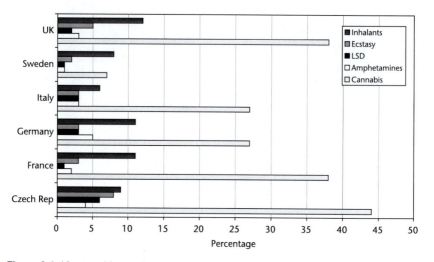

Figure 6.4 16-year-olds ever having used various substances: selected countries
Source: Hibell *et al.* 2004

substances have ever been used by much more than 1 in 10 16-year-olds, and of these few are regular users (Hibell *et al.* 2004).

While overall levels of drug use are highest among middle class youth, when it comes to the use of 'hard' drugs, those from working class families appear to be more likely to use heroin (and are more likely to take drugs intravenously) while those who are more affluent and have higher educational levels are more likely to use cocaine (Leitner *et al.* 1993; Measham 2002). There is also evidence for an increase in the use of 'hard' drugs among young people. In the UK, figures from the British Crime Survey show that between 1996 and 2004/05 the number of people who had used cocaine increased from 0.5 per cent to 2.1 per cent while heroin use remained virtually unchanged at around 0.1 per cent (Roe 2005). Despite popular concerns about young people's use of 'hard' drugs, in Europe the proportion of young people who try them remains small: in most countries, for example, less than one in a hundred 15- to 34-year-olds have used cocaine and even in countries where usage is most prevalent (Spain and the UK) little more than 2 per cent have used it (EMCDDA 2006). Indeed, Mott has argued that despite media coverage of 'increasing' use of 'crack', evidence for an 'epidemic' has mainly been drawn from statistics relating to high risk groups or clinic populations. As Fazey argues 'backgrounds of severe social deprivation and high unemployment characterize a disproportionate number of those with severe enough problems to attend drug treatment clinics' (1991: 23).

Patterns of drug use are affected by opportunities in the form of local supply and fashions (Young 1971; O'Bryan 1989). On some inner city housing estates heroin may be readily available and those without work may be particularly vulnerable (Haw 1985; Plant *et al.* 1985; Peck and Plant 1986; Pearson 1987; Pearson *et al.* 1987; Parker *et al.* 1988; Leitner *et al.* 1993). While there is evidence to suggest that the use of 'hard' drugs has increased, there have been important changes in patterns of usage. While heroin and cocaine use in the 1960s tended to be a rather isolated activity with users being described as 'bohemian' or 'counter-cultural' (Stimson 1987), today's user is less marginalized and will frequently inhale the drug rather than injecting. Young people are also becoming less likely to stick with one drug of choice and select different highs according to mood, environment and occasion. As Deehan and Saville (2003) suggest, the 1990s preference for a single drug of choice has been replaced by a 'cocktail of celebration' in which alcohol, tobacco and a range of 'hard' or 'soft' drugs may be combined in various ways on different occasions.

The other major change in the use of drugs relates to the geographical distribution of users. Whereas in the 1960s users tended to be heavily concentrated in major cities, by the 1980s usage had become common in most conurbations (Giggs 1991). With the increase in HIV/AIDS, the rise in heroin usage, combined with its geographical spread, has frequently caused alarm among politicians and the media (South 1994), even though many new users avoid intravenous methods. The use of drugs has also been associated with other forms of risk taking: drug users often drink heavily, may risk 'unsafe' sex whilst under the influence of drugs (Plant and Plant 1992) may become involved in crime (see Chapter 7) or attempt suicide (Hill 1995). Indeed, Measham and colleagues argue that 'drug use is strongly associated with drinking, smoking, early sexual experience, and various types of deviant and criminal behaviour' (1994: 289).

Sexual behaviour and sexually transmitted infections

Linked to the process of physiological maturation, sexual experimentation is central to the experience of youth and there has been a steady growth in the proportion of young people who engage in teenage sex (Humphries 1991; Waites 2005). In much of Europe and in north America, somewhere between a half and two-thirds of teenagers are sexually active, while in southern Europe rates of activity are somewhat lower; in Italy, for example, around a third of teenagers are sexually active (Wolff *et al.* 1992). In the UK, around a third of 15-year-old males and females will have had sexual intercourse, a figure which increases to about 75 per cent by the age of 19 (Priory 2005).

Despite the availability of contraceptives, one of the main health risks associated with teenage sex is still unwanted pregnancy (which in the 1950s and 1960s carried greater social stigma and was often swiftly followed by increased responsibility as teenage pregnancy tended to be followed by an early marriage). In Europe levels of condom use among sexually active teenagers are relatively high, although teenage sex often occurs under the influence of alcohol and condom use may be inconsistent. There is some evidence suggesting that young men who consume alcohol prior to sexual intercourse are less likely to use condoms (Plant and Plant 1992). However, other studies from Europe and the USA have failed to find strong evidence linking intoxication with risky sex (Leigh and Miller 1995; Cooper 2000; Morrison *et al.* 2003; Traene *et al.* 2003). In the USA, condom use among teenagers is relatively low (56 per cent as compared to 95 per cent in Germany) and rates of teenage pregnancy are double that of many European countries (Wolff *et al.* 1992).

The sharp increase in the incidence of HIV and deaths from AIDS, government sponsored campaigns and the publicity generated by AIDS-related celebrity deaths have all helped encourage condom use (Selzer *et al.* 1989; Sonenstein *et al.* 1989). However, many teenagers who have multiple partners continue to have unprotected sex and it has been argued that few young people routinely use condoms (Plant and Plant 1992). Indeed, Plant and Plant (1992) suggest that coverage of HIV/AIDS by the media has often left young people with the impression that heterosexuals are relatively safe from infection.

While young people have always had to contend with the risk of contracting sexually transmitted infections, there is evidence of an increase since the late 1980s to early 1990s (Centers for Disease Control and Prevention 2004; Public Health Agency of Canada 2005). Potentially life-threatening HIV infections have been a particular cause of concern since the late 1980s and there has been a more recent rise in cases of chlamydia which can damage the reproductive health of young women (Plant and Plant 1992; Centers for Disease Control and Prevention 2004; Public Health Agency of Canada 2005; Waites 2005). Indeed, with an effective cure for gonorrhoea and syphilis only becoming available in the 1940s, sexual activity among young people has tended to involve health risks. Since the 1980s, around 30 million 15- to 24-year-olds have contracted HIV – half of the global total (Blum and Nelson-Mmari 2004).

Although young people are tending to have intercourse at an earlier age than previously, it is important not to portray them as promiscuous. Research from the USA suggests that, compared to the early 1990s, young people today are having fewer sexual partners (Warren *et al.* 1998; Centers for Disease Control and Prevention 2000). Yet casual sexual relationships are not uncommon; in a study of young people in Glasgow, for example, half of the sample reported a sexual relationship in which intercourse had taken place on just one occasion (Wight 1993). While numbers of sexual partners show little variation by social class (Foreman and Chilvers 1989), there is evidence that those living in deprived neighbourhoods tend to have their first sexual encounters at an earlier age (O'Reilly and Aral 1985) and are less likely to use condoms (Bagnall and Plant 1991). Those in the highest educational attainment bands tend to be slightly older when they first have intercourse, and are marginally more likely to use condoms (Breakwell 1992). In this context, sexual activity can be seen as posing a greater health risks for lower working class youths who are more likely to become pregnant whilst teenagers and are more vulnerable to sexual disease.

In recent years relationships with same sex partners have become more socially acceptable, even fashionable, among the younger generation (as reflected in the increased inclusion of gay and lesbian characters in popular television 'soap operas' and legalization of 'marriage' between same sex partners in a range of countries such as Spain, the UK and Canada). While practising gays appear to have a higher risk of contracting HIV, the numbers of young people who experiment with homosexual intercourse has remained small. In a study of 16- to 21-year-olds, just 2 per cent of the sample defined their sexuality as either homosexual or bi-sexual (Ford 1989). Similarly, Foreman and

Chilvers (1989) found that just less than 2 per cent of males reported experience of homosexual intercourse. A 1970 study by the Kinsey Institute (Fay *et al.* 1989) puts the figure slightly higher, with around 4 per cent of males reporting experience of homosexual intercourse and just less than 2 per cent having regular or occasional homosexual relationships. These figures are broadly in line with a those collected in the USA as part of an election exit poll: 4 per cent regarded themselves as gay or lesbian (CNN 2004). While self-reported figures for gay and lesbian activity remain low, heterosexual anal intercourse has also been identified as a potential source of HIV risk: an experience reported by more than one in ten male and female 16- to 20-year-olds (Breakwell 1992).

Conclusion

In this chapter we have highlighted some of the health risks faced by young people and described changes in forms of behaviour which may pose threats to their health. In term of general health, with the absence of reliable trend data it is difficult for us to speculate about whether there has been a weakening in traditional sources of inequality. It is likely that adolescence has always been a period in which the major health inequalities lie dormant and that the differential experiences of young people are reflected in the re-emergence of inequalities based on class and gender as an age cohort moves into adulthood. On the other hand, it is possible that we are witnessing significant changes. Class and gender differences in many health related behaviours are relatively small and this may lead to a process of equalization in adulthood. Although some forms of risky behaviour are more common among working class youth (such as smoking), other risky activities are more prevalent among the middle classes (such as use of alcohol and soft drugs). Similarly, males and females are vulnerable in different ways, but on balance the differences are not striking.

While relatively few young people have to cope with difficulties stemming from diseases or poor physical health during adolescence, there is evidence that the social conditions of high modernity are reflected in a deterioration in mental health which are manifest in different ways among males and females. Depression, eating disorders, suicide and attempted suicide have all become more common and can be seen as reflecting the increased incidence of 'fateful moments' (Giddens 1991) and the ongoing sense of doubt which is a central feature of high modernity and which can be particularly threatening for young people in the process of establishing adult identities. To an extent, these risks have an impact on the lives of all young people, although clearly some are particularly vulnerable to the health risks which stem from labour market marginalization or exclusion. On balance, the evidence on the changing health of young people lends some support for the ideas of Beck and Giddens insofar as the key changes seem to relate to an increase in psychological problems which can linked to a heightened sense of insecurity in late modernity.

7 Crime *and* insecurity

Much of the moralising about young people's behaviour, which was as strident in past centuries as it is today, reveals as much about the frustration with behaviour that they cannot easily control as any deep seated problem in the young people themselves. For most young people, the offensive behaviour passes with the transition to the more stable statuses of employment, partnership and parenthood. . . . A problem may arise when anti-social behaviour coupled with a disadvantaged working class home and low educational achievement leads first to trouble with the police and to subsequent court appearances.

(Bynner *et al.* 2004: 79–80)

Introduction

In the previous chapter we considered the extent to which recent social changes have been associated with increased health risks among young people. In this chapter we focus on crime, which represents a different set of risks. Reports of crime epidemics and civil disorder frequently make the headlines of newspapers and many press reports highlight the involvement of young people, often drawing parallels between an apparent rise in criminal activity and a breakdown in the 'social fabric' of society. In this chapter we attempt to put some of these changes into perspective and examine the implications of processes of social change for young people's involvement in crime. We argue that the sorts of changes which have occurred do not provide support for the idea that there has been a breakdown in traditional social values and suggest that changing patterns of involvement in crime are an inevitable consequence of the extension of youth as a phase in the life cycle. In the context of our discussion about differential patterns of vulnerability in late modernity, we argue that the risks associated with illegal activities continue to be unequally distributed according to 'traditional' social divisions such as class, gender and 'race'. However, this is not to suggest that there are hugely significant differences in overall levels of offending between social groups. On the one hand the differential risks can be seen as reflecting the activities of law enforcement agencies and their assumptions about patterns of involvement;

on the other hand they can be linked to differences in the prevalence of particular forms of offending in different social groups and the level of visibility associated with these acts and groups.

While Durkheim (1964) regarded increasing crime rates as an entirely normal bi-product of social development, some of the key characteristics of late modernity, such as reflexivity of the self and the weakening of collective identities, are processes which might be seen as undermining of the normative order. Indeed, Merton (1969) highlighted the apparent contradiction between social norms which place an emphasis on individual achievement and success, on the one hand, and the maintenance of differential opportunity structures on the other. In this respect, processes of individualization and subjective disembedding, which Beck and Giddens regard as characteristic of late modernity, could be seen as creating the conditions in which crime is likely to rise.

As those without work or domestic responsibilities are more likely to be involved in criminal activities (Rutherford 1992; Flood-Page *et al.* 2000), it can be argued that changing transitional patterns have affected the risk of criminal involvement. Being denied access to the financial rewards of working life and forced into greater dependency on their families, young people may become involved in crime as a way to gain access to consumer culture or simply as part of the quest for excitement or 'kicks' that has long been central to the lives of young people. With a lack of commitments, risk taking and experimentation are considered to be a normal part of adolescent development. Indeed, it has been argued that risk taking and the search for adventure 'help adolescents achieve independence, identity and maturity' (Jack 1989: 337). With a decline in manufacturing employment and as a consequence of the changing structure of opportunities in the youth labour market (especially greater employment insecurity), the involvement of young males in crime can also be interpreted as an attempt to establish masculine identities in a rapidly changing social world (McDowell 2003).

While young people frequently engage in activities which shock or provoke reactions among the adult population, such as drug taking or street violence, in late modernity the weakening of communal ties can be seen as leading to feelings of mistrust and insecurity which can lead to an intensification of generational conflict and may result in extreme reactions such as the introduction of youth curfews. In this context it can be argued that while the evidence for a significant rise in youth crime is, at best, dubious, adults and the criminal justice agencies have become preoccupied with crime prevention (Taylor 1996) and suspicious of young people who are perceived as being more lawless than their own generation (Pearson 1994; Waiton 2006). Summing up popular sentiment, one US Congressman referred to contemporary youth as 'the most dangerous criminals on the face of the earth' (Macallair and Males 2000). In turn, young people also feel vulnerable and express concerns about becoming the victims of violent crime on the streets and in pubs and clubs or subject to unwarranted levels of police surveillance or harassment.

The 'problem' of crime

Concerns about the criminal activities of the young are not a modern phenomenon: Pearson (1994) suggests that politicians and members of the older generation have always tended to regard levels of criminality among the younger generation as abnormal and 'moral panics' about youth crime have surfaced periodically throughout the post-war period in all western societies. Whereas adults tend to think of their own generation as orderly and disciplined, standards of behaviour are constantly perceived as having deteriorated. Pearson (1994) argues that youth crime has often been regarded as a consequence

> of recent social changes, involving a pattern of complaint linking youthful crime to the 'permissive society'; the break-up of the family and community; the dwindling power of parents, teachers, magistrates, and policemen; the lack of respect among the young for authority in all its forms; and the incitements of demoralizing popular entertainments such as television violence and video nasties which lead to imitative 'copy-cat' crime.
>
> (p. 1163)

In recent years, concerns such as these, together with a perception that juvenile crime is a growing problem, have had an impact on criminal justice policy. In particular, in many western societies political parties have tried to improve their positions at the polls by claiming that they could deal effectively with the 'problem' of youth crime through the introduction of harsher sentences and closer surveillance of those given non-custodial punishments. Even parties leaning to the left of the political spectrum, who once placed an emphasis on dealing with the causes of crime, have come to accept there is a need to 'crack down' on youth crime: to be less understanding and more judgmental. Greater emphasis has been placed on the impact of crime on victims, even when the 'impact' stems from fear of crime rather than from actual harm to person or property. Measures have included greater use of imprisonment, the 'short, sharp shock', involving short sentences in institutions run along the lines of military 'boot camps', legislation requiring courts to use financial penalties against the parents of young offenders, as well the electronic tagging of offenders to restrict movement and court orders that threaten jail to those who breach conditions that limit their activities. Youth curfews have been introduced in a number of countries, including the UK and the USA, with the aim of keeping young people below a certain age off the streets at night (although these are frequently restricted to poor neighbourhoods and rarely encroach on the free movement of those from more affluent families). As Ferrell (1997) has argued

> Curfews protect symbolic constructions of adult authority by patrolling the cultural and temporal space of kids . . . they work to unravel cultures and alternative spaces that kids have built around coffee houses, raves, music and style.
>
> (p. 27)

In a USA survey of 347 cities with a population of over 30,000 (US Conference of Mayors 1997) four out of five cities were found to operate a night time curfew of which one in four also had some type of daytime curfew (usually applying to those of school age during school hours). Mayors contacted tended to regard curfews as an effective tool in the fight against crime. The majority saw them as a way of curbing gang violence and youth victimization and, of those operating day-time curfews, most thought they had reduced truancy.

In the UK, civil 'Anti-Social Behaviour Orders' (ASBOs), which can lead to custodial sentences where breached, can be used to regulate young people 'whose behaviour is thought likely to case alarm, distress or harassment' (Muncie 2004: 237). ASBOs (which can be regarded as desperate measures to control young people from working class families whose behaviour is feared) impose a set of conditions on the 'offender', who has not necessarily been found guilty of an offence in a criminal court, and restrict their behaviour in ways laid out by the civil court: they may be banned from socializing with a particular group of friends or from visiting a specific neighbourhood. While ASBOs can be imposed on people of any age, around three-quarters are imposed on young people below the age of 21 (Campbell 2002).

There are significant differences between countries in the minimum age of criminal responsibility (Figure 7.1): as young as 8 in Scotland, but as old as 16 in some USA States (although in North Carolina cases can be considered for a delinquency hearing as young as age 6 (Bishop and Decker 2006)). In the lower age ranges, many countries apply the legal principal of *doli incapax* under which prosecutors have to prove that the offending child was able to tell right from wrong. However, believing that young people are responsible for a 'disproportionate amount of serious and violent crime, in many countries there has been an increased tendency for courts to treat young people as adults' (Macallier and Males 2000: 1).

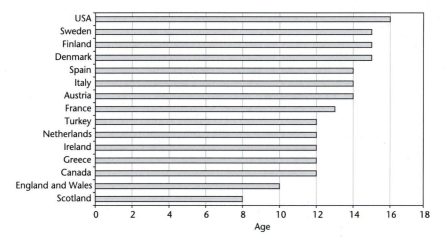

Figure 7.1 Minimum age of criminal responsibility: selected countries
Note: USA is mostly 16, but there is some variation by state.
Source: Scottish Law Commission 2001

Since the 1990s, in most advanced industrial countries, there has been an increase in the rate of incarceration. Between 1992 and 2001, the prison population in the USA rose by 60 per cent while in England and Wales, Germany and Australia, for example, it rose by over 40 per cent (*www.prisonstudies.org*). In many countries the use of custodial sentences for young people has also increased (Muncie 2004) although custodial sentences are largely reserved for those from less advantaged families (Matza 1964). In the UK 40 per cent of young male inmates and 27 per cent of female inmates have been in the care of the local authority for part of their childhood (Esmée Fairbairn Foundation 2005).

In the UK between 1998 and 2003, for example, the number of 15- to 21-year-olds in prison increased by 66 per cent, even though the majority had not been sentenced for violent offences. England and Wales currently incarcerates more young offenders under the age of 18 than any other European country, while for 18- to 21-year-olds Ireland tops the league (Aebi 2002). The imprisonment of young people is relatively rare in the Scandinavian countries, but more common in the north of mainland Europe (Figure 7.2). In the USA (which is one of only two nations not to have ratified the United Nations Convention on the Rights of the Child, 1989) 17 states still permit the execution of 16-year-olds.

The media have tended to play an important role in raising the profile of youth crime and in mobilizing public and political opinion. Inner city disorders, 'riots', have been used by the media as evidence of a rise in the incidence of crime among young people and, in particular, to turn the spotlight on young males (especially asylum seekers and members of ethnic minorities). Here it is suggested that law and order has broken down or that western cultural values may not be shared by recent immigrants. (Disorders in 2005 in Paris, Sydney and Birmingham spring to mind, but the involvement of young British Muslims in the London transport bombings turned the spotlight on the

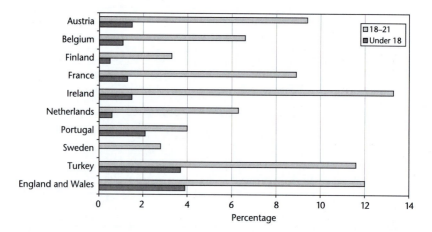

Figure 7.2 Percentage of age group in prison: Europe
Source: Aebi 2002

alienation of the second and third generation children of immigrants.) 'Binge drinking' and street violence on weekend evenings have also been linked and taken as indicative of an increase in antisocial behaviour, sometimes referred to in the press as 'yob culture'. Other significant events which have been used to support this position include, in the UK, the accidental killing of two girls in Birmingham who were victims of a gang-related 'drive by' shooting, and, in the USA, incidents involving shootings of school students by their classmates.

While it is always possible to find examples of serious crime committed by young people, the evidence for a rising crime rate is somewhat contradictory and can reflect the different agendas of those responsible for compiling statistics. Criminologists tend to treat official statistics with caution and often challenge the reliability of the underlying trends. In particular, they suggest that criminal statistics may reflect patterns of policing rather than patterns of offending and therefore exaggerate the relative criminality of groups of people who have traditionally been the focus of police surveillance (Coleman and Moynihan 1996: Muncie 2004). Some observed crimes are frequently not reported to the police (such as street violence), while others remain undetected (especially white collar crimes such as fraud) or are not recorded by the police (such as domestic violence). An increase in surveillance (especially through CCTV), has led to the discovery of more street crime (Christie 2000: Sivarajasingam *et al.* 2003) while new legislation may mean that acts that were once tolerated become re-defined as transgressions: Cohen (2003) points out that in the UK 661 new criminal offences have been created since 1997. Advances in DNA 'fingerprinting' mean that the police are able to secure convictions on evidence that would once have been overlooked.

Although there are difficulties in estimating the relationship between reported and unreported crimes (Pearson 1983), the British Crime Survey shows that nearly six in ten offences go unreported (Nicholas *et al.* 2005), although there are significant differences according to the type of offence. In 2004, for example, it was suggested that of all burglaries in England and Wales, 61 per cent were reported to the police, but just 47 per cent were recorded and ultimately convictions were secured in relation to just 2 per cent of the total (Thorpe and Ruparel 2005). Moreover, in comparison to many crimes, a high proportion of burglaries are reported (with the number of reported burglaries partly reflecting the numbers of people covered by house contents insurance). Much lower levels of reporting and recording occur, for example, in relation to sex crimes and violent behaviour.

Local variations in patterns of reported crime can also reflect differences in the enforcement priorities of local police forces and the recording practices which they adopt (Smith 1995). Although there are significant geographical differentials in levels of crime, with a concentration of police resources in some inner-city areas, working class and ethnic minority youths face a greater risk of arrest than middle class youths who may engage in similar activities in suburban areas with a lower level of policing. In particular, it has been argued that the police are over-zealous when it comes to apprehending black and Asian males and that poor relations between the police and young people from ethnic minorities has been a key factor in explaining 'riots' in cities in Europe and North America (Scarman 1981; Waller 1981; Schostak 1983). In 2005, for example, the civil disorders in Paris, Sydney and Birmingham have been widely interpreted in the press as reflecting hostility to methods of policing in parts of these communities and a lack of sensitivity on the part of the police to the sense of injustice that can arise when a group which suffers economic disadvantage also feels itself to be subject to unjustified surveillance or harassment.

Due to inconsistencies between areas and changing policies relating to prosecutions which affect official statistics, data from victim surveys or self-report studies are often used to provide a more accurate picture of the prevalence of crime. However, while acknowledging that official statistics may provide a distorted picture of levels of involvement among different groups of people, Lea and Young (1993) suggest that in terms of trends, there is actually a close correlation between official statistics and survey data. In the UK, for example, both official statistics and victim surveys indicate a rise in crime which can be traced back to the early 1950s, although this seems to have peaked in the mid-1990s with significant reductions reported in several countries in the mid-1990s (Flood-Page *et al.* 2000; Macallair and Males 2000; Palmer *et al.* 2004; Nicholas *et al.* 2005).

Although we can draw evidence from official statistics and surveys, it is difficult to be conclusive about trends in youth crime. There is evidence to suggest a continued growth in crime in some countries (such as Austria, Belgium, the Netherlands and Portugal) and even evidence to suggest a significant reduction in others (such as Denmark, Germany, Spain, the UK, and the USA) (Macallair and Males 2000; van Kesteren *et al.* 2001; Barclay and Tavares 2002; Muncie 2004; Nicholas *et al.* 2005). The picture for violent crime is somewhat different and suggests a rise in recorded crime between 1996 and 2000 in a wide range of countries. In the EU there was an overall rise in violent crime of around 14 per cent with much higher increases in countries like Spain (38 per cent), France (36 per cent) and Poland (49 per cent). Even in Japan where violent crime is relatively low, over the same period there was an increase of 72 per cent. In the USA and Ireland the numbers of recorded violent crimes fell during this period (Macallair and Males 2000; Barclay and Tavares 2002). The focus on official statistics, though, can be misleading and other commentators have argued that this apparent rise is simply a result of an increased tendency for law enforcement agencies to focus their attention on youth violence (Estrada 2001). To make sense of these trends it is important to be aware that CCTV surveillance may result in a greater tendency to detect and record street crime (Sivarajasingam *et al.* 2003) while an increased tendency to caution young offenders in some countries (such as the UK) may result in a decrease in the numbers of non-violent crimes recorded.

Involvement in crime

Involvement in criminal activities is a normal part of adolescence, although the prevalence of recorded crime is low. In the UK, in 2001, less than 2 per cent of 10- to 17-year-olds were convicted or cautioned for a criminal offence (Bynner *et al.* 2004) with 80 per cent of offenders being male (Muncie 2004). These figures are fairly typical of the northern European countries. Among those without convictions, some will have escaped with a caution, will have evaded arrest or have committed crimes which have not been brought to the attention of the police. Among males and females who have been convicted or cautioned for an offence, the majority have been involved in theft, burglary and the handling of stolen goods (Bynner *et al.* 2004), relatively few indictable crimes involve violence (Muncie 2004). Few females are convicted or cautioned for burglary, yet similar proportions of both sexes are convicted for involvement in violent crimes.

Using self-report data from a study of young people in England and Wales, Beinart and colleagues (2002) describe patterns of participation in a range of criminal activities by young people: almost one in two 11- to 17-year-olds admitted having knowingly broken the law at some point, and a third of 14- to 15-year-olds had stolen goods from a shop. One in five 15- to 16-year-old boys had attacked someone with the aim of causing serious harm. In an earlier study of 14- to 25-year-olds, Graham and Bowling (1995) had found that more than one in five young males admitted having handled stolen goods, shoplifting, participation in group fighting or disorder in a public place, while more than one in ten had been involved in vandalism or theft from work. Females admitted to fewer offences, but more than one in ten had been involved in shoplifting or had handled stolen goods. Both the official statistics and the self-report figures show that involvement in serious crime and persistent offending are relatively rare (Hagell and Newburn 1994; Graham and Bowling 1995; Summerfield and Gill 2005) with most young people being convicted for theft and drug offences (Summerfield and Gill 2005).

Drug offences among young people are relatively common (see Chapter 6), although while the use of some drugs (such as cocaine) has increased since the mid-1990s, the use of many other drugs has declined (such as LSD and amphetamines; Roe 2005). Between 1990 and 2000 the number of drugs seizures by the police increased rapidly in most European countries: the numbers of people per 100,000 population[1] prosecuted for drug offences more than tripled in countries such as Austria, Belgium, Finland, Spain and the UK (United Nations Economic Commission for Europe 2003). Due to the prevalence of drug use (particularly 'soft' drugs), many young people are now cautioned by the police (particularly for first offences) rather than being brought before the courts. In several countries 'soft' drugs have been either formally decriminalized or minor offences of possession are largely ignored by the police. However, use of 'hard' drugs may be associated with an increased likelihood of involvement in other forms of illegal behaviour and drug use (as well as heavy alcohol use) is often regarded as a strong predictor of serious or persistent offending (Flood-Page *et al.* 2000). In particular, rises in property related crimes are frequently associated with increased use of heroin. Parker and colleagues (1988), for example, argue that an increase in burglaries tends to correlate with an increase in heroin use in disadvantaged areas among unemployed youth.

Whilst under the influence of drugs, users may be less aware of the consequences of their activities (Lyon 1996) and habitual drug use may provide the motivation to commit crimes in order to finance an addiction. Indeed, those who are calling for the decriminalization of 'hard' drugs tend to justify their arguments in terms of the impact on levels of crime. Yet Hammersley and colleagues argue that although the use of opioids increased the likelihood of criminal behaviour they 'did not simply and directly cause crime or substantially create criminals from honest citizens' (1990: 19). They concluded that the price of heroin was more related to crime than the addictiveness.

In many countries, young people between the ages of 14 and 25 tend to account for more than half of all indictable offences, with a large proportion of those convicted being young, black males (Farrington 1990; Muncie 2004). Young people from working class families are more likely to be convicted for an offence, with offenders often living in areas of multiple deprivation, having parents who are divorced and with a history of truancy from school (Farrington 1990; Bynner *et al.* 2004). Other factors that have been shown to be associated with convictions include poor educational performance (and especially poor literacy and numeracy), family poverty and neighbourhood deprivation, high rates of local unemployment, chaotic home lives or parental disinterest (Bynner *et al.* 2004).

While official statistics on convictions highlight an association between social class and criminal convictions, these claims are not always supported by survey data pertaining to involvement (Graham and Bowling 1995; Hagan *et al.* 1996). Similarly, the strong differences between male and female involvement in crime indicated by official figures on convictions have been challenged by survey data (Campbell 1981; Graham and Bowling 1995; Hagan *et al.* 1996). Using self-report data, Graham and Bowling (1995) show that in the UK among 14- to 17-year-olds, males and females report similar levels of involvement in offences relating to property and violence (although among older age groups, males reported greater levels of criminal activity). These discrepancies provide support for the view that differential conviction rates reflect patterns of law enforcement rather than underlying gender differences in behaviour.

The higher rates of conviction, prosecution and imprisonment among young people from ethnic minorities that exist in all developed countries are sometimes regarded as a reflection of police activity rather than representing greater involvement in crime. Ethnic minorities frequently live in inner city areas and tend to be subject to higher levels of police surveillance (Fitzgerald 1993). In the USA in 2004, among 20- to 24-year-old males, 6.2 per cent of African Americans were incarcerated as compared with 2.4 per cent of Hispanics and 0.9 per cent of Caucasians (US Department of Justice 2005). In Louisiana, which has one of the highest rates of juvenile imprisonment in the USA, 78 per cent of the youth prison population were African Americans, even though they make up just a third of the population (Juvenile Justice Project of Louisiana 2005). A similar picture emerges in Australia where Aborigines are far more likely to be arrested than non-Aborigines (Ferrante *et al.* 1998) and almost 19 times more likely to be imprisoned (Blagg 1997).

An influential UK report by the Royal Commission on Criminal Justice (Fitzgerald 1993) highlighted a number of factors which were associated with higher levels of conviction and imprisonment among the black population. These included the younger average age of the black population in comparison to that of the white population, the concentration of young blacks in working class families, lower levels of educational attainment, higher levels of unemployment and their geographical distribution: all factors that are associated with criminality among the white population. However, a number of legal factors were also identified which increased their chances of conviction and the severity of the sentence: these included a tendency not to admit guilt (making them ineligible for cautioning and provoking longer sentences if found guilty), the seriousness of offences, the number of previous convictions and the greater tendency for magistrates to refer cases involving black youths to Crown Court. In the USA, black males are far more likely than their white peers to be referred to juvenile court (Bishop and Decker 2006).

While there may be a tendency to exaggerate increases in criminality among the younger generation, there is some evidence that an extension of youth as a stage in the life cycle has led to a prolonged involvement in crime (Rutherford 1992; Graham and Bowling 1995). As Graham and Bowling argue 'If it is true that young people grow out of crime, then many will fail to do so, at least by their mid-twenties, simply because they have not been able to grow up, let alone grow out of crime' (1995: 56). However, as yet we are unable to determine whether longer involvement in crime tends to lead to more serious offences or whether it simply results in more petty offences and, as a consequence, a greater risk of apprehension. Criminologists have shown that young people's involvement in illegal activities tend to decline as they acquire greater responsibilities in work and domestic environments. However, there is also evidence that ageing is associated with a switch from visible crimes committed on the streets (such as violence and car crime) to less visible crime (such as burglary and fraud) (Graham and Bowling 1995). In other words, the lower rates of crime among older youth may partly represent higher rates of apprehension and conviction associated with certain types of juvenile crime rather than the termination of involvement.

Older youths and those with domestic or employment responsibilities are less likely to engage in criminal activities than younger people or those with jobs or family responsibilities (Rutherford 1992; Sampson and Laub 1993). Indeed, there is evidence that commitment to a job or to another person is often associated with a reduction in offending (Parker 1974; Shover 1985; Sampson and Laub 1993). Consequently delays in making key transitions are likely to be reflected in increased levels of criminality. Young people tend to become less involved in criminal activities as they find ways of gaining fulfillment in other areas of their lives and take on responsibilities in a work or domestic sphere. In particular, relationships with girlfriends have been seen as significant in reducing risk taking by males (Coles 1995; Graham and Bowling 1995). However, it has been suggested that with males now facing greater difficulties in obtaining secure positions in the labour market, young women may be less inclined to form steady relationships with young men without secure jobs or obvious prospects (Wallace 1987; Hill 1995). The greater protraction of school to work, domestic and housing transitions for young males is likely to be one of the explanations for the widening gender ratios in offending among the 18-plus age group (Graham and Bowling 1995). In this respect failure to complete a key transition can lead to social marginality and a continuity of the risks associated with criminality.

In this context, transitional experiences are closely related to patterns of involvement in crime and associated with gender differences. Using a multi-variate analysis, Graham and Bowling (1995) show that in the UK the success-ful completion of school to work, domestic and housing transitions was associated with an abrupt and conscious end to offending among females. Males, on the other hand, tended to drift away from crime much more grad-ually and remained susceptible to peer group pressure for some time after making key transitions. Youth unemployment has also been linked to criminal behaviour and unemployed men are more likely to be serious or persistent offenders (Farrington *et al.* 1986; Flood-Page *et al.* 2000). In Aulnay-sous-Bois, one of the Paris suburbs that has been the site of disturbances in the mid-2000s, youth unemployment was reported to have been in the region of 40 per cent (Henley 2005b). Similarly in the impoverished Redfern district of Sydney, which also experienced serous street violence and vandalism after the death of a teenager while being chased by police, more than one in four Aboriginal residents were unemployed even though rates in the city were particularly low.

There is also evidence that those who are involved in crime prior to entering the labour market experience difficulties in finding jobs, largely due to employer discrimination. In these circumstances it has been suggested that unemployment is associated with an intensification and prolongation of crim-inal careers (Hagan *et al.* 1996). While there is some evidence to support the theory that unemployment is associated with increased criminal activity, the association has been explained in a number of different ways (Tarling 1982; Hagan *et al.* 1996). On the one hand, it has been argued that an increasing crime rate reflects the collapse of legitimate opportunity structures; on the other, the 'left realists' associate crime with relative deprivation. Lea and Young (1993), for example, argue that crime rises as a consequence of the discontent and frustration which is the inevitable consequence of economic marginalization. Asked about reasons for involvement in crime, more than eight in ten young people in European Union countries linked crime to unemployment and poverty (European Commission 2003b).

A number of writers have also linked male criminality to difficulties in establishing masculine identities in a changing economic context. With a growth in educational participation, it has been suggested that males who fail to excel academically frequently see schooling as frustrating their masculinity (Messerschmidt 1994; McDowell 2003). Moreover, the decline in manual employment opportunities means that young males today are forced to define their masculinities in new ways with crime offering one route through which positive identities can be established (McDowell 2003). For low educational attainers, involvement in crime may actually result in an increase in self-esteem as a result of gaining kudos with peers (Bynner *et al.* 1981).

Criminal careers

Young people tend to commit their first offences at a relatively young age: in the UK the average age at which males and females start to offend is 13 (Graham and Bowling 1995) with involvement peaking at age 18 for males and 15 for females (Muncie 2004). Those who become involved in car crime, for example, frequently commit their first offence at the age of 13 or 14 (Nee 1993) usually in the company of older peers. In this context, criminologists have argued that patterns of association are particularly significant and that young people become involved in criminal activities in small group settings as they adapt to the norms of peer cultures (Sutherland 1949). Sutherland suggests that individuals engage in criminal acts when such activities are defined as acceptable by their associates while Bynner and colleagues (2004) suggest that boys growing up in fatherless families in high unemployment neighbour-hoods may come to adopt older males who are involved in crime as role models. Although Sutherland's theory of differential association has fre-quently been criticized for suggesting that criminal behaviour is learned (Shoemaker 1990), there is strong evidence that peers have a significant effect on patterns of involvement in crime (Graham and Bowling 1995).

From a different theoretical perspective, Gottfredson and Hirschi (1990) also argue that the amount of time young people spend in the company of their peers has an impact on criminality, with those whose family ties are 'chaotic' tending to spend the greatest amount of time with their friends. Similarly, using self-report data from Northern Ireland, McQuoid suggests that

> juvenile delinquency here is associated with males in their late teens from lower educational and socio-economic groups, who either dislike or who have left school and have no job, have a large circle of 'close' friends, little parental supervision and who do not see the importance of working hard.
>
> (1996: 98)

Control theorists, such as Gottfredson and Hirschi (1990) argue that peer group influence and the lack of close parental supervision provide young people with opportunities to engage in illegal activities either for excitement or financial gain. But opportunities to engage in criminal behaviour are also shaped by the possibilities afforded within a neighbourhood context. In a classic study, Parker (1974), for example, described the ways in which young people living in an inner-city area of Liverpool were provided with opportun-ities for theft in the form of a plentiful supply of cars left by shoppers and city workers. Moreover, young people were easily able to sell stolen car radios due to the existence of a network of 'fences' within the area. The existence of high crime rates in some neighbourhoods has also been seen as reflecting conform-ity to cultural norms rather than a rejection of accepted patterns of behaviour (Mays 1954; Downes 1966). However, subcultural theories are somewhat out of vogue and frequently portrayed as incomplete explanations. Brownfield (1996), for example, argues that the demise of subcultural theories stems from a failure to conceptualize structural and cultural factors within a single explanatory framework.

Criminologists have also highlighted the link between criminal activities and blocked access to legitimate opportunities. In settings where legitimate opportunities are restricted, illegal opportunities may arise which help chan-nel young people into delinquency. Young people who are unable to find jobs or who are forced to occupy precarious positions in the labour market may find that crime provides them with access to consumer goods and leisure lifestyles which they would otherwise be unable to afford. Referring to a group of boys who were involved in car crime, Pearson argues that the lucrative sale of car radios allowed the boys 'to enjoy the "good times" before either settling down to marriage and family life, or going to prison' (1994: 1180). Similarly Hobbs (1989) has described the ways in which young people develop an entrepreneurial approach to crime aided by family and neighbourhood-based social networks. Pryce (1979) described how, for African Caribbean males, 'hustling' was used as a means to overcome frustrations caused by the lack of legitimate opportunities (Pearson 1994). In his report on the Brixton disorders, Lord Scarman (1981) drew attention to the ways in which young blacks shared the material expectations encouraged within advanced capitalism, yet as a result of racism and high rates of unemployment often experienced status frustrations. These explanations underline Merton's (1969) arguments about the gap between social norms and aspirations and differential access to opportunities as well as the views of the 'left realists' regarding the consequences of relative deprivation.

Although the association between relative deprivation and crime has merit, it is important to stress that young criminals are often opportunists and frequently lack a profit motive. Many young people become involved in criminal activities as a consequence of seeking new ways of relieving boredom: financial incentives are often of little importance (Nee 1993). Coles, for example, argues that 'early youth crime is often spontaneous, unskilled, committed by a peer group having a bit of a laugh together, and acted out as a piece of hooliganism rather than as a piece of calculated or instrumental rationality' (1995: 185).

Young people as victims of crime

While there is evidence that a substantial proportion of crimes are committed by young people, it is also important to stress that young people are frequently the victims of crime and express concerns about perceived personal risks of crime. Much of the research on youth and crime has focused on young people as perpetrators of crime; relatively few writers have explored the implications of fear of crime among the young or analysed the extent to which they are the victims of police harassment or of crimes committed by adults and other young people. Given that a high proportion of criminal acts are committed against young people, this represents a serious bias.

There are a number of studies that have explored aspects of fear of crime among young people and its implications (Anderson *et al.* 1994; Maung 1995; Lemos 2004; Muncie 2004). In the UK, for example, around a third of secondary school students feel unsafe when walking out after dark, around one in four worry about theft and about five per cent are concerned about crimes involving weapons (Lemos 2004). The fear of attack is a particular concern of females. Using evidence from the British Crime Survey, Maung (1995) found that the possibility of sexual pestering or assault by a stranger were the chief concerns of female 12- to 15-year-olds: 56 per cent said that they were very worried about the chances of sexual pestering while 48 per cent were very worried about assault by a stranger. A number also expressed concerns about mugging or burglary (35 per cent and 22 per cent respectively). Boys in the same age range were somewhat less concerned about the possibility of crime: 31 per cent were very worried about sexual pestering, 28 per cent about assault by a stranger, 24 per cent about mugging and 15 per cent about burglary. For each of these crimes, African Caribbean and Asian youth were significantly more likely to express concern about becoming a victim, as were those living in urban areas and areas in which levels of recorded crime were high. These concerns affected the ways in which young people spent their time and the places they visited. In particular, young women are much more likely than young men to feel unsafe when out alone and often felt the need to take precautions against crime, such as making special transport arrangements or going out with friends (Hough 1995).

While fears of crime are not necessarily related to the chances of victimization, young people's behaviour may be affected by the fear of crime. Young people may avoid visiting places they perceive as risky, or may defend themselves against possible attack. In a survey of 14,000 secondary school students in the UK, almost one in four 16-year-olds admitted that they had carried a knife or other weapon while nearly one in five had used a weapon (Lemos 2004). Statistics on victims of crime compiled for 17 industrialized countries by van Kesteren and colleagues (2001) show that overall weapons were used (as a threat or otherwise) in just less than one in four recoded cases of assault or threat (rising to more than four in ten where the victim was a male).

Indeed, studies of young people's experiences of crime show that many of their fears are well founded. Half of the 11- to 15-year-olds interviewed by Anderson and colleagues (1994) had been victims of a crime with members of ethnic minorities being most likely to be the victims of street robbery (BSC 2000). In cases where the offender could be identified, less than half were under the age of 16: 10 per cent of offences against boys and 17 per cent of offences against girls were committed by people over the age of 21 (Anderson *et al.* 1994). Indeed, two-thirds of the girls reported having been harassed by adults, sometimes being followed by people either in cars or on foot. In a 2002 study of 5,000 UK school children, over a third had been physically attacked and almost half threatened: a third had had things stolen from them at school (MORI 2002a).

Compared to older age groups, UK males aged 16 to 24 were four times more likely to have been the victim of a violent incident over the last year while females of the same age were almost twice as likely to have been victims (Nicholas *et al.* 2005) (Figure 7.3). Other factors associated with a significant increase in risk include being single, unemployed, living in an area characterized by high levels of disorder and visiting a pub more than three times a week (Nicholas *et al.* 2005).

There are wide variations in the risk of violence between countries. In the USA, the National Crime Victimization Survey has shown that 12- to 17-year-olds represent around one in five victims of serious criminal violence and are twice as likely as adults to be victims of assault (Bishop and Decker 2006) while Blacks are almost twice as likely as Whites to be victims of serious violent crimes (US Department of Justice 2005). A study of criminal victimization in 17 industrialized countries (van Kesteren *et al.* 2001) show relatively high

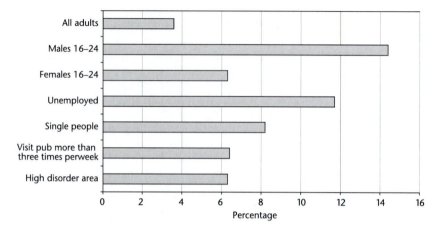

Figure 7.3 Self-reported victims of violence: UK 2004/05
Source: Nicholas *et al.* 2005

levels of victimization in countries like Australia, England and Wales and Canada but much lower levels in Japan, Portugal and the USA (Figure 7.4).

While crimes committed against young people are a common occurrence, relatively few incidents are reported to the police. Whereas more than a third of adults will tend to report offences such as assaults, robberies, personal threats and thefts, among 16- to 19-year-olds just 14 per cent would make a formal complaint (Maung 1995). Similarly, Anderson and colleagues (1994) showed that 14 per cent of 11- to 15-year-olds would report an assault to the police. Asian and African Caribbean youths are less likely than white youths to report crimes committed against them, although Maung (1995) argues that ethnic differences are not significant once characteristics of areas are taken into consideration. While young people are hesitant about reporting offences

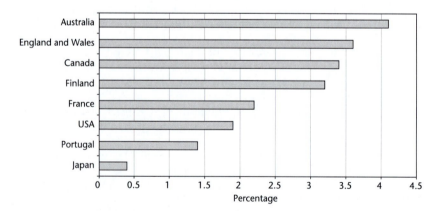

Figure 7.4 Victims of robbery, sexual assault, and assault with force: selected countries, 1999
Source: van Kesteren *et al.* 2001

to the police, they frequently tell their friends and, depending on the nature of the offence, are likely to bring the matter to the attention of their parents (Anderson *et al.* 1994; Maung 1995). However, females experiencing sexual harassment are frequently unwilling to discuss events with their parents and child abuse is sometimes regarded as an 'invisible' crime.

In many respects, the concentration on young people as the perpetrators of crimes has left us blind to the extent to which young people are victims; they frequently have crimes committed against them and their fears have an impact on their day-to-day behaviour. In particular, young women frequently experience harassment which they are reluctant to report and which restricts their freedom to go out alone. Moreover, while adults express concerns about 'lawless' youth, many crimes are also committed against young people by adults.

Conclusion

Although many young people engage in criminal activities and while significant numbers will be the victims of crime, it would be wrong to suggest that the patterns of criminality which we have described in this chapter represent a breakdown in the social fabric of society. Young people have always indulged in risky behaviour and in activities which are illegal. The youth of previous generations engaged in similar types of activities and also found themselves to be the focus of police attention and the source of anguish to adults (Pearson 1983). There is, however, little evidence that the numbers of serious crimes committed by young people are rising, although criminal careers are perhaps becoming longer.

In many respects, the 'problem' of crime today relates more to its amplification by the media than to actual risk. Indeed, Hough has suggested that by the 1980s, 'the fear of crime was running ahead of substantive crime problems' (1995: 4). The media focus on abnormal youth crimes has perhaps led to an increased perception of a lawless younger generation and to calls for tougher sanctions against offenders. However, the increased fear of crime has implications for everyone, as Box and colleagues (1988) suggest, the fear of crime can fracture communities as people move away from the cities and restrict their movements: it can also promote the introduction of measures that curtail the feedoms of young people who are not engaged in criminal acts. In this context, Giddens (1991) is wrong to suggest that place loses its significance in the age of high modernity: both the fear of crime, the chances of becoming a victim of crime and the risks of apprehension for involvement in crime continue to reflect social geographies. While Giddens would argue that through the mass media we are all exposed to the consequences of crime and develop a heightened sense of insecurity and mistrust, perceptions of risk are differentially distributed. Viewers contextualize television violence and are more concerned when the risks highlighted by the media are shown to affect their own locality or areas with similar characteristics (Gunter 1987). As such, those who live in deprived inner city areas with visible signs of decay are more frightened to go out alone than those living in non-urban areas (Hough 1995).

Our discussion of young people and crime also highlights the continued association between deprivation and risk of crime in late modernity. Although the evidence suggests that those groups whose members are most often apprehended for crimes (working class males and black and Asian males) are not significantly more likely to be involved in crime than members of other social groups, the activities of the police are organized on the premise that criminality is a subcultural phenomenon and very much related to place. One of the consequences of patterns of police surveillance is that members of disadvantaged social groups are more likely to be charged with offences and, as a result, can face difficulties in the labour market, thus increasing the odds that criminal careers will continue.

While young people are more likely to commit certain types of criminal offences than adults, many offences are relatively trivial and criminal careers usually end as young people acquire responsibilities and commitments through jobs and relationships. The main change that we have witnessed here concerns the implications of extended transitions. Delayed transitions are likely to result in an extension of criminality (albeit mainly of a minor nature) as young people have fewer responsibilities and spend greater periods of time in the company of their peers.

The other key change which is likely to have had an impact on criminality relates to the growing closeness of the relationship between youth cultures and consumerism. Whereas during the 1950s and 1960s youth was a period of affluence, especially for young people from working class families who had relatively high disposable incomes soon after leaving school, today fewer young people have access to the same sort of disposable income and some are in danger of long-term exclusion from consumer society. Although most juvenile crime is expressionistic rather than instrumental, criminologists have argued that the relative deprivation which stems from exclusion can lead to the development and prolongation of criminal careers as young people begin to appreciate that crime provides the potential for the enhancement of lifestyles and the means of access to consumer culture.

8 Politics *and* participation

To young people such as myself, the two major parties locked in seemingly endless arm-wrestling for electoral supremacy, offer little more
than a choice between Fruit Loops and Coco Pops – both saccharine,
hollow in the middle and of dubious nutritional value.
(Youth journalist following the 2004 electoral campaign in Australia:
www.onlineopinion.com.au/view.asp?article=3012)

Introduction

Although young people's lives have changed quite significantly, the evidence
presented in previous chapters shows that traditional forms of social stratification still hold the key to an understanding of life chances in the age of high
modernity. At the same time, we have suggested that subjective awareness of
the influence of social structures has diminished as experiences and lifestyles
become increasingly individualized. If it is true that young people today lack a
developed awareness of the significance of collective experiences, then we
would expect to find these changes reflected in political orientations.

On the surface, the task of describing changes in the political orientations of youth appears straightforward. Yet while there is a wealth of information on changes in the political behaviour of adults, political scientists have
largely neglected the study of youth[1] partly because compared to some older
groups of voters (such as pensioners), the youth vote has not tended to sway
election results (Bynner and Ashford 1994; Park 1996, 2004). In fact in many
countries comprehensive inter-generational comparisons of the political
orientations of young people cannot be easily supported by the available data.

Political commentators have frequently drawn attention to young
people's lack of political awareness, to political apathy, to a disinterest in politics and to their lack of participation in the political process (Stradling 1977;
Cochrane and Billig 1983; Furnham and Stacey 1991; Bynner and Ashford
1994; Park 2004; Print *et al.* 2004). In turn, these concerns have sometimes
been seen as posing a threat to democratic traditions as young people have
little basic knowledge about political processes and remain unconvinced about
the commitment of politicians to deal with issues which concern them or to

act in ways which will lead to an improvement in their circumstances (Bynner and Ashford 1994; Print *et al.* 2004; Electoral Commission 2005; Saha *et al.* 2005). Voicing concerns that have been expressed in many countries, in 2005 in his Australia Day address, the Governor-General of Australia talked about a crisis of democracy and argued that it had become necessary to find new ways of interesting young people in politics.

Low levels of political participation among youth have been a cause for concern in a number of industrialized countries and various attempts have been made to encourage greater involvement, including a range of initiatives that have attempted to capitalize on young people's interest in popular music. An early example from the UK was the Red Wedge concert tour which various artists performed with the aim of encouraging young people to vote for the Labour Party. The politically neutral, Rock the Vote campaign also aimed to persuade young people to exercise their voting rights. In the USA, similar initiatives have been launched, including the Vote for Change tour led by Bruce Springsteen, the Dixie Chicks and Pearl Jam which explicitly set out to promote an anti-Bush vote among young (and not so young) voters.

While young people's lack of involvement in the formal political process is not a new phenomenon, recent changes in the experiences of adolescents and young adults may well have an impact on forms of political engagement. In particular, given evidence showing a significant relationship between educational participation and political involvement (Bynner and Ashford 1994; Haerpfer *et al.* 2002), changes in patterns of schooling could have an impact on political awareness which we might hope to see reflected in an increase in political participation. Indeed, Emler (1996) has argued that the experiences of 16- to 25-year-olds can have a lasting and significant impact on political orientations. However, changes in the circumstances faced by young people in the modern world can also have negative political consequences. A greater individualization of experiences in education and in the workplace can lead to a weakening of the mechanisms of political socialization, while the experience of unemployment or job insecurity can lead to a lack of faith in the political system, to a rise in support for extreme right and left wing parties and even to a willingness to consider violent political action (Breakwell 1986; Banks and Ullah 1987). There is also evidence suggesting that the shift from a political agenda shaped by concerns for social justice towards neo-liberalism and a preoccupation with fiscal matters have alienated young people from national politics (Adsett 2003).

There has been some debate about the extent to which young people's apparent lack of interest in politics represents a significant generational shift (Park 2000, 2004; Blias *et al.* 2001; Adsett 2003) and, while the research remains inconclusive, there is a growing body of evidence that suggests a weakening of participation in the formal political process. As Jowell and Park note 'the trend towards less engagement in politics among the young . . . appears to signal a generational change' (1998: 14). At the same time, Adsett (2003) has cautioned that any decline in political participation among the current generation of young people has to be set against what was perhaps a relatively high level of involvement among the 'baby-boomers' generation who were particularly active in youth counter-cultures.

In the context of generational change, sociologists writing in the late-modernist tradition would argue the social changes currently taking place do not simply involve a quantitative shift in political orientations within a 'traditional' framework, but imply a fundamental qualitative change in political values which will impact on political involvement. Giddens (1991) has suggested that in high modernity an increasing emphasis is placed on 'life politics' rather than the 'emancipatory politics' which were associated with traditional social orders. Whereas emancipatory politics involve a struggle for liberation and the enhancement of collective life chances, life politics is the 'politics of self-actualisation in a reflexively ordered environment' (Giddens 1991: 214). In other words, the problems associated with the reflexive construction of self identity and lifestyles involve a new set of issues and priorities which have a political nature but which link the individual to the social world in a different way – connecting the individual to the political world directly rather than via the collective mediation of social groups.

It is important here to stress that Giddens is not suggesting that there is no place for emancipatory politics in late modernity. The point is that with processes of self-actualization raising fundamental moral issues, the personal sphere is increasingly linked to political issues. Items high on the agenda for life politics include issues related to environmentalism and animal rights: those which concern many young people (Inglehart 1990; Bennie and Rüdig 1993; Scarbrough 1995; Bynner *et al.* 2003; Haste 2005b).

In any discussion about young people and politics it is important to be aware of the different levels at which political engagement can be measured. Young people can express an interest in politics without being active in the formal institutions of party politics, they may be involved in political action while not voting or expressing a strong party affiliation, or may be knowledgeable about political issues while remaining cynical about their ability to influence the political agenda (Gauthier 2003). Moreover, they may engage in actions which are political in the broader sense of the word without expressing any interest or having any involvement in the politics of emancipation. As one young activist put it, 'there are things we do every day that are very political, like taking the subway instead of the car, or buying coffee that has been fair traded, or eating tangerines from Morocco – they are all political acts' (Queniart and Jacques 2000, quoted in Gauthier 2003).

In this chapter we explore these different levels of involvement. We argue that although young people may lack an involvement in formal politics, they do have a concern with broader issues which may be construed as political and, in particular, are frequently involved in single issue political campaigns on issues which are perceived as having a relevance to their lives. Despite these claims, we are sceptical of the tendency to regard the political priorities of youth as indicative of the ascendancy of 'post-materialist' values (Inglehart 1977, 1990) or as signalling the demise of emancipatory politics. Indeed, on some levels it can be argued that the political values of the younger generation are not so very different from those of the previous generation.

Political interest and knowledge

In most advanced countries there is a wealth of evidence showing that, compared to older citizens, young people currently have little interest or involvement in party politics (Roberts and Parsell 1990; Bhavanani 1991; Furnham and Stacey 1991; MacDonald and Coffield 1991; Bynner and Ashford 1994; Adsett 2003; Print *et al.* 2004; Saha *et al.* 2005). Party politics are perceived as boring and as something which has little relevance to their lives (Banks and Ullah 1987; Roberts and Parsell 1990; Bhavanani 1991; Print *et al.* 2004; Saha *et al.* 2005). 'Politics for most young people means a drab world of grey, besuited, middle-aged, middle-class, male MPs, compulsory party political broadcasts and strange, heated arguments about which they know little' (MacDonald and Coffield 1991: 217).

In Europe, the majority of young people do not express an interest in politics: in an EU survey (EUYOUPART 2005), just 37 per cent of 15- to 25-year-olds said that they had an interest. The highest levels of interest were recorded in Germany where 51 per cent said that they were interested in politics and the lowest recorded in France and Finland (36 and 35 per cent respectively).

In the UK changing levels of interest in party politics can be traced using the regular British Social Attitudes Survey. Among all of those of voting age, the numbers saying that they have some interest in politics has not fallen below 60 per cent since 1986 (Figure 8.1). Yet throughout this period those aged 18 to 24 were less likely to express any interest in politics, with the gap between young people and the all age sample becoming wider since 1994. By 2003 just 41 per cent of young people were willing to concede that they had any interest in politics – with 36 per cent of 18- to 24-year-olds saying that they had no interest in politics at all (compared to 13 per cent of the overall

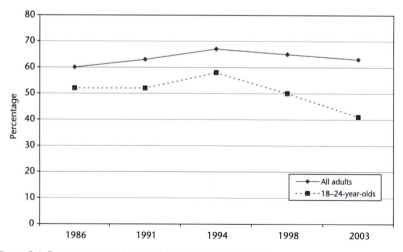

Figure 8.1 Persons expressing some interest in politics: UK
Source: Park 2004

sample). Just one in twenty young people under the age of 25 are members of a UK political party (Fahmy 1999). Interest in politics tends to be greater among males than females (Roberts and Parsell 1990; Park 2004); young people from non-manual families show a greater interest than those from manual backgrounds (Roberts and Parsell 1990; Bynner and Parsons 2003); and political interest tends to increase with length of education and age (Emler 1996; Bynner and Parsons 2003; Park 2004).

Faced with a lack of political interest among the younger generation, politicians have tried to 'sell themselves' in a variety of ways and have attempted to increase their profile by appearing at events which appeal to young people. Given the high average age of politicians, these efforts often look like a cynical attempt to win votes. Tony Blair, following in the tradition of Harold Wilson (who tried to curry favour with younger members of the electorate by appearing on television with the Beatles), was keen to be associated with 'Britpop'. His early days in office were marked by the frequent reporting of drinks parties at 10 Downing Street with the likes of the Gallagher brothers and Jarvis Cocker. Such attempts have not been confined to British politicians. Both Bill Clinton and George W. Bush, used celebrities to try and bolster election campaigns. The politically inspired Rock the Vote campaign, which claimed to have registered 1.2 million new voters for the 2004 Presidential election, celebrated its fifteenth anniversary in 2005. Using the slogan, 'piss off a politician by voting', and involving artists like Joss Stone and Snoop Dogg, Rock the Vote has been accredited with boosting the youth vote.

Young people's lack of interest in party politics is partly linked to a lack of knowledge about the process, policies and the implications of decisions. In the UK, a survey carried out for *The Times* newspaper found that just 23 per cent could name their MP (MORI 2002b). Similarly, in a study of 11- to 21-year-olds carried out in 2005, nearly one in five (17 per cent) did not know that Tony Blair was Prime Minister while almost one in ten (8 per cent) still thought that Margaret Thatcher was PM (Haste 2005b). A short quiz about politics was also used in the teenage sample (12- to 19-year-olds) linked to the British Social Attitudes Survey. Analysis of the results showed that males knew more about party politics than females, and those from non-manual social classes performed better than those from manual families. There was no significant difference in the political knowledge of Labour and Conservative supporters, but supporters of the Liberal Democrats displayed the greatest knowledge of the political system (Park 1996).

In a recent study of senior school students in Australia (Print *et al.* 2004) it was argued that young people did not feel well prepared to vote and lacked a solid understanding of the political system. Around one in two lacked the knowledge to be able to vote effectively, to make decisions when voting, to understand political parties or political issues (Figure 8.2). Males were more confident in the adequacy of their knowledge than females.

Expressing concerns about the lack of useful political knowledge among young people, Stradling argues that

> There is something essentially paradoxical about a democracy in which some eighty to ninety per cent of the future citizens (and present

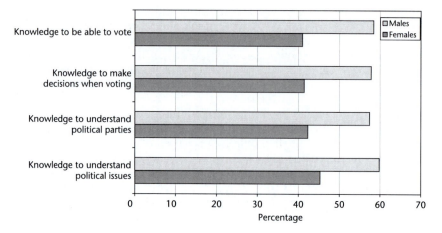

Figure 8.2 Political knowledge of young Australians
Source: Print *et al.* 2004

citizenry) are insufficiently well-informed about local, national and international politics to know not only what is happening but also how they are affected by it and what they can do about it. Most of the political knowledge which they do have is of a rather inert and voyeuristic kind and of little use to them either as political consumers or as political actors.

(Stradling 1977: 57, quoted in Furnham and Gunter 1989: 19)

There is also evidence that political knowledge among young people has declined: in the USA in the postwar era there has been a decline in the numbers who can recognize key political figures and even a sharp reduction in the number of Americans who can locate Europe on a world map (down from 45 per cent in 1947 to 25 per cent in 1988) (Buckingham 2000). Here Putnam (2000) makes a link between political disengagement among the younger generation, a decline in interest in current affairs and falling levels of civic engagement.

While political knowledge may be poor (and perhaps deteriorating) apathy and cynicism are also rife (Bhavnani 1991; MacDonald and Coffield 1991; Bynner and Ashford 1994; Print *et al.* 2004). Some feel that politics doesn't affect their day-to-day lives or they have little confidence that politicians will listen to them or take any account of their concerns. As one 16-year-old put it, 'You are always getting different people saying that they're going to do this and that and whatever, and nothing happens, nothing really changes' (quoted in White *et al.* 2000).

The decision to go to war with Iraq and the failure to be swayed by a high level of youth involvement in anti-war demonstrations can be used to justify the view that young people's political voices tend to fall on deaf ears (Print *et al.* 2004) as has the failure to prevent changes in funding arrangements for students in the UK. Rare exceptions include the U-turn in proposals to reduce employment security for young workers in France and the political influence of the Make Poverty History protest organized to coincide with the G8 summit in Scotland. In general, western politicians rarely focus on matters that directly concern young people except when they withdraw benefits or impose new restrictions on their actions (Wallace 2003). Here the British Youth Council has suggested that

> rather than young people being apathetic it is in fact the politicians and parties that are indifferent, uninterested and complacent as they do not seem to give consideration to the extremely difficult positions that young people are facing, or contemplate how young people will be affected by the proposals in the legislation they produce.
>
> (1995: 1)

Politics may be seen as a 'dirty business' and, like many adults, young people may feel that politicians are out of touch, out for their own ends or simply don't care what voters think until it comes to the next round of elections. A study commissioned by the Australian Electoral Commission (Print *et al.* 2004) concluded that young people did not trust politicians. Less than three in ten males and around one in five females thought that most people in government are honest and less than one in two thought that the government could be trusted to do what is right for the country. Added to the feeling that politicians were dishonest and perhaps untrustworthy, only around a third of young people thought that their representatives were smart enough to know what they were doing. In the UK politicians were seen as biased with fewer than one in two 11- to 21-year-olds (48 per cent) trusting the government to 'make laws that ensure that people are treated fairly whatever their background' (Haste 2005b: 8).

Political apathy and a lack of engagement with party politics can also be linked to the feeling that the main parties have few real differences in their priorities for policy and that therefore there is little at stake in elections. In the UK, for example, 18- to 24-year-olds were fairly evenly divided as to whether they personally felt it was important who won the next general election (MORI 2002b). In part, this can be linked to a lack of detailed knowledge about the policies of different parties and the ways that these affect their lives. Indeed, the decline in political interest and participation of young people may reflect the weakening of class-based politics. Not too long ago, in the main industrial nations, class and politics were inextricably linked. As Clarke and colleagues put it 'when voters cast their ballots, they expressed their "tribal loyalties". These loyalties were stable products of deeply engrained, class-based partisan allegiances' (2004: 175). Consequently a detailed knowledge of party politics was unnecessary as long as you knew which party was aligned to the class to which you belong or aspire.

Without a detailed knowledge of policies and lacking an informed view about many of the issues discussed in a political campaign, young people sometimes feel that it is not right to vote. As one young woman interviewed by MORI (2002b: 5) put it

> I have never voted because I don't think it's fair that I should use my vote and I don't know anything about it. And if I did vote, I would probably

find out a couple of months later, 'oh, I didn't know they did that, I voted for them and I wish I hadn't'.

For those who fear that they don't know enough about the complex range of polices being developed by a particular political party, the safest option might be to support a limited number of single issue pressure groups in areas where they hold strong views: a strategy that is popular with young people.

For some, political cynicism has been linked to a disaffection brought about as a result of a lack of opportunities for young people, to changing transitional experiences and to an extension in dependency (Marsh 1990; Kimberlee 2002; Thomson *et al.* 2004). Others though, have argued that political apathy is largely unaffected by post-16 experiences (Bynner and Ashford 1994). Bynner and Ashford argue that political disaffection is something which develops as a response to negative school experiences among the under-16s: among those who remain at school beyond the age of 16, interest in party politics tends to increase (Haerpfer *et al.* 2002). Educational performance has also been linked to political liberalism (Colby and Kohlberg 1987) and to lack of cynicism about politics (Emler 1996).

If patterns of interest in party politics among young people reflect their knowledge of the workings of the political system, then for a democracy to function effectively greater emphasis needs to be placed on the provision of citizenship and political education and an interest in current affairs needs to be stimulated. There may also be a case to be made for introducing young people to democracy through involvement in decisions that affect them: through allowing them to vote on school policies or in elections for school governors. Indeed, involvement in democratic organizations in the school is associated with a willingness to get involved in national and community politics (Print *et al.* 2004).

Political participation

Reflecting relatively low levels of interest in party politics, young people are less likely than adults to register a vote and tend to have a weaker commitment to any political party (Heath *et al.* 1991; Fahmy 1999; Print *et al.* 2004). In Australia, where registration and voting is compulsory with non-compliance leading to an automatic fine, young people are still less likely than adults to register or vote. In 2004, 82 per cent of 17- to 25-year-olds were registered to vote compared to 95 per cent of the overall adult population. In a survey of senior school students Print and colleagues (2004) asked respondents if they intended to vote in Federal elections when they reached 18: 87 per cent said that they would definitely or probably vote, with females being more inclined to vote than males. Asked if they would vote if it were not compulsory, one in two said that they would not. In the UK, of those eligible to vote, just 36 per cent said that they were 'absolutely certain' to vote in the next General Election (Haste 2005b).

In the UK, there has been an increase in those who claim not to have voted in General Elections since 1992: a trend that is particularly sharp among younger members of the electorate (Figure 8.3). In a recent poll commissioned

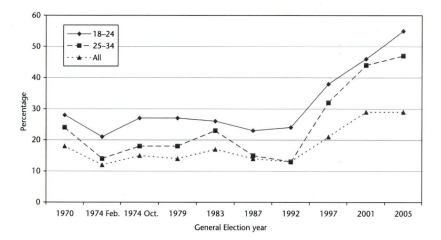

Figure 8.3 UK electorate who claim not to have voted in general elections, by age group
Source: Electoral Commission 2005

by the UK Electoral Commission (MORI 2005) 31 per cent of 18- to 24-year-olds said that they never or rarely vote in General Elections compared to 9 per cent of the voting age population. While levels of voting tend to be similar among males and females, rates of participation are higher among non-manual employees compared to manual workers and lowest among those who had never had a job (Bynner and Parsons 2003). In the UK, levels of voting are particularly low among 18–24-year-old African Caribbean's with members of ethnic minority groups swayed by politicians willingness to address minority issues (Sagger 2000).

The sharp decline in voting among young people, which in the UK has been particularly noticeable since the 1997 election, is common in a number of other countries (such as Canada and the USA), although there are significant differences in the timing (Buckingham 2000; O'Neill 2001). In Canada, for example, a sharp fall occurred between 1980 and 1984. While in the 1970s around seven in ten 18- to 24-year-olds typically voted, by the mid-1980s turnout was down to around four in ten (Gauthier 2003). Gauthier explains the downturn as reflecting the end of a political era in which there had long been a relatively weak government and a strong opposition which made for lively and responsive party politics. The 1984 election of the Progressive Conservatives signalled the emergence of neo-liberalism, a preoccupation with the economy and a shift away from concerns with social justice. With young people being attracted by issues of equality and alienated by fiscal matters, these changes were directly responsible for a reduction in the youth vote. Gauthier's argument has its attractions and can be applied to other countries where the ending of a political era was also marked by changes in young people's voting behaviour. It also suggests that changes in the political agenda could re-mobilize young people.

Low levels of participation in elections among younger members of the electorate may partly mean that adult concerns differ from their own priorities. It may also reflect a lack of knowledge about contemporary political issues, or may simply describe the extent to which many simply cannot see the point of voting. There are no obvious rewards, although in Australia the incentive to vote may simply be the negative inducement of penalty avoidance. In the Australian study carried out by Print and colleagues (2004) two-thirds of the young people thought that voting was boring while a further six in ten regarded it as a hassle: more than four in ten resented the fact that voting interrupted normal Saturday activities. In many respects, the biggest incentive to vote comes from a belief in the ability to influence a political agenda: it is the main opportunity for citizens to have their voices heard and to affect policy. Yet young people were often cynical about the chances of their having an impact on national agendas. As one of the Australian respondents put it 'They will do what they want. Their promises mean nothing. So what's the point?'

Cynicism among young people in regard to the political process is widespread and seems to have been heightened by an invasion of Iraq that took place despite the mobilization of vast numbers of young people who took part in demonstrations, often for the first time. However, as Bhavanani argues, cynicism does not necessarily imply apathy or a lack of interest in broader political issues. Indeed, she argues that cynicism 'may even act as an impetus for political activity' (1991: 13) by citing a study showing that among black law students in America, the most cynical were the most politically active.

Nevertheless, in terms of participation in the formal political process, young people's professed lack of interest in politics is reflected in levels of party membership and their voting behaviour. Statistics on the membership of the main political parties in Britain show that young people's impression that party politics is largely the preserve of the middle aged is correct. In 2004, less than 8 per cent of UK Members of Parliament were under the age of 40 with the median age having remained fairly stable since 1951 (House of Commons 2004). In Australia and some Eastern European countries the age profile of elected representatives is more balanced, although there is no direct evidence of a link between the ages of elected representatives and young people's interest in politics.

While political scientists once argued that young people were more likely to vote for left wing parties than older members of the electorate, voting statistics from the UK 2001 General Election suggest that it is 25- to 34-year-olds rather than new voters who were most likely to vote for the Labour Party (it is this group who, as younger voters, displayed the largest swing to Labour in 1997) (Harrison and Deicke 2001). Whereas 18- to 24-year-olds gave Labour a 14 per cent lead over the Conservatives, 25- to 34-year-olds gave Labour a 27 per cent lead and 35- to 44-year-olds a 17 per cent lead (House of Commons 2004). With the UK Labour Party having held office since 1997 and with an agenda that many regard as lacking a radical edge, it could be that younger voters associate Labour with the status quo rather than as a party of radical change. It is also likely that some of the policies implemented in terms of student finance are received negatively by younger voters. Among 18- to 21-year-olds who intended voting in 2005, support for the Liberal Democrats was almost double that of the Labour or Conservative parties (Haste 2005b), perhaps reflecting the strong association between the policies of that party and young people's own priorities (anti-Iraq war, pro-environment, supportive of student grants).

The political orientations of different age groups has been explored by Inglehart and colleagues (2004) using data from the 1999–2002 human beliefs and values surveys that were carried out in more than eighty countries. The results are complex but, in relation to first world countries, tend to show that the oldest people (over 50) are less likely to hold left wing values than those who are younger. However, countries vary as to whether 16- to 29-year-olds or 30- to 49-year-olds are more left leaning. In Canada, Germany, France, Japan and the USA, for example, it is the younger age group whose values are more likely to be classed as left wing while in Australia and France it is the 30–49-year-olds (Figure 8.4). As such, it is difficult to be clear about the relationship between generation and political change.

Political scientists frequently regard age-related differences in voting behaviour as being part of a 'life-cycle' effect whereby older people are seen as becoming more conservative (Sanders 1992). Indeed, a comparison of party support among parents and their children showed that although teenagers were more likely than their parents to support the Labour Party and less likely to support the Conservatives, differences were quite small (Park 1996) and recent trends seem to highlight strong similarities. Indeed, Park (1996) shows that almost two-thirds of young people with a parent who identified with the Conservatives held the same political allegiances, while nearly three-quarters of teenage Labour supporters had a parent who supported Labour. Although a significant proportion of young people hold different allegiances to those of their parents, Himmelweit and colleagues (1985) have argued that in cases where parents hold political views which are in line with their class member-ship, young people tend to follow their parents' political views. Evidence from several countries also show that traditional socio-economic differences are still evident in modern forms of political engagement among younger members of

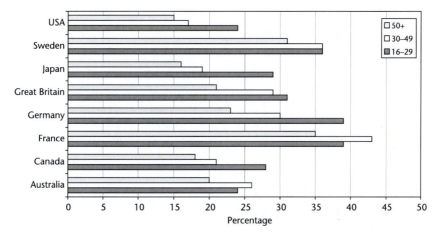

Figure 8.4 Orientation to left of centre political views, by age group: selected countries
Source: Inglehart *et al.* 2004

the electorate: class, education, employment status and gender remain powerful predictors of political attitudes (Haerpfer *et al.* 2002).

With evidence that the main predictors of partisanship among adults (such as social class, level of education, gender and 'race') still help us to understand the party affiliation of young voters, it is tempting to argue that sources of continuity in the political system are more powerful than sources of change. However, there have been important changes in patterns of political socialization which could serve to weaken these links. Franklin (1985) studied the effect of parents' social class and parents' party affiliation on voting behaviour and argued that, in Britain, such effects became weaker between the 1960s and late 1970s. Heath and colleagues (1991) undertook a similar analysis for voting patterns between 1964 and 1987 and argued that children had become less likely to adopt the political perspectives of their parents. As yet there is no evidence to show whether this trend is continuing, although changing levels of educational participation may have an ongoing impact on processes of political socialization (Scarborough 1995; Emler 1996).

While the increase in educational participation may have an impact on party allegiances, changes in processes of political socialization have also been affected by the re-structuring of the youth labour market. Traditionally, working class youth received a swift initiation into the world of politics on the factory floor through conversations with older workmates and through union membership. However, as MacDonald and Coffield point out

> the cultural inheritance of collectivism, trade union membership and Labour Party support, traditionally bound to apprenticeships into manual labour, are swiftly being eroded by the new cultural identities constructed over the past decade through youth traineeships.
>
> (1991: 220)

Greater insecurity in the labour market and the uncertainties which characterize early careers can mean that young people's work experiences are more individualized as they are forced to compete with each other in the hope of remaining in employment. As young workers become less able to identify collectivist solutions to negative workplace experiences traditional, class-based, political allegiances may weaken as employees become sceptical of the willingness or ability of governments to address the issues that concern them most.

In this context, although evidence of a link between educational participation and political involvement has been interpreted as a factor leading to a greater and more informed participation in the political process (Heath and Topf 1987; Bynner and Ashford 1994), some would argue that benefits are partly dependent on opportunities in the youth labour market. Indeed, if the efforts young people make in the education system are not rewarded through entry into highly paid or high status jobs, the likely outcome of this status inconsistency will be a rise in dissatisfaction leading to political unrest and protest among those who consider that they have been denied access to appropriate opportunities (Runciman 1966; Emler 1996). However, this interpretation has been challenged by Abrams (1990) who argues that Runciman's theory of a causal link between the relative deprivation of individuals and social protest is flawed. Abrams suggests that on an individual level, thwarted ambition (even if perceived as unfair or unjustified) leads to stress rather than political unrest. Drawing on the work of Tajfel and Turner (1979), Abrams (1990) suggests that it is *group*, rather than *individual*, relative deprivation that leads to social change. In other words, for political action to occur, people have to develop an awareness that a group to which they belong is being illegitimately disadvantaged (as was the case in France where the proposed changes in employment legislation applied only to young workers). Linking this theory to potential for political action among youth, Abrams suggests that current trends in education and the labour market may actually have weakened the potential for collectivism by strengthening individualist sentiments.

In communities characterized by high unemployment and urban decline, some young people may develop an awareness that the group to which they belong has been unfairly disadvantaged. While the French government does not collect statistics in ethnicity and unemployment, it has been suggested that in the estates most affected by recent troubles, up to 40 per cent of minority groups may be unemployed (*Sunday Times* 2005). Indeed, those faced with insecurity in the labour market who are deprived of traditional sources of political socialization, and who maintain a cynical attitude to mainstream political parties may come to identify with parties on the extreme right or left. In particular, the popularity of extreme right wing parties in countries like the UK, France and Australia among working class males has been associated with the increase in unemployment with members tending to be drawn from the least educated sections of the population. Supporters of extreme right wing parties tend to be more politically alienated than supporters of the mainstream parties and tend to feel that politicians take no notice of the concerns of ordinary people (Cochrane and Billig 1983).

Despite claims that rising unemployment is likely to lead to political extremism, a number of writers have been critical of the idea that negative labour market experiences are leading to a new radicalism (Banks and Ullah 1987; Roberts and Parsell 1990). Roberts and Parsell (1990) argue that unemployment is more likely to lead to 'passive alienation', which can be manifest in vandalism and conflicts with the police (see Chapter 7) rather than political unrest. While the 2005 disturbances in France may involve widespread vandalism, the burning of cars and battles with the police, it is perhaps a bit of an understatement to refer to it as 'passive alienation'. Although there are many instances of links between unemployment and unrest, Roberts and Parsell suggest that experiences in the post-school period have little impact on political orientations. Indeed, responses to unemployment are more likely to be individualist (such as stress and self-blame) rather than collectivist and young people may fail to identify a collective solution to their problems. With increasing levels of unemployment in the UK in the 1980s, the Conservatives were hated by the vast majority of the long-term unemployed (McRae 1987), although the majority of young unemployed voted for the Labour Party rather than for extreme parties of the left or right.

Post-materialist politics

Another theme which has been pursued by political scientists relates quite closely to Giddens' distinction between emancipatory politics and life politics. Inglehart (1977, 1990) has claimed to be able to detect a shift from 'materialist' to 'post-materialist' value orientations within advanced industrial societies and suggests that these changes have had an impact on the political agenda and on forms of political affiliation which can be seen as 'displacing the polit-ics of class' (Scarborough 1995: 123). These ideas are based on the theory that individuals become more concerned with self-actualization (post-modernist values) once concerns about basic needs and securities (materialism) have been fulfilled. Thus materialist values are centred around the need for physical sustenance and safety, whereas post-materialist values stress the need for belonging, self-expression and quality of life. These writers claim to be able to identify a 'silent revolution' which 'originates in the different value priorities as between older and younger generations, which, as younger generations replace older generations, result in a slow but steady shift in the cultural character of a society' (Scarborough 1995: 125).

Both Inglehart (1990) and Scarborough (1995) have attempted to exam-ine the extent to which a shift from materialist to post-materialist values can be detected empirically through an examination of the value orientations of members of different birth cohorts. Both writers detected a growth in post-materialist values which they linked, in part, to rising levels of education. In this respect, differences between the values of younger and older generations are not simply understood as representing 'youthful idealism' (Abramson and Inglehart 1992: 200), but reflect the material circumstances of the 'unprecedented' historical period (Scarborough 1995: 148) in which the current generation of young people spent their formative years. Although the ideas of Inglehart are controversial, they are central to our discussion of young people and politics in late modernity insofar as Giddens has suggested that political priorities have changed in the light of global insecurities.[2]

If we were to accept Giddens' interpretation of trends in high modernity, we would stress young people's relative lack of involvement in 'emancipatory' politics, as represented by the mainstream political parties, and would high-light their interest and involvement in 'lifestyle politics'. While young people may express an interest in single issue campaigns, such as environment issues, animal rights and anti-war and anti-globalization movements (Bennie and Rüdig 1993; Mulgan and Wilkinson 1997; Print *et al.* 2004; Haste 2005b), we do not regard this as a generational shift. In the 1950s and 1960s, for example, young people were active in CND and in protests against American involve-ment in Vietnam. Today's young people have been active in protests against the war in Iraq, against the introduction of GM crops and against globalization and first world policies towards third world debt.

Here the argument that young people lack an engagement with political issues starts to crumble. While there seems to have been some withdrawal from party politics and voting, young people display different forms of civic engagement and often prefer the simplicity of single issue politics where they both know what they are buying into and can judge progress towards specific goals. Often the issues they support are not ones that have been fully (or convincingly) adopted by mainstream political parties – issues such anti-vivisection, blood sports and student finance, for example. In Europe, more young people lend their support to a non-governmental organization than a political party (Generation Europe 2004). In a sense, this can be regarded as an individualized form of political engagement which leaves people free to support those issues they feel strongly about, without explicitly supporting a package of issues that include things with which they disagree. As one young person put it 'I think that belonging to a political party is something that, in a way, traps you. I want to be free according to the issues at any given time' (Generation Europe 2004: 4).

Forms of individualized political participation that are popular among young people include activities such as joining demonstrations, boycotting products and signing petitions (Carle 2001; Haerpfer *et al.* 2002; Vromen 2003; Haste 2005b; Saha *et al.* 2005). Several studies have shown that signing petitions tends to be the most popular political activity among young people: the numbers involved vary according to the country in question and the age group surveyed, but between 30 and 70 per cent will have signed a petition while around two-thirds would do so if they wanted to have their views heard (Carle 2001; Haste 2005b; Saha *et al.* 2005). Around one in five young people will have taken part in demonstrations while between 5 and 10 per cent will have occupied a building, participated in a strike or damaged property as part of a protest (Carle 2001; Saha *et al.* 2005). Yet engagement in these forms of activity are structured in the same way as more traditional forms of political participation with factors such as age and education being powerful predictors of involvement (Haerpfer *et al.* 2002). Young people are also willing to pay more in taxes or prices to achieve their aims: around 70 per cent of young people in Europe, for example, are willing to pay higher taxes to prevent environmental damage (Haerpfer *et al.* 2002).

While these trends support the idea that political participation has become more individualized, the evidence to support the idea that there has been a shift from the politics of emancipation to life politics is less convincing. Environmental and anti-globalization movements do have a vision of a new society in which capitalistic expansion would be limited and which revolve around a post-materialist philosophy. Indeed, the interest of young people in environmental politics has been interpreted by some as part of this intergenerational shift from 'materialist' to 'post-materialist' values identified by Inglehart (1977, 1990). Inglehart (1977) suggests that whereas the older generation regard re-industrialization and re-armament as important, shifts in values would lead to the emergence of a new type of political protest based on issues surrounding the quality of life and resulting in a reduction in class conflict. In terms of translating these interests into party politics, in Europe the Green Party has had some success in involving young people (Bennie and Rüdig 1993). However, although there was a large increase in young members of the Green Party in the late 1980s and early 1990s, many subsequently left what they came to perceive (correctly) as an adult dominated organization (Banks 1993). Indeed, Bennie and Rüdig (1993) suggested that membership frequently represented a fashion statement rather than reflecting serious involvement. In this respect it can be argued that young people's involvement in post-materialist politics is somewhat limited. Bennie and Rüdig (1993) also examined the views of young people and adults on a wide range of issues related to the local, national and global environments: concern was widespread, but the differences between adults and young people tended to be small. However, on a practical level, there were interesting differences in emphasis: young people were more likely to purchase 'green' products, while adults were more concerned with conserving resources.

The involvement of young people in 'new social movements' can also be used to test the proposition that 'life politics' are becoming more important than emancipatory politics. Since the 1980s, a number of seemingly diverse movements have developed which have been seen as sharing similar underlying values. The term 'new social movements' has been used by a number of sociologists (e.g. Cohen 1983; Touraine 1985; Lash and Urry 1987; Scott 1990) to draw attention to the ways in which a range of groups (such as CND, Friends of the Earth, Animal Liberation Front, Gay Rights; New Age Travellers and the anti-globalization movement) have emerged which pose a challenge to the established political, social and economic order of advanced capitalist societies. Those who are a part of the 'new social movements' are frequently young, often have parents employed in the public or service sectors of the economy and many participants occupy peripheral positions in the labour market (such as students and the unemployed) (Hallsworth 1994).[3]

Hallsworth (1994) has argued that two distinct categories of new social movements can be identified: those which seek to defend the natural and social environment against perceived threats (such as environmental and anti-nuclear movements) and which have sought to politicize such issues, and those which seek the extension of social rights to groups which have been repressed by state action (such as gay rights and feminist movements). For Lash and Urry (1987), new social movements reflect the emergence of a set of values and political standpoints which are critical of the state and of its ability to promote meaningful social change. Thus the politics of the new generation are seen as highlighting the disintegration of older forms of collective identity, a politicization of the 'personal' and a rejection of forms of politics rooted in the old social order rather than a disinterest in politics *per se.*

On the other hand, it is important to keep these changes in perspective. In a recent UK survey of 11- to 21-year-olds, just 3 per cent said that they would vote for the Green Party: of those who knew which way they would vote, a large majority said they would cast their votes in favour of one of the 'mainstream' political parties (Haste 2005b). In other words, while young people may get involved in political causes, especially where proposed action is seen as affecting their personal security (e.g. nuclear weapons) freedom (e.g. the Criminal Justice Bill) or finances (student support) we do not predict a significant weakening of collective, emancipatory politics. Indeed, the politics of self-actualization are unlikely to thrive in an economic context characterized by uncertainty.

Conclusion

If young people are to be regarded as a vanguard of social change (Feuer 1969), then the evidence we have reviewed in this chapter suggests that the future is essentially conservative. The family remains central to processes of political socialization and to a large extent young people come to share the political concerns of their parents (Allatt and Benson 1991; Park 1996; Haerpfer *et al.* 2002). At the same time, with a weakening of the link between class and voting (which has been encouraged by the main political parties who appreciate the need to secure the votes of the 'centre') young people often want to know what issues they are supporting and may be reluctant to buy into packages of policies.

Although there is some evidence that the younger generation has a weaker commitment to traditional party politics, existing data does not support the conclusion that political orientations among the young have become individualized. Young people still express collective concerns, although they frequently seek personal solutions to problems which are largely a consequence of their socio-economic positions and expect politicians to act in accord with their interests and values. In this context Abrams (1990) is correct to suggest that disadvantage which is interpreted individually leads to stress rather than political unrest. On the other hand, the disadvantages faced by some groups of young people are so strong that they cannot fail to link them to the broader economic structure: in these circumstances, parties of the extreme right or left may be seen as offering the only real solution.

Although we reject the claim that in late modernity 'life politics' come to assume a central position, we suggest that some of the political priorities which have emerged in recent years reflect the new risks and global insecurities which Giddens (1991) has highlighted. However, these are concerns which call for emancipation from perceived threats to the quality of life in high modernity rather than being linked to processes of self-actualization. Nevertheless, life politics and empancipatory politics are closely intertwined and, as Beck (1992) suggests, political movements can simultaneously engage in struggles to reduce global risks as well as promoting the right to develop alternative lifestyles.

9 *The* epistemological fallacy *of* late modernity

> Class location is a basic determinant of the matrix of objective possibilities faced by individuals, the real alternatives people face in making decisions.
>
> (Wright 1985: 144)

> The social world is increasingly fragmented, less structured in terms of institutions or class, increasingly decentred.
>
> (McDonald 1999: 210)

Introduction

The experiences of young people growing up in the contemporary world are quite different from those encountered by earlier generations, but we are not convinced that recent social changes have been conceptualized in ways that fully enlighten us about the nature of these developments. Life in late modernity involves subjective discomfort and uncertainty. Young people can struggle to establish adult identities and maintain coherent biographies and may develop strategies to overcome various obstacles. But can their life chances still be regarded as being highly structured, with social class and gender being crucial to an understanding of experiences in a range of life contexts, or are we witnessing the emergence of a 'kaleidoscope of microcultures' (McDonald 1999: 1) that cannot be understood using conventional sociological tools and concepts?

In our view, late modernity involves an essential continuity with the past: economic and cultural resources are still central to an understanding of differential life chances and experiences. In this context we have suggested that life in late modernity revolves around a epistemological fallacy. The paradox of late modernity is that although the collective foundations of social life have become more obscure, they continue to provide powerful frameworks which constrain young people's experiences and life chances. Contrary to the ways in which some social scientists have (mis)interpreted our views (e.g. Evans 2002), we do not seek to deny the importance of subjectivity: any re-conceptualization of social class must account for agency which is an important resource in late modern contexts. Reflexivity is a key component in the dynamics of class, not a challenge to class-based perspectives.

In this book we have described a number of changes that have occurred that have helped obscure the essential continuities in the structure of social life and which often mask processes of social reproduction. These changes have promoted individual responsibilities and weakened collectivist traditions and have made the language of class appear antiquated. In this chapter, we review the main sources of change and continuity in the lives of young people and discuss some of the ways in which their subjective understanding of the world can be seen to misrepresent these underlying structures.

The crossroads of social reproduction

If there is empirical evidence to support the claim that we are currently witnessing an historical transformation of the social world, then we would expect to find the most advanced representations of these changes in the experiences of young people at the crossroads of the process of social reproduction. If structural analysis has lost its explanatory power, then we would expect to gain little mileage from attempts to understand young people's lives using concepts such as class and gender.

In our view young people's life contexts have changed quite significantly since the 1980s: changes which are closely linked to the transformation of the youth labour market, which was part of a broader process of economic change in western economies, involving a shift from manufacturing to service industries and the establishment of much more fragmented labour market experiences. In Europe, the recession of the late 1970s and early 1980s was a turning point, signifying a shift from a Fordist to a post-Fordist industrial structure, which was marked by a radical change in the demand for youth labour. During the Fordist era, there was a demand for relatively unqualified school-leavers in large industrial units: since the mid-1980s patterns of labour demand have changed significantly and opportunities for young workers are increasingly located in small work units. The demand for 'flexible specialization', the increased use of part-time and temporary employment contracts and the entrenchment of what Beck (2000) refers to as 'nomadic multi-activity' are all processes that have weakened collective employment experiences and are associated with a process of individualization and a sense of insecurity and risk.

The restructuring of the youth labour market during the 1980s also led to demands for more advanced educational qualifications and different types of skills which, in turn, meant that the average age at which young people entered the labour market increased. These changes led to a greater protraction and diversification of transitions from school to work so that by the late 1980s, young people tended to follow a wider and very different set of routes into the labour market. Unemployment, underemployment and insecurity of tenure became part of the transitional experiences of a growing proportion of young people. Although transitional routes remained highly stratified, these changes again affected subjective orientations as the range of experiences encountered at this stage in the life cycle became much more individual. Moreover, with an increase in educational participation, especially at the tertiary level, and the establishment of an educated workforce in low-skill service environments, young workers were being encouraged to regard themselves as middle class, even when an objective analysis would suggest otherwise. Again this is a process that promotes the epistemological fallacy.

Although changing school to work transitions have led to an increased risk of marginalization, risks continued to be broadly distributed in ways that reflect social divisions characteristic of the 'traditional' order. In other words, despite the fragmentation of experiences and the growth of non-linear routes, it is still possible to predict labour market outcomes fairly accurately on the basis of social class (via educational performance) and gender. Indeed, while the breakdown of collective transitions created the illusion of individuality, we have argued that these changes had little effect on processes of social reproduction.

In both Fordist and post-Fordist economies, patterns of social reproduction are mediated through educational attainment and, partly as a result of changes in the youth labour market, educational experiences have been transformed. Young people remain in full-time education for significantly longer periods and follow a more diverse set of educational routes in which consumer 'choice' is seen as playing an increasingly significant part. This increased emphasis on credentials, 'choice', and the greater social mix within educational institutions can be seen as having weakened collective responses to the school and can also be associated with a process of individualization. Despite the far-reaching nature of changing educational experiences, the relationship between social class and scholastic performance has not weakened significantly. In a wide range of countries, class-based inequalities have been maintained, and have even grown, despite the development of mass systems of higher education. Forms of stratification have been developed which keep cross-class interactions in higher education to a minimum and the establishment of educational markets provide another effective barrier to inclusivity.

While associations between social class and educational outcomes remain strong, in many countries there has been a marked improvement in the educational prospects of females. These trends are likely to have been influenced by changing expectations of parents and teachers and reflect the growth of opportunities for females in the service sector.

With the rapid expansion in post-compulsory educational participation and the protraction of school to work transitions, young people today spend longer periods of time in a state of semi-dependency. In recent years, legislative changes have been introduced in many countries which have served to reinforce the extension of semi-dependency, making it more difficult for young people to make early housing or domestic transitions.

These changing patterns of dependency have helped promote a greater diversity of experiences. Males and females from all social classes tend to marry later and are increasingly likely to spend time living in intermediary households, alone and cohabiting. New arrangements have opened up a space where relationships are renegotiated. In this context it has been argued that the protraction of young adulthood is often driven by the choices of young people who are attempting to strike new balances between life and work and avoid the compartmentalized and predictable lives experienced by their parents.

Despite these changes, the timing of domestic and housing transitions and patterns of completion still reflect 'traditional' class and gender divisions. Independence is limited by structures of opportunity. Whereas the protraction of domestic and housing transitions has created the potential for young people to develop as individuals and experiment with different living arrangements, new forms of vulnerability have also been introduced due to the removal of state support and the increasing unreliability of access to family resources. In this context we have suggested that the establishment of adult identities has become more problematic.

While experiences of the three main youth transitions continue to reflect class and gender divisions, in other areas of young people's lives differences are not so clear cut and there is evidence of a degree of convergence. In particular, a number of writers have drawn attention to the lack of significant differences in leisure and lifestyles and it has been argued that the relationship between class and youth cultures has all but vanished and gender differences have weakened. In so far as most young people tend to participate in a similar range of activities, this argument is correct. Scratch beneath the surface, and it becomes clear that access to resources affect both levels and patterns of participation.

Changing leisure patterns and lifestyles highlight the extent to which preferences have been manufactured through mass marketing techniques. Lifestyles are increasingly shaped by the market and those who lack the resources to participate in consumer markets face cultural as well as financial exclusion. The consumption of leisure, patterns of socialization, sub-cultural affiliation and involvement in the night-time economy are all structured activities and our evidence highlights a polarization of social life in which those occupying disadvantaged socio-economic positions face the prospect of total exclusion.

The evidence we reviewed on changes in the health and health related behaviour of young people also highlighted a relative absence of significant class-related differences, although we suggested that youth could be viewed as a period of dormancy. We were not convinced that the relative lack of class-related differences in youth would be manifest in health equality in adulthood. Moreover, there is evidence that the uncertainties which stem from changing transitional experiences are having a negative impact on young people's mental health. Suicidal thoughts and parasuicide have increased, especially among young women, while eating disorders can be seen as an attempt to control identity and body image in a period when scope for meaningful action is limited.

The protraction of youth transitions can also be linked to a prolongation of involvement in criminal activity. Although survey evidence suggests a lack of pronounced class and gender differentials in patterns of participation in illegal activities, apprehensions and convictions remain heavily concentrated among working class males and members of ethnic minorities. In turn, the extension of criminal careers, which can result from exclusion from labour markets and fashions relating to lifestyle consumption, can lead to the increased vulnerability of those occupying disadvantaged positions within traditional social structures.

Changes in education and the labour market can also be linked to changes in political orientations. In particular, the weakening of collective traditions is likely to have an impact on processes of political socialization and it has been argued that these changes have already been manifest in decline in involvement in traditional party politics and in reduced participation in the political process. The evidence on trends in young people's political behaviour is somewhat weak and we believe that it would be premature to predict trends in left or right wing affiliation. However, we noted that in the past political affiliations often related to the almost tribal loyalties of class and suggested that a lack of awareness of class affiliation may impact on traditional linkages between class and voting behaviour.

While young people tend to display a lack of interest in politics and while their knowledge of formal political processes is underdeveloped, political knowledge, interest and affiliation still reflects their location within traditional social structures. A number of writers, including Anthony Giddens, have suggested that the growth of new social movements represents a shift away from emancipatory politics based on class divisions and the emergence of life politics in which priority is given to processes of self-actualization. However, although young people frequently become involved with single issue political campaigns, we are sceptical of the way in which the political priorities of young people have been seen as indicative of a greater emphasis on post-materialist values. Indeed, in our view young people's political involvement and orientations reveals important continuities with the past.

Conceptualizing late modernity

The existence of powerful continuities which link the experiences of this generation to those of earlier ones mean that we are cautious about attaching too much significance to changes which have occurred since the 1980s. Throughout this book we have argued that the social divisions which were seen as shaping life chances in modernity are still central to an understanding of structured inequalities in late modernity. Young people's experiences are strongly affected by gender divisions, and even though we have focused on the lives of young people in a period of rapid social change, there is little evidence to suggest that the effect of social class on life chances is diminishing. At the same time, we are convinced that social divisions have become more obscure due to a greater individualization of experiences. The explicit lines of social stratification that were evident across virtually all activities in Fordist societies have been replaced by forms of stratification that are much more covert. The increasing lack of awareness of the significance of social interdependencies leads us to share the conclusions of Goldthorpe and Marshall (1992) who have argued that social classes should no longer be seen as the basis for collective action and consciousness or regarded as an engine of social change. However, for us, capitalism without classes is inconceivable because some groups are always able to monopolize scarce resources and ensure that these advantages are reproduced across generations.

While we have rejected suggestions that 'traditional' social divisions are becoming less powerful determinants of life chances, we do accept Beck's conclusion that one of the central characteristics of late modernity is a weakening of collective social identities. Indeed, in our view the process of individualization represents a subjective weakening of social bonds due to a growing diversity of life experiences. These changes are reflected in an individualization of lifestyles and a convergence of class cultures. However, we are critical of the significance which both Beck and Giddens attach to changes in the ways individuals interpret the world and subjectively construct social realities. In our view, Giddens and, to a lesser extent, Beck, have failed to capture the essence of late modernity due to an over-emphasis on the significance of individual reflexivity. While we can identify many common concerns and points of agreement between Beck and Giddens, we share the concern that in Giddens' work 'subjects appear ... to be disconnected from their "real" social and political contexts' as a result of an over-estimation of the extent to which individuals are able to construct their identities (May and Cooper 1995: 75).

In many ways, these difficulties are being worked through very effectively by social scientists studying youth. The development of biographical perspectives, that draw on interpretations of lived experiences while showing how structures are recreated both through actions and interpretations, offers an appropriate tool that can be used to understand modern life contexts. Within Fordist contexts the reconciliation between objective experiences and subjective interpretations was relatively straightforward. In late modernity the fragmentation of experiences make such reconciliations much more difficult, but to work with biographical perspectives does not require the abandonment of structural perspectives on life.

Giddens' susceptibility to the epistemological fallacy of late modernity is particularly evident in his argument about the declining significance of area. Giddens suggests that the worlds young people inhabit are no longer bounded by space and argues that their experiences are broadened by continual access to mass communications systems. Consequently, place loses much of its significance as experiences are shaped by much broader social processes in time and space. As Giddens puts it, 'place becomes phantasmagoric ... [it] ... becomes thoroughly penetrated by disembedding mechanisms which recombine the local activities into time-space relations of ever-widening scope' (1991: 146). While we accept that mediated experiences are central to an understanding of late modernity, in our view its main significance is derived from its power to *distort* reality. The television, for example, can open a window on a world which is remote from our lived experiences; programmes can help shape our opinions and may make us feel a part of broader community. At the same time, our opportunities and our life chances continue to be structured by our lived rather than our mediated experiences. The country we live in and the neighbourhood where we reside powerfully shape life experiences.

In contrast to the work of Giddens, Beck constantly draws attention to the ways in which processes of individualization are tightly constrained. Thus he argues that coupled with this interest in 'the individual solution' there is however considerable pressure to conform and behave in a standardized way; the means which encourage individualism also induce sameness. . . . The situations which arise are contradictory because double-faced: individual decisions are heavily dependent on outside influences.

(Beck and Beck-Gernsheim 1995: 40)

Thus the process of individualization can be linked to long-term developmental trends. In education and in the labour market, young people are forced to take greater individual responsibility and to assess appropriate courses of action. Risk and uncertainty are the consequences of pressures to adopt individualistic perspectives in a society characterized by interdependency.

The contradiction which Beck highlights here has been examined in detail by Norbert Elias (1978, 1982). In rejecting the dualism between the self and the outside world, Elias argued that individuals are tied together by chains of mutual dependence to form changeable social figurations. Thus individuals are inseparable from their social contexts and as social figurations change, similar changes are manifest in the constituent parts. According to Elias, the idea that the individual represented a separable, independent, social entity is a product of long-term historical trends which have involved an increase in self-control and a reduction in externally imposed discipline. In this sense, individualization can be regarded as an historical extension of a process which led first to the emergence of what Elias refers to as *homo clausus*, or closed-off individualism. Building on these ideas, late modernity can be seen as representing a further step along a continuum leading from collectivized to individualized social identities. Seen in these terms, social change does not involve a weakening of social structures; the chains of interdependence remain intact, but 'the entire complex of intermeshing processes of change eludes the control and even the comprehension of the individuals who partake in it' (Goudsblom 1977: 148).

In other words, life in high modernity revolves around an epistemological fallacy in which feeling of separation from the collectivity represents part of a long-term historical process which is closely associated with subjective perceptions of risk and uncertainty. Individuals are forced to negotiate a set of risks which impinge on all aspects of their daily lives, yet the intensification of individualism means that crises are perceived as individual shortcomings rather than the outcome of processes which are largely outwith the control of individuals. In this context, we have seen that some of the problems faced by young people in modern societies stem from an attempt to negotiate difficulties on an individual level. Blind to the existence of powerful chains of interdependency, young people frequently attempt to resolve collective problems through individual action and hold themselves responsible for their inevitable failure.

Notes

1 The risk society

1 The terms 'late modernity' and 'high modernity' are used here interchangeably.
2 Giddens uses the term 'ontological security' to refer to 'a sense of continuity and order in events' (1991: 243).
3 Recognizing the ways in which racial categories are socially constructed and accepting the problems associated with using 'race' as an analytic concept, many writers place the word in inverted commas (Miles 1989).

2 Change and continuity in education

1 Indeed, in many countries due to the existence of highly localized systems of educational delivery, especially at the primary level, many young people spend most of their educational careers in the company of pupils who share a similar social background.
2 Rates of participation in France and Germany partly reflect their higher minimum leaving age (17).

3 Social change and labour market transitions

1 In the UK between 1980 and 1988, long-term unemployment (a year or more) among 18- to 24-year-olds fell from 260 000 to 63,100 (ONS 2000).
2 Sweden is acknowledged as providing the first genuine youth guarantee in 1984 (OECD 2002b).
3 The graduate premium is calculated by comparison with a young person with A levels who chooses not to progress to university.
4 It is noted that in countries where degree programmes are longer, returns tend to be lower. Returns to German graduates, for example, are uniformly lower than in the UK.
5 The contemporary interpretation of transitions in the 1960s has been challenged by Goodwin and O'Connor (2005) who, in a re-analysis of data collected by Norbert Elias and colleagues, suggest that transitions were never as straightforward as implied.

4 Changing patterns of dependency

1 Fifteen countries.

5 Leisure and lifestyles

1 While leisure can be defined in a variety of ways, here we adopt one of the most common definitions in which leisure is equated with time which is free from other obligations (Roberts 1983; Rojek 1985).
2 Given that most leisure activities are commercialized and involve monetary exchange, we regard leisure and consumption as being closely linked.

6 Health risks in late modernity

1 Specific conditions included cerebral palsy, cystic fibrosis, respiratory problems, ear infections, hearing and visual impairment.
2 It is likely that differences in reporting practices between countries will help to under-state suicide rates in some countries. In England, for example, a suicide verdict is only recorded when there is no doubt about suicidal intention (Eckersley and Dear 2002).
3 The term parasuicide was coined by Kreitman (1977) to refer to suicidal behaviour with a non-fatal outcome. The term us used in preference to attempted suicide as intention is treated as problematic. Diekstra and colleagues (1995) argue that motives can be difficult to determine as the majority of young people who come close to dying by their own hand will subsequently deny intention.
4 Defined here as having more than five drinks on one occasion, a quantity that many of those outside of the health professions would regard as entirely normal.

7 Crime and insecurity

1 All age figures.

8 Politics and participation

1 While this is true in much of Europe and North America, in Australia much more attention has been given to young people and politics.
2 One of the major criticisms of Inglehart relates to the tendency for the shift from materialist to post-materialist values to continue irrespective of fluctuations in economic prosperity.
3 Many new social movements appeal to a broad age range and many have significant numbers of middle-aged members.

References

Aamodt, P.O. and Kyvik, S. (2005) 'Access to higher education in the Nordic countries', in T. Tapper and D. Palfreyman (eds) *Understanding Mass Higher Education: Comparative Perspectives on Access*. Abingdon: Routledge.

Aassve, A., Billari, F. C., Mazzuco, S. and Ongaro, F. (2002) 'Leaving home: a comparative analysis of ECHP data', *Journal of European Social Policy*, 12, 259–75.

Abma, R. (1992) 'Working class heroes. A review of the youth subculture theory of the Centre for Contemporary Cultural Studies', in W. Meeus, M. de Goede, W. Kox and K. Hurrelman (eds) *Adolescent Careers and Cultures*. Berlin and New York: de Gruyter.

Abrams, D. (1990) *Political Identity. Relative Deprivation, Social Identity and the Case of Scottish Nationalism*, ESRC 16–19 Initiative Occasional Papers, no. 24. London: City University.

Abrams, M. (1961) *The Teenage Consumer*. London: London Press Exchange.

Abramson, P.A. and Inglehart, R. (1992) 'Generational replacement and value change in eight West European societies', *British Journal of Political Science*, 22, 183–228.

Adams, J. (1995) *Risk*. London: UCL.

Adsett, M. (2003) 'Change in political era and demographic weight in explanations of youth "disenfranchisement" in federal elections in Canada, 1965–2000', *Journal of Youth Studies*, 6, 247–64.

Aebi, M. F. (2002) *Space 1 Council of Europe Annual Penal Statistics*. Strasbourg: Council of Europe, Strasbourg.

Agerbo, E., Nordentoft, M. and Mortwensen, O.P.B. (2002) 'Familial psychiatric and socioeconomic risk factors for suicide in young people: nested case control study', *British Medical Journal*, 317, 74–7.

Ainley, P. (1991) *Young People Leaving Home*. London: Cassell.

Allatt, P. and Benson, L. (1991) *Family Discourse. Political Socialization Amongst Teenagers and their Families*. ESRC 16–19 Initiative Occasional Papers, no. 37. London: City University.

Anderson, I., Kemp, P. and Quilgars, D. (1993) *Single Homeless People*. London: HMSO.

Anderson, S., Kinsey, R., Loader, I. and Smith, C. (1994) *Cautionary Tales. Young People, Crime and Policing in Edinburgh*. Aldershot: Avebury.

Anisef, P., Axelrod, P., Baichman-Anisef, E., James, C. and Turrittin, A. (2000) *Opportunity and Uncertainty: Life Course Experiences of the Class of '73*. Toronto: University of Toronto Press.

Aries, P. (1962) *Centuries of Childhood. A Social History of Family Life*. London: Cape.

Arnett, J.J. (2004) *Emerging Adulthood: The Winding Road Through the Late Teens to the Twenties*. New York: Oxford University Press.

Arnett, J.J. (2006) 'Emerging adulthood in Europe: A response to Bynner', *Journal of Youth Studies*, 9, 111–23.

Arrowsmith, J. (2006) *Temporary Agency Work in an Enlarged European Union*. Dublin: European Foundation for the Improvement of Living and Working Conditions.

Arum, R. and Shavit, Y. (1995) 'Secondary vocational education and the transition from school to work', *Sociology of Education*, 68, 187–204.

Ashton, D.N. and Field, D. (1976) *Young Workers*. London: Hutchinson.

Ashton, D.N. and Maguire, M.J. (1983) *The Vanishing Youth Labour Market*. London: Youthaid.

Ashton, D.N., Maguire, M.J. and Spilsbury, M. (1990) *Restructuring the Labour Market. The Implications for Youth*. Basingstoke: Macmillan.

Atkinson, J. (1984) 'Manpower strategies for flexible organizations', *Personnel Management*, August.

Babb, P. and Bethare, A. (1995) 'Trends in births and marriage', *Population Trends*, 81, 17–22.

Bagguley, P. and Mann, K. (1992) 'Idle thieving bastards? Scholarly representations of the underclass', *Work, Employment and Society*, 6, 113–26.

Bagnall, G. and Plant, M.A. (1991) 'AIDS risks, alcohol and illicit drug use amongst young adults in areas of high and low rates of HIV infection', *AIDS Care*, 3, 355–61.

Ball, S.J. (1981) *Beachside Comprehensive. A Case Study of Secondary Schooling*. Cambridge: Cambridge University Press.

Ball, S.J. (2003) *Class Strategies in the Educational Market: The Middle Classes and Social Advantage*. London: Routledge Falmer.

Ball, S.J., Maguire, M. and Macrae, S. (2000) *Choice, Pathways and Transitions Post-16*. London: Routledge-Falmer.

Banks, M., Bates, I., Breakwell, G., Bynner, J., Emler, N., Jamieson, L. and Roberts, K. (1992) *Careers and Identities*. Milton Keynes: Open University Press.

Banks, M.H. and Jackson, P.R. (1982) 'Unemployment and risk of minor psychiatric disorders in young people. Cross sectional and longitudinal evidence', *Psychological Medicine*, 12, 789–98.

Banks, M.H. and Ullah, P. (1987) 'Political attitudes and voting among unemployed and employed youth', *Journal of Adolescence*, 10, 201–16.

Banks, M. and Ullah, P. (1988) *Youth Unemployment in the 1980s. Its Psychological Effects*. Beckenham: Croom Helm.

Banks, S. (1993) 'Young People and the environment', *Youth and Policy*, 42, 1–5.

Barclay, G. and Tavares, C. (2002) *International Comparisons of Criminal Justice Statistics, 2000*. London: Home Office.

Barclay's Bank (2005) *Eleventh Barclay's Annual Graduate Survey*. http://www.newsroom.barclays.com/content/detail.asp?ReleaseID=276&NewsAreaID=2 (accessed 18 April 2006).

Baron, S., Field, J. and Schuller, T. (2000) *Social Capital: Critical Perspectives*. Oxford: Oxford University Press.

Baudrillard, J. (1988) *Selected Writings*. Oxford: Oxford University Press.

Bauman, Z. (2001) *The Individualized Society*. Cambridge: Polity.

Beck, U. (1992) *Risk Society. Towards a New Modernity*. London: Sage.

Beck, U. (1994) 'The reinvention of politics. Towards a theory of reflexive modernization', in U. Beck, A. Giddens and S. Lash (eds) *Reflexive Modernization, Politics, Tradition and Aesthetics in the Modern Social Order*. Oxford: Polity.

Beck, U. (2000) *The Brave New World of Work*. Cambridge: Polity.

Beck, U. and Beck-Gernsheim, E. (1995) *The Normal Chaos of Love*. Oxford: Polity.

Beinart, S., Anderson, B., Lee, S. and Utting, D. (2002) *Youth at Risk? A National Survey of Risk Factors, Protective Factors and Problem Behaviour Among Young People in England, Scotland and Wales*. London: Communities that Care.

Bell, D. (1973) *The Coming of Post-Industrial Society*. New York: Basic Books.

Benn, T. (2005) ' "Race", physical education, sport and dance', in K. Green and K. Hardman (eds) *Physical Education: Essential Issues*. London: Sage.

Bennett, A. (1999) 'Subcultures or neo-tribes? Rethinking the relationship between youth, style and musical taste', *Sociology*, 33, 599–617.

Bennett, A. (2000) *Popular Music and Youth Culture: Music, Identity and Place*. Basingstoke: Macmillan.

Bennett, D. and Williams, M. (1994) 'Adolescent health care: The international context', in R.S. Tonkin (ed.) *Current Issues in the Adolescent Patient*. London: Bailliére Tindall.

Bennie, L. and Rüdig, W. (1993) 'Youth and the environment: Attitudes and actions in the 1990s', *Youth and Policy*, 42, 1–5.

Berger, P.L., Berger, B. and Kellner, H. (1974) *The Homeless Mind*. Harmondsworth: Penguin.

Bernhardt, E. and Gähler, M. (2001) Cohabitation or residential independence in Sweden? The impact of childhood family structure and conflict on routes out of the parental home. Paper presented at the annual meeting of the Population Association of America, Washington, DC, 29–31 March.

Bernhardt, E., Gähler, M. and Goldscheider, F. (2005) 'Childhood family structure and routes out of the parental home in Sweden', *Acta Sociologica*, 48, 99–115.

Bernstein, N. (2004) Young love, new caution: Behind the fall in pregnancy, a new teenage culture of constraint, *New York Times*, 7 March.

Bhavanani, K.-K. (1991) *Talking Politics. A Psychological Framing for Views from Youth in Britain*. Cambridge: Cambridge University Press.

Biggart, A. (2002) 'Attainment, gender and minimum-aged school leavers' early routes in the labour market', *Journal of Education and Work*, 15, 145–62.

Biggart, A. and Furlong, A. (1996) 'Educating "discouraged workers". Cultural diversity in the upper secondary school', *British Journal of Sociology of Education*, 17, 253–66.

Bishop, D. and Decker, S. (2006) 'Juvenile justice in the United States: A review of policies, programs and trends', in J. Junger-Tas (ed) *Improving Juvenile Justice*. Berlin: Springer.

Blackburn, R.M. and Jarman, J. (1993) 'Changing inequalities in access to British universities', *Oxford Review of Education*, 9, 197–215.

Blackman, S. (2005) 'Youth sub-cultural theory: A critical engagement with the concept, its origins and politics, from the Chicago school to postmodernism', *Journal of Youth Studies*, 8: 1–20.

Blagg, H. (1997) 'A just measure of Shame? Aboriginal youth and conferencing in Australia', *The British Journal of Criminology*, 37, 481–501.

Blias, A., Gidengil, E., Nevitte, N. and Nadeau, R. (2001) 'The evolving nature of non-voting evidence from Canada'. Paper presented to the American Political Science Association, San Francisco, 30 August to 2 September.

Blum, R.W. and Nelson-Mmari, K. (2004) 'The health of young people in a global context', *Journal of Adolescent Health*, 35, 402–18.

Bonoli, G., George, V. and Taylor-Gooby, P. (2000) *European Welfare Futures*. Cambridge: Polity.

Bóse, M. (2003) ' "Race" and class in the post-industrial economy', in D. Muggelton and R.Werinzierl (eds) *The Post-subcultures Reader*. Oxford: Berg.

Boudon, R. (1973) *Education, Opportunity and Social Inequality*. New York: Wiley.

Bourdieu, P. (1977) 'Cultural reproduction and social reproduction', in J. Karabel and A.H. Halsey (eds) *Power and Ideology in Education*. New York: Oxford University Press.

Bourdieu, P. and Passeron, J.C. (1977) *Reproduction in Education, Society and Culture*. London: Sage.

Box, S., Hale, C. and Andrews, G. (1988) 'Explaining the fear of crime', *British Journal of Criminology*, 28, 340–56.

Bradley, S. and Taylor, J. (2004) 'Ethnicity, educational attainment and the transition from school', *Manchester School*, 72, 317–46.

Brain, K. (2000) *Youth, Alcohol and the Emergence of the Post-Modern Alcohol Order*. London: Institute for Alcohol Studies.

Breakwell, G. (1986) 'Political and attributional responses of the young short-term unemployed', *Political Psychology*, 7, 265–78.

Breakwell, G. (1992) 'Changing patterns of sexual behaviour in 16–29-year-olds in the UK. A cohort-sequential longitudinal study', in W. Meeus, M. de Goede, W. Kox and K. Hurrelmann (eds) *Adolescent Careers and Cultures*. Berlin and New York: de Gruyter.

Brettschneider, W.D. and Naul, R. (2004) *Study of Young People's Lifestyles and Sedentariness and the Role of Sport in the Context of Education as a Means of Restoring the Balance*. Brussels: European Commission.

British Crime Survey (2000) *British Crime Survey*. London: Home Office.

British Heart Foundation (2005) Alcohol consumption by country of adults aged 15 and above, 1970–2001, Europe. www.heartstats.org/datapage.asp?id=4597 (accessed 3 March 2006).

British Youth Council (1995) *Politics: In Brief*. London: British Youth Council.

Brown, P. (1987) *Schooling Ordinary Kids*. London: Tavistock.

Brownfield, D. (1996) 'Subcultural theories of crime and delinquency', in J. Hagan, A.R. Gillis and D. Brownfield (eds) *Criminological Controversies*. Oxford: Westview.

Bryson, A. and Gomaz, R. (2002) 'Marching on together? Recent trends in union membership', in A. Park, J. Curtice, K. Thomson, L. Jarvis and C. Bromley (eds) *British Social Attitudes: The 19th Report*. London: Sage.

Büchner, P. (1990) 'Growing up in the eighties. Changes in the social biography of childhood in the FRG', in L. Chisholm, P. Büchner, H.-H. Krüger and P. Brown (eds) *Childhood, Youth and Social Change. A Comparative Perspective*. London: Falmer.

Buckingham, D. (2000) *The Making of Citizens: Young People, News and Politics*. London: Routledge.

Bühler, C. (1921) *Das Seelenleben*. Quoted in J. Coleman and T. Husen (1985) *Becoming an Adult in a Changing Society*. Paris: OECD.

Burke, K.C., Burke, J.D. (Jr), Regier, D.A. and Rae, D.S. (1990) 'Age at the onset of select mental disorders in five community populations', *Archive of General Psychiatry*, 5, 511–18.

Burnhill, P., Garner, C. and McPherson, A. (1990) 'Parental education, social class and entry into higher education 1976–86', *Journal of the Royal Statistical Society*, Series A, 153, 233–48.

Button, E.J. and Whitehouse, A. (1981) Subclinical anorexia nervosa, *Psychological Medicine*, 11, 509–16.

Bynner, J. (2005) 'Rethinking the youth phase of the life-course: The case for emerging adulthood', *Journal of Youth Studies*, 8, 367–84.

Bynner, J. and Ashford, S. (1994) 'Politics and participation. Some antecedents of young people's attitudes to the political system and political activity', *European Journal of Social Psychology*, 24, 223–36.

Bynner, J., Bachman, J.G. and O'Malley, P. (1981) 'Self esteem and delinquency revisited', *Journal of Youth and Adolescence*, 10, 407–41.

Bynner, J., Chisholm, L. and Furlong, A. (eds) (1997) *Youth, Citizenship and Social Change in a European Context*. Aldershot: Ashgate.

Bynner, J., Londra, M. and Jones, G. (2004) *The Impact of Government Policy on Social Exclusion Among Young People*. London: The Office of the Deputy Prime Minister.

Bynner, J. and Parsons, S. (2003) 'Social participation, values and crime', in E. Ferri, J. Bynner and M. Wadsworth (eds) *Changing Britain, Changing Lives*. London: Institute of Education.

Bynner, J. and Roberts, K. (1991) (eds) *Youth and Work: Transitions to Employment in England and Germany*. London: Anglo-German Foundation.

Bynner, J., Romney, D.M. and Emler, N.P. (2003) 'Dimensions of political and related facets of identity in late adolescence', *Journal of Youth Studies*, 6, 319–35.

Callender, C. (2003) 'Student financial support in higher education', in M. Tight (ed) *Access and Exclusion*. Oxford: Elsevier.

Campbell, A. (1981) *Girl Delinquents*. Oxford: Blackwell.

Campbell, S. (2002) *Review of Anti-social Behaviour Orders*. Home Office Research Study 236. London: Home Office.

Caradec, V. (1996) 'Les formes de la vie comjugale des "jeunes" couple âgés', *Population*, 51, 897–928.

Carle, J. (2001) 'Social and political activity among unemployed young people in six northern European countries', in A. Furlong and T. Hammer (eds) *Youth Unemployment and Marginalisation in Northern Europe*. Oslo: Norwegian Social Research.

Carter, M.P. (1962) *Home, School and Work*. London: Pergamon.

Cashmore, E.E. (1984) *No Future. Youth and Society*. London: Heinemann.

Centers for Disease Control and Prevention (2000) 'Youth risk behavior surveillance – United States 1999', *Morbidity and Mortality Weekly Report*, 49 (SS-5).

Centers for Disease Control and Prevention (2004) SRD Surveillance 2004. www.cdc.gov/std/stats/trends2004.htm (accessed 1 May 2006).

Chan, T.W. and Goldthorpe, J.H. (2005) 'The social stratification of theatre, dance and cinema attendance', *Cultural Trends*, 14, 193–212.

Chase, E., Douglas, N., Knight, A., Rivers, K., Warwick, I. and Aggleton, P. (2003) *Teenage Pregnancy and Parenthood Among Young People Looked after by Local Authorities: Determinants and Support. A Research Review*. London: Thomas Corum Research Unit, Institute of Education.

Chatterton, P. and Hollands, R. (2003) *Urban Nightscapes: Youth Cultures, Pleasure Spaces and Corporate Power*. London: Routledge.

Cheek, N. and Burch, W. (1976) *The Social Organization of Leisure in Human Societies*. New York: Harper and Row.

Chitty, C. (1987) (ed) *Aspects of Vocationalism*. London: Institute of Post-16 Education.

Chitty, C. (1989) *Towards a New Educational System. The Victory of the New Right?* London: Falmer.

Christie, N. (2000) *Crime Control Industry*. London: Routeledge.

Clarke, C. and Critcher, C. (1985) *The Devil Makes Work. Leisure in Capitalist Britain*. Basingstoke: Macmillan.

Clarke, H.D., Sanders, D., Stewart, M.C. and Whiteley, P. (2004) *Political Choice in Britain*. Oxford: Oxford University Press.

CLS (Centre for Longitudinal Studies) (2006) *Obesity, diet and exercise*, CLS Briefing, May. London: Institute of Education.

CNN (2004) *US Election Exit Poll*. http://www.exitpollz.org/cnn2004epolls/Pres_epolls/1A_P.html (accessed 12 December 2005).

Coakley, J. and White, A. (1992) 'Making decisions: Gender and sport participation among British adolescents', *Sociology of Sport Journal*, 9, 20–35.

Cochrane, R. and Billig, M. (1983) 'Youth and politics in the 80s', *Youth and Policy*, 2, 31–4.

Coffield, F., Borrill, C. and Marshall, S. (1986) *Growing up at the Margins*. Milton Keynes: Open University Press.

Cohen, J. (1983) 'Rethinking social movements', *Berkeley Journal of Sociology*, 28, 97–113.

Cohen, S. (1972) *Folk Devils and Moral Panics*. Oxford: Blackwell.

Cohen, S. (2003) '661 New Crimes – and counting'. *New Statesman*, 7 July.

Colby, A. and Kohlberg, L. (1987) *The Measurement of Moral Judgement, Vol.1. Theoretical Foundations*. Cambridge: Cambridge University Press.

Coleman, C. and Moynihan, J. (1996) *Understanding Crime Data. Haunted by the Dark Figure*. Buckingham: Open University Press.

Coles, B. (1995) *Youth and Social Policy*. London: UCL.

Collins, M. (1998) *Altered State: The Story of Ecstasy Culture and Acid House*. London: Serpent's Tail.

Cooper, L. (2000) 'Alcohol use and risky sexual behavior among college students and youth: Evaluating the evidence', www.collegedrinkingprevention.gov/supportingresearchjournal/cooper.aspx (accessed 6 March 2006).

Côté, J. (2000) *Arrested Adulthood: The Changing Nature of Maturity and Identity*. New York: New York University Press.

Côté, J.E. and Allahar, A.L. (1996) *Generation on Hold. Coming of Age in the Late Twentieth Century*. New York: New York University Press.

Courtenay, G. and McAleese, I. (1993) *England and Wales Youth Cohort Study. Report on Cohort 5, Sweep 1*. Sheffield: Employment Department.

Craig, G. (1991) *Fit for Nothing? Young People, Benefits and Youth Training*. London: The Children's Society.

Craine, S. (1997) 'The black magic roundabout: cyclical transitions, social exclusion and alternative careers', in R. MacDonald (ed) *Youth, the 'Underclass' and Social Exclusion*. London: Routledge.

Croghan, R., Griffin, C., Hunter, J. and Phoenix, A. (2006) 'Style failure: Consumption, identity and social exclusion', *Journal of Youth Studies*, 9: 467–82.

Croxford, L., Howieson, C., Ianelli, C. and Ozga, J. (2002) *Educational Maintenance Allowance (EMAs): Evaluation of the East Ayrshire Pilot*. Edinburgh: Scottish Executive.

Croxford, L., Howieson, C., Ianelli, C., Raffe, D. and Shapira, M. (2006) Trends in education and youth transitions across Britain 1984–2002. Working paper presented to the conference Education and Social Change in England Wales and Scotland 1984–2002. University of Edinburgh.

Croxford, L. and Raffe, D. (2005) 'Education markets and social class inequality: A comparison of trends in England, Scotland and Wales'. Working paper, Edinburgh, Centre for Educational Sociology, University of Edinburgh.

Currie, C., Roberts, R., Morgan, A., Smith, R., Settertobulte, W., Samdal, O. and Rasmussen, V.B. (eds) (2004) *Young People's Health in Context, Health Behaviour in School Aged Children (HBSC) Study, International Report From the 2001–02 Survey*. Geneva: World Health Organisation Regional Office for Europe.

D'Attilio, J.P., Campbell, B.M., Lubold, P., Jacobson, T. and Richard, J. A. (1992) 'Social support and suicide potential: Preliminary findings for adolescent populations', *Psychological Reports*, 70, 76–8.

DaVanzo, J. and Goldscheider, F.K. (1990) Coming home again. Returns to the family home of young adults, *Population Studies*, 44, 241–55.

Davis, J. (1990) *Youth and the Condition of Britain. Images of Adolescent Conflict*. London: Athlone.

Deehan, A. and Saville, E. (2003) *Calculating the Risk: Recreational Drug Use Among Clubbers in the South East of England*. London: Home Office.

Deem, R. (1986) *All Work and No Play. The Sociology of Women and Leisure*. Milton Keynes: Open University Press.

Delamont, S. (1980) *Sex Roles and the School*. London: Methuen.

Dennis, N., Henriques, F. and Slaughter, C. (1956) *Coal is Our Life*. London: Eyre and Spottiswoode.

Department of Education Training and Youth Affairs (1999) *Equity in Higher Education*. Canberra: Higher Education Division.

Department of Health (2005) *Smoking, Drinking and Drug Use Among Young People in England in 2004: Headline Figures*. London: Department of Health.

de Vaus, D. and Qu, L. (1998) 'Intergenerational transfers across the lifecourse', *Family Matters*, 50, 27–30.

DfEE (Department for Education and Employment) (2000) *Labour Market Trends*, 108. July.

DfES (Department for Education and Science) (2005) *Youth Cohort Study: The Activities of 16 year-olds: England and Wales, 2004*. London: DfES.

Devine, F. (2004) *Class Practices: How Parents Help Their Children to Get Good Jobs*. Cambridge: Cambridge University Press.

de Wilde, E.J., Kienhorst, C.W.M., Diekstra, R.F.W. and Wolters, W.H.G. (1992) 'The relationship between adolescent suicidal behaviour and life events in childhood and adolescence', *American Journal of Psychiatry*, 1, 45–51

Diekstra, R.F.W., Garnefski, N., Heus, P. de, Zwart, R. de, Praag, B. van, and Warnaar, M. (1991) *Scholierenonderzoek 1990. Gedrag en gezondheid*. Den Haag: NIBUD.

Diekstra, R.F.W., Kienhorst, C.W.M. and de Wilde, E.J. (1995) 'Suicide and suicidal behaviours among adolescents', in M. Rutter and D.J. Smith (eds) *Psychological Disorders in Young People. Time Trends and their Causes*. John Wiley and Sons: Chichester.

Dobson, I. (2003) 'Access to university in Australia: Who misses out?', in M. Tight (ed) *Access and Exclusion*. Oxford: Elsevier.

Donovan, C. (1990) 'Adolescent sexuality', *British Medical Journal*, 30, 1026–7.

Douglas, J.W.B. (1967) *The Home and the School*. St. Albans: Panther.

Douvan, A. and Adelson, J. (1966) *The Adolescent Experience*. New York: Wiley.

Downes, D. (1966) *The Delinquent Solution. A Study in Subcultural Theory*. London: Routledge and Kegan Paul.

du Bois Reymond, M. (1998a) 'I don't want to commit myself yet: young people's life concepts', *Journal of Youth Studies*, 1, 63–79.

du Bois Reymond, M. (1998b) 'Negotiation strategies in modern families: What does it mean for global citizenship?', in K. Mattijis and A. Van den Troost (eds) *The Family: Contemporary Perspectives and Challenges*. Leuven: Leuven University Press.

Durkheim, E. (1947) *The Division of Labour in Society*. New York: Macmillan.

Durkheim, E. (1964) *The Rules of Sociological Method*. New York: Free Press.

Dwyer, P. and Wyn, J. (2001) *Youth, Education and Risk: Facing the Future*. London and New York: Routledge-Falmer.

Eckersley, R. and Dear, K. (2002) 'Cultural correlates of youth suicide', *Social Science and Medicine*, 55, 1891–4.

Egerton, M. and Halsey, A.H. (1993) 'Trends in social class and gender in access to higher education in Britain', *Oxford Review of Education*, 19, 183–96.

EGRIS (European Group for Integrated Social Research) (2001) 'Misleading trajectories: Transitions dilemmas of young adults in Europe', *Journal of Youth Studies*, 4, 101–19.

Electoral Commission (2005) *Election 2005: Turnout*. London: Electoral Commission.

Elias, N. (1978) *The History of Manners. The Civilising Process, Volume I.* Oxford: Blackwell.

Elias, N. (1982) *State Formation and Civilization. The Civilising Process, Volume II.* Oxford: Blackwell.

Elias, P. and Purcell, K. (2004) *The Earnings of Graduates in their Early Careers,* Research Paper no. 5. Warwick: Institute of Employment.

EMCDDA (European Monitoring Centre for Drugs and Drug Addiction) (2006) *Statistical Bulletin 2005.* Lisbon: EMCDDA.

Emler, N. (1996) A new agenda for youth politics research? The contribution of a social psychological perspective. Conference paper, University of Glasgow 'British Youth Research: The New Agenda', 26–28 January.

Erikson, E.H. (1968) *Identity, Youth and Crisis.* New York: Norton.

Ermisch, J. (1997) *Prices, Parents and Young People's Household Formation,* ISER working paper no. 97–18. Colchester: University of Essex.

Ermisch, J. (2000) *Personal Relationships and Marriage Expectations: Evidence from the 1998 British Household Panel Survey,* ISER working paper no. 2000–27. Colchester: University of Essex.

Ermisch, J. and Francesconi, M. (2000) 'Patterns of household and family formation', in R. Berthoud and J. Gershuny (eds) *Seven Years in the Lives of British Families: Evidence on the Dynamics of Social Change from the British Household Panel Survey.* Bristol: Policy Press.

Esmée Fairbairn Foundation (2005) *Re-thinking Crime and Punishment.* London: Esmée Fairbairn Foundation.

ESPAD (European School Survey on Alcohol and Other Drugs) (2003) *Summary of the 2003 Findings.* www.espad.org/summary.html (accessed 19 December 2005).

Estrada, F. (2001) 'Juvenile violence as a social problem: Trends, media attention and societal responses', *British Journal of Criminology,* 41, 639–55.

European Commission (1999) *Employment in Europe 1998: Jobs for People, People for Jobs.* Luxembourg: Office for the Official Publications of the European Communities.

European Commission (2002) *Higher Education and Graduate Employment in Europe: New Perspectives for Learning.* Briefing Paper 10. Brussels: European Commission.

European Commission (2003a) *Time Use at Different Stages of Life: Results from 13 European Countries.* Luxembourg: Office for Official Publications of the European Community.

European Commission (2003b) *Results of Eurobarometer 58.* Brussels: European Commission.

European Commission (2004a) *Employment in Europe 2004: Recent Trends and Prospects.* Luxembourg: Office for the Official Publications of the European Communities.

European Commission (2004b) *The Citizens of the European Union and Sport.* Eurobarometer 213. Brussels: European Commission.

Eurostat (2005) *Employment in Hotels and Restaurants.* Eurostat News Release 127/2005, 11 October 2005.

EUYOUPART (2005) Political participation of young people in Europe (http://europa.e-u.int/comm/research/headlines/news/article_05_09_14_en.html) (accessed 10 November 2005).

Evans, K. (2002) 'Taking control of their lives? Agency in young adult transitions in England and the New Germany', *Journal of Youth Studies,* 5, 245–71.

Evans, K. and Furlong, A. (1997) 'Metaphors of youth transitions. Niches, pathways, trajectories or navigations', in J. Bynner, L. Chisholm and A. Furlong (eds) *Youth, Citizenship and Social Change in a European Context.* Aldershot: Avebury.

Fahmy, E. (1999) 'Youth and political participation: Findings from a 1996 MORI survey', *Radical Statistics,* 18–26.

Farrell, L. and Shields, M.A. (2002) 'Investigating the economic and demographic determinants of sporting participation in England', *Journal of the Royal Statistical Society*, 165, 335–48.

Farrington, D.P. (1990) 'Implications of criminal career research for the prevention of offending', *Journal of Adolescence*, 13, 93–113.

Farrington, D., Gallagher, B., Morley, L., St Ledger, R. and West, D.J. (1986) 'Unemployment, school-learning and crime', *British Journal of Criminology*, 26, 335–56.

Fay, R.E., Turner, C.F., Klassen, A.D. and Gagnon, J.H. (1989) Prevalence and patterns of some gender sexual contact among men, *Science*, 243, 338–48.

Fazey, C. (1991) 'The consequences of illegal drug use', in D. Whynes and P. Bean (eds) *Policing and Prescribing: The British System of Drug Control*. London: Macmillan.

Featherstone, M. (1991) *Consumer Culture and Postmodernism*. London: Sage.

Federation of European Employers (2005) http://fedee.com/tradeunions.html (accessed 28 July 2005).

Ferchoff, W. (1990) 'West German youth cultures at the close of the eighties', in L. Chisholm, P. Büchner, H.-H. Krüger and P. Brown (eds) *Childhood, Youth and Social Change. A Comparative Perspective*. Basingstoke: Falmer.

Ferrante, A.M., Loh, N.S.N. and Maller, M. (1998) *Crime and Justice Statistics for Western Australia: 1996*. Crime Research Centre: University of Western Australia.

Ferrell, J. (1997) 'Cultural criminology', *Annual Review of Sociology*, 25, 395–418.

Ferri, E. and Smith, K. (2003) 'Partnerships and parenthood', in E. Ferri, J. Bynner and M. Wadsworth (eds) *Changing Britain Changing Lives*. London: Institute of Education.

Feuer, L.S. (1969) *The Conflict of Generations. The Character and Significance of Student Movements*. New York: Basic Books.

Field, J. (2003) *Social Capital*. London: Routledge.

Finch, J. (1989) *Family Obligations and Social Change*. Cambridge: Polity.

Fitzgerald, M. (1993) *The Royal Commission on Criminal Justice. Minorities and the Criminal Justice System*. London: HMSO.

Fitzpatrick, S. (2000) *Young Homeless People*. London: Macmillan.

Flintoff, A. and Scraton, S. (2005) 'Gender and physical education', in K. Green and K. Hardman (eds) *Physical Education: Essential Issues*. London: Sage.

Flood-Page, C., Campbell, S., Harrington, V. and Miller, J. (2000) *Youth Crime: Findings from the 1998/99 Youth Lifestyles Survey*. Home Office Research Study 209. London: HMSO.

Fombonne, E. (1995) 'Eating disorders. Time trends and possible exploratory mechanisms', in M. Rutter and D.J. Smith (eds) *Psychological Disorders in Young People. Time Trends and their Causes*. Chichester: Wiley.

Fombonne, E. (1998) 'Suicide behaviours in vulnerable adolescents. Time trends and their correlates'. *British Journal of Psychiatry*, 173, 154–59.

Forcese, D. (1997) *The Canadian Class Structure*, 4th edition. Toronto: McGraw-Hill.

Ford, J. (1969) *Social Class and the Comprehensive School*. London: Routledge and Kegan Paul.

Ford, N. (1989) 'Urban-rural variations in the level of heterosexual activity of young people', *Area*, 21, 237–48.

Foreman, D. and Chilvers, C. (1989) 'Sexual behaviour of young and middle aged men in England and Wales', *British Medical Journal*, 298, 1137–42.

Forsyth, A. (1997) A Qualitative Exploration of Dance Drug Use. Unpublished PhD thesis, University of Glasgow.

Forsyth, A. and Furlong, A. (2000) *Socioeconomic Disadvantage and Access to Higher Education*. Bristol: Policy Press.

Fossey, E., Loretto, W. and Plant, M. (1996) 'Alcohol and youth', in L. Harrison (ed) *Alcohol Problems in the Community*. London: Routledge.

Franklin, M.N. (1985) *The Decline in Class Voting in Britain*. Oxford: Clarendon.

Franzén, E.M. and Kassman, A. (2005) 'Longer-term labour market consequences of economic activity during young adulthood: A Swedish national cohort study', *Journal of Youth Studies*, 8, 403–25.

Frédéric, L. (2005) *Japan Encyclopaedia*. Cambridge, MA: Harvard University Press.

Frith, S. (1978) *The Sociology of Rock*. Constable: London.

Fryer, D. and Payne, R. (1986) 'Being unemployed. A review of the literature on the psychosocial experience of unemployment', in C.L. Cooper and I. Robertson (eds) *International Review of Industrial and Organisational Psychology*. Chichester: Wiley.

Furlong, A. (1992) *Growing Up in a Classless Society*. Edinburgh: Edinburgh University Press.

Furlong, A. (2005) 'Cultural determinants of decisions about educational participation among 14–19 year-olds: The parts Tomlinson doesn't reach', *Journal of Educational Policy*, 20, 379–89.

Furlong, A. and Cartmel, F. (2001) 'The relationship between youth unemployment and social and economic marginalisation: A comparative perspective', in B. Furaker (ed) *Employment, Unemployment and Marginalisation*. Stockholm: Almqvist and Wiksell.

Furlong, A. and Cartmel, F. (2004) *Vulnerable Young Men in Fragile Labour Markets*. York: York Publishing.

Furlong, A. and Cartmel, F. (2005) *Graduates from Disadvantaged Families: Early Labour Market Experiences*. Bristol: Policy Press.

Furlong, A., Cartmel, F., Biggart, A., Sweeting, H. and West, P. (2003) *Reconceptualising Youth Transitions: Patterns of Vulnerability and Processes of Social Exclusion*. Edinburgh: Scottish Executive.

Furlong, A. and Cooney, G. (1990) 'Getting on their bikes. Early home leaving among Scottish youth', *Journal of Social Policy*, 19, 535–51.

Furlong, A. and Kelly, P. (2005) 'The Brazilianization of youth transitions in Australia and the UK?', *Australian Journal of Social Issues*, 40, 207–25.

Furlong, A. and McNeish, W. (2000) *Integration Through Training*. Report to the European Commission. Glasgow: University of Glasgow.

Furnham, A. and Gunter, B. (1989) *The Anatomy of Adolescence*. London: Routledge.

Furnham, A. and Stacey, B. (1991) *Young People's Understanding of Society*. London: Routledge.

Futureskills Scotland (2006) *The Labour Market for Graduates in Scotland*. Glasgow: Futureskills Scotland.

Garasky, S. (2002) 'Where are they going? A comparison of urban and rural youths' locational choices after leaving the parental home', *Social Science Research*, 31, 409–31.

Garasky, S., Haurin, R.J. and Haurin, D.R. (2001) 'Group living decisions as youth transition to adulthood', *Journal of Population Economics*, 14, 329–49.

Gard, M. and Wright, J. (2005) *The Obesity Epidemic: Science, Morality and Ideology*. Routledge: London.

Garfinkel, P.E. and Garner, D.M. (1982) *Anorexia Nervosa. A Multidimensional Perspective*. New York: Brunner/Mazel.

Garton, A.F. and Pratt, C. (1991) 'Leisure activities of adolescent school students. Predictors of participation and interest', *Journal of Adolescence*, 14, 305–21.

Gauthier, M. (2003) 'The inadequacy of concepts: The rise of youth interest in civic participation in Quebec', *Journal of Youth Studies*, 6, 265–77.

Generation Europe (2004) *Findings of the Second Pan-European Survey of Youth Opinions and European Politics*.
www.generation-europe.eu.com/images/files/geapathysurvey2004.pdf
(accessed 11 February 2006).

Gewirtz, S. (1996) 'Market discipline versus comprehensive education. A case study of a London comprehensive school struggling to survive in the education market place', in J. Ahier, B. Cosin and M. Hales (eds) *Diversity and Change. Education, Policy and Selection*. London: Routledge.

Giddens, A. (1990) *The Consequences of Modernity*. Oxford: Polity.

Giddens, A. (1991) *Modernity and Self Identity. Self and Society in the Late Modern Age*. Oxford: Polity.

Giggs, J. (1991) 'The epidemiology of contemporary drug abuse', in D. Whynes and P. Bean (eds) *Policing and Prescribing. The British System of Drug Control*. London: Macmillan.

Gillett, N. (2005) 'The Warriors', *Guardian*, 26 November.

Glendinning, A., Love, J.G., Hendry, L.B. and Shucksmith, J. (1992) 'Adolescence and health inequalities. Extensions to Macintyre and West', *Social Science Medicine*, 35, 679–87.

Goldscheider, F.K. and DaVanzo, J. (1986) 'Pathways to independent living in early adulthood. Marriage, semi-autonomy and pre-marital residential independence', *Demography*, 26, 597–614.

Goldscheider, F.K. and Goldscheider, C. (1993) *Leaving Home Before Marriage. Ethnicity, Familism, and Generational Relationships*. Madison, Wisconsin: University of Wisconsin Press.

Goldthorpe, J.H. and Marshall, G. (1992) 'The promising future of class analysis. A response to recent critiques', *Sociology*, 26, 381–400.

Goodwin, J. and O'Connor, H. (2005) 'Exploring complex transitions: Looking back at the "Golden Age" of youth transitions', *Sociology*, 39, 201–21.

Gorard, S. and Smith, E. (2004) 'An international comparison of equity in education systems', *Comparative Education*, 40, 16–28.

Gorz, A. (1999) *Reclaiming Work: Beyond the Wage-based Society*. Cambridge: Polity.

Gottfredson, M.R. and Hirschi, T. (1990) *A General Theory of Crime*. Stanford: Stanford University Press.

Goudsblom, J. (1977) *Sociology in the Balance*. Oxford: Blackwell.

Gowers, S.G. and Shore, A. (2001) 'Development of weight and shape concerns in the aetiology of eating disorders', *British Journal of Psychiatry*, 179, 236–42.

Graham, J. and Bowling, B. (1995) *Young People and Crime*, Home Office Research Study 145. London: Home Office.

Green, A., Wolf, A. and Leney, T. (1999) *Convergence and Divergence in European Education and Training Systems*. London: University of London Institute of Education.

Green, E., Hebron, S. and Woodward, D. (1990) *Women's Leisure, What Leisure?* Basingstoke: Macmillian.

Green, G., Macintyre, S., West, P. and Ecob, R. (1991) 'Like parent like child? Associations between drinking and smoking behaviour of parents and their children', *British Journal of Addiction*, 86, 745–58.

Green, K., Smith, A. and Roberts, K. (2005) 'Social class, young people, sport and physical education', in K. Green and K. Hardman (eds) *Physical Education: Essential Issues*. London: Sage.

Greener, T. and Hollands, R. (2006) 'Beyond subculture and post-subculture? The case of virtual psytrance', *Journal of Youth Studies*, 9, 393–418.

Guardian (2006) 'Child obesity has doubled in a decade', 22 April.

Gunter, B. (1987) *Television and Fear of Crime*. London: Libbey.

Haerpfer, C., Wallace, C., and Spannring, R. (2002) *Young People and Politics in Eastern and Western Europe*. Vienna: Reighe Soziologie.

Hagan, J., Gillis, A.R. and Brownfield, D. (1996) (eds) *Criminological Controversies*. Oxford: Westview.

Hagell, A. and Newburn, T. (1994) *Persistent Young Offenders*. London: Policy Studies Institute.

Hall, G. S. (1904) *Adolescence. Its Psychology and its Relations to Physiology, Anthropology, Sociology, Sex, Crime, Religion and Education*, 2 Vols. New York: Appleton.

Hall, S. and Jefferson, T. (1976) (eds) *Resistance Through Rituals. Youth Subcultures in Post-War Britain*. London: Hutchinson.

Hallsworth, S. (1994) Understanding new social movements, *Sociology Review*, 4, 7–10.

Halsey, A.H. (1992) *Opening Wide the Doors of Higher Education*, Briefing Paper No. 6. London: National Commission on Education.

Halsey, A.H., Heath, A.F. and Ridge, J.M. (1980) *Origins and Destinations. Family, Class and Education in Modern Britain*. Oxford: Clarendon.

Hammarström, A. (2000) 'Is unemployment correlated with ill-health? A comparative analysis between six northern European countries', in A. Furlong and T. Hammer (eds) *Youth Unemployment and Marginalisation in Northern Europe*. Oslo: Norwegian Social Research.

Hammer, T. (1992) 'Unemployment and the use of drugs and alcohol among young people', *British Journal of Addiction*, 87, 1571–81.

Hammersley, R., Morrison, V., Davies, J.B. and Forsyth, A. (1990) *Heroin Use and Crime*. Edinburgh: Scottish Office. Central Research Unit Papers.

Hargreaves, D. (1967) *Social Relations in a Secondary School*. London: Routledge and Kegan Paul.

Harris, A. and Ranson, S. (2005) 'The contradictions of educational policy: disadvantage and achievement', *British Educational Research Journal*, 31, 571–87.

Harris, C. (1983) *The Family and Industrial Society*. London: Allen and Unwin.

Harris, N. (1990) 'Social security and the transition to adulthood', *Journal of Social Policy*, 17, 501–23.

Harrison, L. and Deicke, W. (2001) 'Capturing the first time voters', *Youth and Policy*, 67, 167–92.

Haskey, J. (2001) 'Cohabitation in Great Britain: past, present and future trends and attitudes', *Population Trends*, 103. London: The Stationery Office.

Haskey, J. (2005) 'Living arrangements in contemporary Britain: Having a partner who usually lives elsewhere and Living Apart Together (LAT)', *Population Trends*, 122, 35–45.

Haste, H. (2005a) *Joined-up Texting*. London: Nestlé Social Research Programme.

Haste, H. (2005b) *My Voice, My Vote, My Community: A Study of Young People's Civic Action and Inaction*. London: Nestlé Social Research Programme.

Haw, S. (1985) *Drug Problems in Greater Glasgow*. London: Chamelion.

Hawton, K., Arensman, E., Townsend, E., Bremner, S., Feldman, E., Goldney, R., Gunnell, D., Hazell, P., van Heeringen, K., House, A., Owens, D., Sakinofsky, I. and Träskman-Bendz, L. (1998) 'Deliberate self harm: a systematic review of psychosocial and pharmacological treatments in preventing repetition', *British Medical Journal*, 317, 441–47.

Hawton, K., Houston, K. and Shepperd, R. (1999) 'Suicide in young people of 174 cases aged under 25 years, based on coroners and medical records', *British Journal of Psychiatry*, 175, 271–6.

Hayward, G., Hodgson, A., Johnson, J., Keep, E., Oancea, A., Pring, R., Spours, K. and Wright, S. (2004) *The Nuffield Review of 14–19 Education and Training: Annual Report 2003–04*. Oxford: Department of Educational Studies, University of Oxford.

HEA (Health Education Authority) (1992) *Tomorrow's Young Adults. 9–15 Year-olds Look at Alcohol, Drugs, Exercise and Smoking*. London: Health Education Authority.

Heath, A., Curtice, J., Jowell, R., Evans, G., Field, J. and Witherspoon, S. (1991) *Understanding Political Change. The British Voter 1964–1987*. Oxford: Pergamon.

Heath, A. and Topf, R. (1987) 'Political culture in social attitudes', in R. Jowell, S. Wither-spoon and L. Brook (eds) *British Social Attitudes Survey. The 1987 Report*. Aldershot: Gower.

Heath, S. and Cleaver, E. (2003) *Young, Free and Single? Twenty-Somethings and Household Change*. Basingstoke: Palgrave/Macmillan.

Hebdige, D. (1979) *Subculture. The Meaning of Style*. London: Methuen.

Hebdige, D. (1988) *Hiding in the Light*. London: Comedia.

Heikkinen, M. (2001) 'Social networks of the marginal young: a study of young people's social exclusion in Finland', *Journal of Youth Studies*, 3, 389–407.

Heinz, W. (1987) 'The transition from school to work in crisis. Coping with threatening unemployment', *Journal of Adolescent Research*, 2, 127–41.

Heinz, W. (1991) *Theoretical Advances in Life Course Research*. Weinheim: Deutscher Verlag.

Hendry, L. and Raymond, M. (1983) 'Youth unemployment and lifestyles. Some educational considerations', *Scottish Educational Review*, 15, 28–40.

Hendry, L., Shucksmith, J., Love, J.G. and Glendinning, A. (1993) *Young People's Leisure and Lifestyles*. London: Routledge.

Henley, J. (2005a) 'Teenage double suicide shocks France', *Guardian*, 27 September.

Henley, J. (2005b) 'Worlds apart: Paris suburb on the divide between hope and despair', *Guardian*, 7 November.

Hess, L.E. (1995) 'Changing family patterns in Western Europe. Opportunity and risk factors for adolescent development', in M. Rutter and D.J. Smith (eds) *Psychological Disorders in Young People. Time Trends and their Causes*. Chichester: Wiley.

Hibell, B., Andersson, B., Bjarnasson, T., Alstrom, S., Balakireva, O., Kokkevi, A. and Morgan, M. (2004) *The ESPAD Report 2003: Alcohol and Other Drug Use Among Students in 35 European Countries*. Stockholm: The Swedish Council for Information on Alcohol and Other Drugs (CAN) and the Pompidou Group at the Council of Europe.

Hill, K. (1995) *The Long Sleep. Young People and Suicide*. London: Virago.

Himmelweit, H.T., Humphreys, P. and Jaeger, M. (1985) *How Voters Decide*. Milton Keynes: Open University Press.

Hobbs, D. (1989) *Doing the Business*. Oxford: Oxford University Press.

Hodkinson, P. (2002) *Goth: Identity, Style and Subculture*. Oxford: Berg.

Hogan, D. Hao, L. and Parish, W. (1990) 'Race, kin networks and assistance to mother headed families', *Social Forces*, 68, 797–812.

Holdsworth, C. (2000) 'Leaving home in Britain and Spain', *European Sociological Review*, 16, 201–22.

Hollands, R. (1990) *The Long Transition*. Basingstoke: Macmillan.

Hollands, R. (1995) *Friday Night, Saturday Night. Youth Cultural Identification in the Post-Industrial City*. Newcastle: University of Newcastle.

Holm, G., Daspit, T. and Young, A.J.K. (2005) 'The sky is always falling: [Un]changing views on youth in the US', in C. Leccardi and E. Ruspinin (eds) *A New Youth? Young People, Generations and Family Life*. Aldershot: Ashgate.

Holt, M. and Griffin, C. (2005) 'Students versus locals: Young adults' constructions of the working class Other', *British Journal of Social Psychology*, 44, 241–67.

Horkheimer, M. and Adorno, T. (1972) *Dialectic of Enlightenment*. New York: Herder and Herder.

Horner, M.S. (1971) 'Femininity and successful achievement', in M.H. Garskof (ed) *Roles Women Play*. California: Brooks Cole.

Hough, M. (1995) *Anxiety About Crime. Findings from the 1994 British Crime Survey*, Home Office Research Study 147. London: Home Office.

House of Commons (2004) *UK Election Statistics 1918–2004*, House of Commons Research Paper 04/61. London: House of Commons.

Hsu, L.K.G. (1990) 'Body image disturbance. Time to abandon the concept for eating disorders', *International Journal of Eating Disorders*, 10, 15–30.

Huisman, J., Kaiser, F. and Vossensteyn, H. (2003) 'The relationship between access, diversity and participation: Searching for the weakest link', in M. Tight (ed) *Access and Exclusion*. Oxford: Elsevier.

Humphries, S. (1991) *The Secret World of Sex*. London: Sidgwick and Jackson.

Hurrelmann, K. (1990) Basic issues and problems of health in adolescence, in K. Hurrelmann and F. Lösel (eds) *Health Hazards in Adolescence*. Berlin and New York: de Gruyter.

Iacovou, M. (2001) 'Leaving Home in the European Union'. Institute for Social and Economic Research working paper no 2001–18. Colchester: University of Essex.

Iacovou, M. and Berthoud, R. (2001) *Young People's Lives: A Map of Europe*. Colchester: University of Essex, Institute for Social and Economic Research.

Iannelli, C. (2003) 'Young people's social origin, educational attainment and labour market outcomes in Europe: Youth transitions from education to working life in Europe (Part III)', in Eurostat (ed) *Statistics in Focus: Population and Social Conditions*. Luxembourg: Eurostat.

ILO (International Labour Office) (2003) *Key Indicators of the Labour Market*, 3rd edition. Geneva: ILO.

Inglehart, R. (1977) *The Silent Revolution. Changing Values and Political Styles Among Western Publics*. Princeton, NJ: Princeton University Press.

Inglehart, R. (1990) *Culture Shift in Advanced Industrial Society*. Princeton, NJ: Princeton University Press.

Inglehart, R., Basáñez, M., Díez-Medrano, J., Halman, L. and Luijkx, R. (2004) *Human Beliefs and Values: A Cross-Cultural Sourcebook Based on the 1999–2002 Values Surveys*. Mexico: Siglo Veintiuno Editores.

Institute of Alcohol Studies (2005) *Alcohol and Young People: International Comparisons*. London: Institute of Alcohol Studies.

Inui, A. (2005) 'Why Freeter and NEET are Misunderstood: Recognizing the New Precarious Conditions of Japanese Youth', *Social Work and Society*, 3, 244–51.

Jack, M.S. (1989) 'Personal fable. A potential explanation for risk-taking behaviour in adolescents', *Journal of Paediatric Nursing*, 4, 334–8.

Jacobs, J. (1971) *Adolescent Suicide*. London: Wiley Interscience.

Jansen, T. and Van der Veen, R. (1992) 'Reflexive modernity, self-reflexive biographies. Adult education in the light of the risk society', *International Journal of Lifelong Learning*, 11, 275–86.

Jencks, C. and Phillips, M. (1998) 'The black-white test score gap; an introduction', in C. Jencks and M. Phillips (eds) *The Black-White Test Score Gap*. Washington, DC: Brookings Institute.

Jones, G. (1995) *Leaving Home*. Buckingham: Open University Press.

Jones, G. (1987) 'Leaving the parental home. An analysis of early housing careers', *Social Policy*, 16, 49–74.

Jones, G. (2000) 'Experimenting with households and inventing "home" ', *International Social Sciences Journal*, 164, 183–94.

Jones, G. and Wallace, C. (1990) 'Beyond individualization. What sort of social change?', in L. Chisholm, P. Büchner, H.-H. Krüger and P. Brown (eds) *Childhood, Youth and Social Change. A Comparative Perspective*. London: Falmer.

Jones, G. and Wallace, C. (1992) *Youth, Family and Citizenship*. Milton Keynes: Open University Press.

Jones, G.W. (2004) 'A risky business: Experiences of leaving home among rural women', *Journal of Youth Studies*, 7, 209–21.

Jowell, R. and Park, A. (1998) *Young People, Politics and Citizenship: A Disengaged Generation?* London: Citizenship Foundation.

Julkunen, I. and Malmberg-Heimonen, I. (1998) *The Encounter of High Unemployment Among Youth: A Nordic Perspective.* Helsinki: Työministeriö.

Juvenile Justice Project of Louisiana (2005) What's happening to our kids?: Youth in prison http://www.jjpl.org/whatshappeningtoourkids/youthinprison/youthinprison.html (accessed 9 October 2006).

Kagan, C., O'Reilly, J. and Halpin, B. (2005) *Job Opportunities for Whom? Labour Market Dynamics and Service Sector Employment Growth in Germany and Britain.* London: Anglo-German Foundation.

Kao, G. and Thompson, J.S. (2003) 'Racial and ethnic stratification in educational achievement and attainment', *Annual Review of Sociology*, 29, 417–42.

Kaufman, L. (1980) 'Prime-time nutrition', *Journal of Communication*, Summer, 37–46.

Kellner, D. (1992) 'Popular culture and the construction of postmodern identity', in S. Lash and J. Friedman (eds) *Modernity and Identity.* Oxford: Blackwell.

Kerckhoff, A.C. and McRae, J. (1992) 'Leaving the parental home in Great Britain. A comparative perspective', *Sociological Quarterly*, 33, 281–301.

Kiernan, K.E. (1986) 'Leaving home. A comparative analysis of six western European countries', *European Journal of Population*, 2, 177–84.

Kiernan, K.E. (1992) 'The impact of family disruption in childhood on transitions made in young adult life', *Population Studies*, 46, 213–34.

Kiernan, K. (1999) 'Cohabitation in western Europe', *Population Trends*, 96, 25–34.

Kimberlee, R. (2002) 'Why don't British young people vote at General Elections?', *Journal of Youth Studies*, 5, 85–98.

Kirkby, D., Coyle, K. and Gould, J.B. (2001) 'Manifestations of poverty and birthrates among young teenagers in California zip code areas', *Family Planning Perspectives*, 33, 63–9.

Klein, N. (2000) *No Logo.* London: Flamingo.

Kogan, I. and Jungblut, J-M. (2004) 'Labour market entry, early employment careers and prospects for further education and training among the low educated youth in Europe', www.nuff.ox.ac.uk/projects/changequal/papers/public/conf/4/theme_1_414_jungblutkogan.doc (accessed 16 February 2006).

Krahn, H.J. and Lowe, G.S. (1993) *Work, Industry and Canadian Society.* Scarborough, Ontario: Nelson.

Kreitman, N. (1977) *Parasuicide.* London: Wiley.

Kumar, K. (1995) *From Post-Industrial to Post-Modern Society.* Oxford: Blackwell.

Kutcher, S. (1994) 'Adolescence. Normal development and some important psychiatric conditions onsetting in the teenage years', in R.S. Tonkin (ed) *Current Issues in the Adolescent Patient.* London: Bailliére Tindall.

Lader, D. and Matheson, J. (1991) *Smoking Among Secondary School Children in 1990.* London: OPCS.

Langman, L. (1992) 'Neon cages. Shopping for subjectivity', in R. Shields (ed) *Shopping. The Subject of Consumption.* London: Routledge.

Lash, S. (1992) *Modernity and Identity.* Oxford: Blackwell.

Lash, S. and Urry, J. (1987) *The End of Organised Capital.* Cambridge: Polity.

Lash, S. and Urry, J. (1994) *Economies of Signs and Space.* London: Sage.

Lea, J. and Young, J. (1993) *What is to be Done About Law and Order? Crisis in the Nineties.* London: Pluto.

Leigh, B.C. and Miller, P. (1995) 'The relationship of substance use with sex with the use of condoms in two urban areas of Scotland', *AIDS, Education and Prevention*, 7, 278–84.

Leitner, M., Shapland, J. and Wiles, P. (1993) *Drug Usage and Prevention. The Views and Habits of the General Public*. London: HMSO.

Lemos, G. (2004) *Fear and Fashion: The Use of Knives and Other Weapons by Young People*. London: Lemos and Crane.

Leonard, D. (1980) *Sex and Generation. A Study of Courtship and Weddings*. London: Tavistock.

Livingstone, S., Bober, M. and Helsper, E. (2004) *Active Participation or just More Participation? Young People's Take Up of Opportunities to Act or Interact on the Internet*. Research report. London: London School of Economics.

Loader, I. (1996) *Youth, Policing and Democracy*. Basingstoke: MacMillan.

Love, J.F. (1995) *McDonald's: Behind the Arches*. New York: Bantam.

Lucey, H. (1996) Transitions to womanhood. Constructions of success and failure for middle and working class young women. Conference paper, University of Glasgow, 'British Youth Research: The New Agenda', 26–8 January.

Lyon, J. (1996) 'Adolescents who offend', *Journal of Adolescence*, 19, 1–4.

Lyotard, J.-F. (1984) *The Postmodern Condition. A Report on Knowledge*. Minneapolis: University of Minnesota Press.

Macallair, D. and Males, M. (2000) *Dispelling the Myth: An Analysis of Youth and Adult Crime Patterns in California over the Past 20 Years*. San Francisco, CA: Centre on Juvenile and Criminal Justice.

McClure, G.M.G. (2001) 'Suicide in children and adolescents in England and Wales 1970–1998', *British Journal of Psychiatry*, 178, 469–74.

McDonald, K. (1999) *Struggles for Subjectivity: Identity, Action and Youth Experience*. Cambridge: Cambridge University Press.

MacDonald, R. and Coffield, F. (1991) *Risky Business? Youth and the Enterprise Culture*. London: Falmer.

MacDonald, R. and Marsh, J. (2005) *Disconnected Youth? Growing Up in Britain's Poor Neighbourhoods*. London: Palgrave.

McDonough, P.M. (1997) *Choosing Colleges: How Social Class and Schools Structure Opportunity*. New York: SUNY Press.

McDowell, L. (2003) *Redundant Masculinities? Employment Change and White Working Class Youth*. London: Blackwell.

Macintyre, S. (1988) 'Social correlates of human height', *Science Progress Oxford*, 72, 493–510.

MacKenzie, D. and Chamberlain, C. (2003) *Counting the Homeless 2001*. Canberra: Australian Bureau of Statistics.

McPherson, M. and Schapiro, M. (1991) *Keeping Colleges Affordable: Government and Educational Opportunity*. Washington, DC: Brookings Institution.

McPherson, M. and Schapiro, M. (1999) *Reinforcing Stratification in American Higher Education: Some Disturbing Trends*. Stanford, Stanford University, National Center for Postsecondary Improvement.

McQuoid, J. (1996) 'The ISRD study. Self report findings from Northern Ireland', *Journal of Adolescence*, 19, 95–8.

McRae, S. (1987) 'Social and political perspectives found among young unemployed men and women', in M. White (ed) *The Social World of the Young Unemployed*. London: Policy Studies Institute.

Maffesoli, M. (1996) *The Time of Tribes: The Decline of Individualism in Mass Society*. London: Sage.

Maguire, M. (1991) 'British labour market trends', in D.N. Ashton and G. Lowe (eds) *Making Their Way. Education, Training and the Labour Market in Canada and Britain*. Milton Keynes: Open University Press.

Makeham, P. (1980) *Youth Unemployment*. Department of Employment Research Paper, No.10. London: HMSO.

Mann, A.H., Wakeling, A., Wood, K., Monck, E., Dobbs, R. and Szmakler, G. (1983) 'Screening for abnormal eating attitudes and psychiatric morbidity in an unselected population of 15 year old schoolgirls', *Psychological Medicine*, 13, 573–88.

Markus, H. and Nurius, P. (1986) 'Possible selves', American Psychologist, 41, 954–69.

Marsh, A. (1990) *Political Action in Europe and the USA*. London: Macmillan.

Marsh, A., Dobbs, J. and White, A. (1986) *Adolescent Drinking*. London: HMSO.

Marshall, G. and Swift, A. (1993) 'Social class and social justice', *British Journal of Sociology*, 44, 187–211.

Massey, D. (1994) *Space, Place and Gender*. Cambridge: Polity Press.

Matza, D. (1964) *Delinquency and Drift*. New York: Wiley.

Maung, N. (1995) *Young People, Victimisation and the Police. British Crime Survey Findings on Experiences and Attitudes of 12 to 15 Year Olds*. Home Office Research Study 140. London: HMSO.

May, C. and Cooper, A. (1995) 'Personal identity and social change. Some theoretical considerations', *Acta Sociologica*, 38, 75–85.

Mays, J.B. (1954) *Growing Up in the City. A Study of Juvenile Delinquency in an Urban Neighbourhood*. Liverpool: Liverpool University Press.

Measham, F. (2002) ' "Doing Gender" – "Doing Drugs": Conceptualising the gendering of drug cultures', *Contemporary Drug Problems*, 29, 335–73.

Measham, F. (2004) 'The decline of ecstasy, the rise of "binge drinking" and the persistence of pleasure', *Probation Journal*, 51, 309–26.

Measham, F., Newcombe, R. and Parker, H. (1994) 'The normalisation of recreational drug use amongst young people in north-west England', *British Journal of Sociology*, 45, 287–312.

Meeus, W. (1994) 'Psychosocial problems and support', in F. Nestmann and K. Hurrelmann (eds) *Social Networks and Social Support in Childhood and Adolescence*. Berlin and New York: de Gruyter.

Melucci, A. (1992) 'Youth silence and voice. Selfhood and commitment in the everyday experiences of adolescents', in J. Fornas and G. Bolin (eds) *Moves in Modernity*. Stockholm: Almqvist and Wiskell.

Mennell, S., Murcott, A. and van Otterloo, A.H. (1992) *The Sociology of Food. Eating, Diet and Culture*. London: Sage.

Merton, R.K. (1969) 'Social structure and anomie', in D.R. Cressey and D.A. Ward (eds) *Delinquency, Crime and Social Processes*. New York: Harper and Row.

Messerschmidt, J.W. (1994) 'Schooling, masculinities and youth crime', in T. Newburn and E.A. Stanko (eds) *Just Boys Doing the Business? Men, Masculinities and Crime*. London: Routledge.

Miles, R. (1989) *Racism*. London: Routledge.

Miles, S. (1998) *Consumerism as a Way of Life*. London: Sage.

Miles, S. (2000) *Youth Lifestyles in a Changing World*. Buckingham: Open University Press.

Miles, S. (1996) Use and consumption in the construction of identities. Conference paper, University of Glasgow, 'British Youth Research: The New Agenda', 26–28 January.

Miles, S. (1995) Pleasure or pressure. Consumption and youth identity in the contemporary British shopping centre. Conference paper, University of Leicester, British Sociological Association, 3–5 April.

Millward, C. (1998) 'Later life parents helping adult children', *Family Matters*, 50, 38–42.

Mission Australia (2001) *Youth Suicide Factsheet*. Sydney: Mission Australia.

MORI (2002a) *Youth Survey: Summary*. London: Youth Justice Board.

MORI (2002b) *Young People and Citizenship*. http://www.mori.com/mrr/2002/c020906.shtml (accessed 14 September 2005).

MORI (2005) Being young in Scotland 2005. www.scotland.gov.uk/publications/2005/ 09/02151404/14051 (accessed 7 April 2006).

Morrison, D.M., Gillmore, M.R., Hoppe, M.J., Gaylord, J., Leigh, B.C. and Rainey, D. (2003) 'Adolescent drinking and sex: Findings from a daily diary study', *Perspectives on Sexual and Reproductive Health*, 35, 4.

Mulder, C.H. and Clark, W.A.V. (2002) 'Leaving home for college and gaining independence', *Environment and Planning*, 34, 981–99.

Mulgan, G. and Wilkinson, H. (1997) 'Freedom's children and the rise of generational politics', in G. Mulgan (ed) *Life After Politics: New Thinking for the Twenty First Century*. London: Fontana.

Müller, W. and Karle, W. (1993) 'Social selection in educational systems in Europe', *European Sociological Review*, 9, 1–22.

Muncie, J. (2004) *Youth and Crime*. London: Sage.

Murdock, G. and McCron, R. (1976) 'Youth and class. The career of a confusion', in G. Mungham and G. Pearson (eds) *Working Class Youth Culture*. London: Routledge and Kegan Paul.

Murray, C. (1990) *The Emerging British Underclass*. London: Institute of Economic Affairs.

Naidoo, B., Warm, D., Quigley, R. and Taylor, I. (2004) *Smoking and Public Health: A Review of Interventions to Increase Smoking Cessesion, Reduce Smoking Initiation and Prevent Further Uptake of Smoking*. London: Health Development Agency.

Nee, C. (1993) *Car Theft. The Offenders Perspective*. London: Home Office.

Nicholas, S., Povey, D., Walker, A. and Kershaw, C. (2005) *Crime in England and Wales 2004/2005*. London: Home Office.

Nicoletti, C. and Tanturri, M.L. (2005) *Differences in Delaying Motherhood Across European Countries: Empirical Evidence from the ECHP*. Colchester: Institute for Social and Economic Research, University of Essex.

O'Bryan, L. (1989) 'Young people and drugs', in S. MacGregor (ed) *Drugs and British Society*. London: Routledge.

OECD (Organisation for Economic Co-operation and Development) (1995) *Employment Outlook*. Paris: OECD.

OECD (1998) *Employment Outlook*. Paris: OECD.

OECD (1999) *Employment Outlook*. Paris: OECD.

OECD (2002a) *Reading for Change*. Paris: OECD.

OECD (2002b) *Employment Outlook*. Paris: OECD.

OECD (2004) *Education at a Glance*. Paris: OECD.

OECD. (2005a) *From Education to Work: A Difficult Transition for Young Adults with Low Levels of Education*. Paris: OECD.

OECD (2005b) *Employment Outlook*. Paris: OECD.

Offer, D., Ostrov, E., Howard, K. and Atkinson, R. (1988) *The Teenage World*. New York: Plenum.

O'Higgins, N. (2001) *Youth Unemployment and Employment Policy: A Global Perspective*. Geneva: ILO.

Oksman, V. and Rautiainen, P. (2002) 'I've got my whole life in my hand', *Revista de Estudias Juventud*, 57, 25–33.

Olk, T. (1988) 'Gesellschaftstheoretissche Ansätze in der Jungendforschung', quoted in L. Chisholm, P. Büchner, H.-H. Krüger, and P. Brown (1990) (eds) *Childhood, Youth and Social Change. A Comparative Perspective*. London: Falmer.

One plus One (2004) *Relationships Today*, 5 (May). www.oneplusone.org.uk (accessed 9 August 2005).

O'Neill, B. (2001) 'Generational patterns in the political opinions and behavior of Canadians: Separating the wheat from the chaff', *Policy Matters*, 2, 5 www.irpp.org/pm/ (accessed 4 October 2005).

ONS (Office of National Statistics) (2000) *Annual Abstract of Statistics*. London: Office for National Statistics.

ONS (2003) *Social Trends 33*. London: Office for National Statistics.

ONS (2005) *Social Trends 35*. London: Office for National Statistics.

ONS (2006) *Social Trends 36*. London: Office for National Statistics.

O'Reilly, K.R. and Aral, S.O. (1985) 'Adolescent and sexual behaviour', *Journal of Adolescent Health Care*, 6, 262–70.

Osgerby, B. (1998) *Youth in Britain Since 1945*. Oxford: Blackwell.

Pahl, R.E. (1989) 'Is the emperor naked? Some comments on the adequacy of socio-logical theory in urban and regional research', *International Journal of Urban and Regional Research*, 15, 127–9.

Pahl R.E. (1993) 'Does class analysis without class theory have a promising future?', *Sociology*, 27, 253–8.

Pakulski, L. and Waters, M. (1996) *The Death of Class*. London: Sage.

Palmer, G., Carr, J. and Kenway, P. (2004) *Monitoring Poverty and Social Exclusion 2004*. York: Joseph Rowntree Foundation.

Park, A. (1994) *England and Wales Youth Cohort Study Cohort 4. Young People 18–19 Years Old in 1991. Report on Sweep 3*. London: Employment Department.

Park, A. (1996) 'Teenagers and their politics', in R. Jowell, J. Curtice, A. Park, L. Brook and D. Ahrendt (eds) *British Social Attitudes Survey, the 12th Report*. Dartmouth: Aldershot.

Park, A. (2000) 'The generation gap', in R. Jowell, J. Curtice, A. Park, K. Thompson, L. Jarvis, C. Bromley, and N. Stratford (eds) *British Social Attitudes, the 17th Report: Focusing on Diversity*. London: Sage.

Park, A. (2004) 'Has modern politics disenchanted the young?', in A. Park, J. Curtis, K. Thompson, C. Bromley and M. Phillips (eds) *British Social Attitudes, the 21st Report*. London: Sage.

Parker, H.J. (1974) *View From the Boys*. Newton Abbot: David and Charles.

Parker, H., Bakx, K. and Newcombe, R. (1988) *Living with Heroin*. Milton Keynes: Open University Press.

Parry-Jones, W. Ll. (1988) 'Obesity in children and adolescence', in G.B. Burrows, P. Beumont and R.C. Casper (eds) *Handbook of Eating Disorders. Part 2, Obesity*. Amsterdam: Elsevier.

Payne, J. (1995) *Routes Beyond Compulsory Schooling*, Youth Cohort Paper No.31. London: Employment Department.

Pearson, G. (1983) *Hooligan. A History of Respectable Fears*. Basingstoke: Macmillan.

Pearson, G. (1987) *The New Heroin Users*. Oxford: Blackwell.

Pearson, G. (1994) 'Youth, crime and society', in M. Maguire, R. Morgan and R. Reiner (eds) *The Oxford Handbook of Criminology*. Oxford: Clarendon.

Pearson, G., Gilman, M. and McIver, S. (1987) *Young People and Heroin Use in the North of England*. London: Gower.

Peck, D.F. and Plant, M.A. (1986) 'Unemployment and illegal drug use. Concordant evidence from a prospective study and from national trends', *British Medical Journal*, 293, 929–32.

Penhale, B. (1990) *Living Arrangements of Young Adults in France, England and Wales*, LS working paper no. 68. London: SSRU, City University.

Phoenix, A. and Tizard, B. (1996) 'Thinking through class: The place of social class in the lives of young Londoners', *Feminism and Psychology*, 6, 427–42.

Plant, M.A. (1989) 'The epidemiology of illicit drug-use and misuse in Britain', in S. MacGregor (ed) *Drugs and British Society*. London: Routledge.

Plant, M.A., Peck, D.F. and Samuel, E. (1985) *Alcohol, Drugs and School Leavers*. London: Tavistock.

Plant, M.A. and Plant, M. (1992) *Risk-Takers. Alcohol, Drugs, Sex and Youth.* London: Routledge.

Pleace, N. and Fitzpatrick, S. (2004) *Centrepoint Youth Homelessness Index: An Estimate of Youth Homelessness for England.* York: Centre for Housing Policy, University of York.

Polman, J. and Vitone, E. (2004) 'The scope of youth homelessness', Texas Homeless Network News, March. www.thn.org/newsletters/mar04/featureyouth.htm (accessed 3 April 2006).

Poole, M.E. (1989) 'Adolescent transitions. A life-course perspective', in K. Hurrelman and U. Engel (eds) *The Social World of Adolescents. International Perspectives.* Berlin and New York: de Gruyter.

PricewaterhouseCoopers (2005) *The Economic Benefits of Higher Educational Qualifications,* Report to the Royal Society of Chemistry and the Institute of Physics. London: Royal Society of Chemistry and the Institute of Physics.

Print, M., Saha, L.J. and Edwards, K. (2004) *Youth Electoral Study – Report 1: Enrolment and Voting.* Sydney: Australian Electoral Commission.

Priory, The (2005) Adolescent Angst. Leatherhead: The Priory.

Pryce, K. (1979) *Endless Pressure: A Study of West Indian Lifestyles in Bristol.* Harmonds-worth: Penguin.

Public Health Agency of Canada (2005) *2002 Canadian Sexually Transmitted Infections Surveillance Report.* Ottowa: Public Health Agency of Canada.

Putnam, R.D. (2000) *Bowling Alone: The Collapse and Revival of American Community.* New York: Simon and Schuster.

Quéniart, A. and Jacques, J. (2000) 'L'engagement politique des juenes femmes au Que-bec: de la responsatilité au pouvoir d'agir pour un changement de société', *Lein social et Politiques,* 46, 45–53.

Raffe, D. (1992) *Participation of 16–19 Year-Olds in Education and Training, Briefing Paper No. 3.* London: National Commission on Education.

Raffe, D., Brannen, K., Fairgrieve, J. and Martin, C. (2001) 'Participation, inclusiveness, academic drift and parity of esteem: a comparison of post-compulsory education and training in England, Scotland, Wales and Northern Ireland', *Oxford Review of Education,* 27, 173–203.

Raffe, D. and Shapira, M. (2005) 'Has the work-based route gained status?', working paper. Edinburgh: Centre for Educational Sociology, University of Edinburgh.

Raffe, D. and Willms, J.D. (1989) 'Schooling the discouraged worker. Local labour-market effects on educational participation', *Sociology,* 23, 559–81.

Raftery, A.E. and Hout, M. (1990) *Maximally Maintained Inequality. Expansion, Reform and Opportunity in Irish Education, 1921–75.* Madrid: ISA Research Committee on Social Stratification.

Rattansi, A. and Pheonix, A. (1997) 'Rethinking youth identities: modernist and post-modernist frameworks', in J. Bynner, L. Chisholm, and A. Furlong (eds) *Youth, Citizenship and Social Change in a European Context.* Aldershot: Ashgate.

Rifkin, J. (1996) *The End of Work: The Decline of the Global Labor Force and the Dawn of the Post-Market Era.* New York: Tarcher-Penguin.

Rindfuss, R.R., Swicegood, C.G. and Rosenfeld, R.A. (1987) 'Disorder in the life course. How common and does it matter?', *American Sociological Review,* 52, 785–801.

Roberts, K. (1968) 'The entry into employment. An approach towards a general theory', *Sociological Review,* 16, 165–84.

Roberts, K. (1983) *Youth and Leisure.* London: Allen and Unwin.

Roberts, K. (1985) 'Youth in the 1980s: A new way of life', *International Social Science Journal,* 37, 427–40.

Roberts, K. (1995) *Youth and Employment in Modern Britain.* Oxford: Oxford University Press.

Roberts, K. (1999) *Leisure in Contemporary Society*. Wallingford: CABI Publishing.

Roberts, K., Brodie, D.A., Campbell, R., Lamb, K., Minten, J. and York, C. (1989) 'Indoor sports centres. Trends in provision and usage', in Health Promotion Research Trust (ed) *Fit for Life*. London: Health Promotion Research Trust.

Roberts, K., Dench, S. and Richardson, D. (1987) *The Changing Structure of Youth Labour Markets*. London: Department of Employment.

Roberts, K. and Parsell, G. (1990) 'The political orientations, interests and activities of Britain's 16 to 18 year olds in the late 1980s', *ESRC 16–19 Initiative Occasional Papers*, No. 26. London: City University.

Roberts, K. and Parsell, G. (1992a) 'Entering the labour market in Britain. The survival of traditional opportunity structures', *Sociological Review*, 30, 727–53.

Roberts, K. and Parsell, G. (1992b) 'The stratification of youth training', *British Journal of Education and Work*, 5, 65–83.

Roberts, K. and Parsell, G. (1994) 'Youth cultures in Britain. The middle class take-over', *Leisure Studies*, 13, 33–48.

Roe, S. (2005) *Drug Misuse Declared: Finding from the 2004/05 British Crime Survey*. London: Home Office.

Rojek, C. (1985) *Capitalism and Leisure Theory*. London: Tavistock.

Rose, M. (1996) 'Still life in Swindon. Case-studies in union survival and employer policy in a "Sunrise" labour market', in D. Gallie, R. Penn and M. Rose (eds) *Trade Unionism in Recession*. Oxford: Oxford University Press.

Rudat, K., Ryan, H. and Speed, M. (1992) *Today's Young Adults. An In-depth Study into the Lifestyles of 16 to 19 Year Olds*. London: Health Education Authority.

Runciman, W.G. (1966) *Relative Deprivation and Social Justice*. Berkeley, CA: University of California Press.

Rutherford, A. (1992) *Growing out of Crime. The New Era*. London: Waterside Press.

Rutter, M. and Smith, D.J. (eds) (1995) *Psychosocial Disorders in Young People. Time Trends and their Causes*. Chichester: Wiley.

Ryan, P. (2001) 'The school-to-work transition: A cross-national perspective', *Journal of Economic Literature*, 39, 34–92.

Ryland, D. and Kruesi, M. (1992) 'Suicide among adolescents', *International Review of Psychiatry*, 4, 185–95.

Sagger, S. (2000) *Race and Representation*. Manchester: Manchester University Press.

Saha, L.J., Print, M. and Edwards, K. (2005) *Youth Electoral Study – Report 2: Youth Political Engagement and Voting*. Sydney: Australian Electoral Commission.

Saito, T. (1998) *Shakaiteki Hikikomori: Owarani Shisyun (Social Withdrawal: Unfinished Puberty)*. Tokyo: PHP-Kenkyu-jo.

Sampson, R.J. and Laub, J.H. (1993) *Crime in the Making. Pathways and Turning Points Through Life*. Cambridge, MA: Harvard University Press.

Sanders, D. (1992) 'Why the Conservative Party won – again', in A. King, I. Crewe, D. Denver, K. Newton, P. Norton, D. Sanders and P. Seyd (eds) *Britain at the Polls, 1992*. New Jersey: Chatham House.

Saunders, P. (1995) 'Might Britain be a meritocracy?', *Sociology*, 29, 23–41.

Savage, M. (2000) *Class Analysis and Social Transformation*. Buckingham: Open University Press.

Scarborough, E. (1995) 'Materialist-postmaterialist value orientations', in J.W. Van Deth and E. Scarbrough (eds) *Beliefs in Government, Volume Four. The Impact of Values*. New York: Oxford University Press.

Scarman, The Rt. Hon. The Lord (1981) *The Brixton Disorders*, Cmnd 8427. London: HMSO.

Schömann, K. and O'Connell, P.J. (2002) 'From the market for qualifications to the transitional market for learning and working: summary and conclusion', in K.

Schömann and P.J. O'Connell (eds) *Education, Training and Employment Dynamics.* Northampton: Edward Elgar.

Schostak, J.F. (1983) 'Race, riots and unemployment', in R. Fiddy (ed) *In Place of Work.* New York: Falmer.

Scott, A. (1990) *Ideology and the New Social Movements.* London: Unwin Hyman.

Scottish Law Commission (2001) *Discussion Paper on Age of Criminal Responsibility.* Discussion Paper No.115. Edinburgh: Scottish Law Commission.

Seabrook, J. (1983) *Unemployment.* London: Granada.

Seabrook, T. and Green, E. (2004) 'Streetwise or safe? Girls negotiating time and space', in W. Mitchell, R. Bunton, and E. Green (eds) *Young People, Risk and Leisure: Constructing Identities in Everyday Life.* London: Palgrave Macmillan.

Selman, P. (2003) 'Scapegoating and moral panics: Teenage pregnancy in Britain and the United States', in S. Cunningham-Burley and L. Jamieson (eds) *Families and the State: Changing Relationships.* Basingstoke: Palgrave.

Selzer, V.L., Rabin, J. and Benjamin, F. (1989) 'Teenagers' awareness of acquired immunodeficiency syndrome and the impact on their sexual behaviour', *Obstetrics and Gynaecology*, 74, 55–8.

Sennett, R. (1998) *The Corrosion of Character: The Personal Consequences of Work in the New Capitalism.* New York and London: Norton.

Shafii, M. (1989) 'Completed suicide in children and adolescents. Methods of psychological autopsy', in C.R. Pfeffer (ed) *Suicide Among Youth. Perspectives on Risk Prevention.* Washington: American Psychiatric Press.

Shavit, Y. and Blossfeld, H.P. (1993) *Persistent Inequality.* Boulder, CO: Westview.

Shavit, Y. and Müller, W. (1998) 'The institutional embeddedness of the stratification process', in Y. Shavit and W. Müller (eds) *From School to Work: A Comparative Study of Educational Qualifications and Occupational Destinations.* Oxford: Clarendon Press.

Shavit, Y. and Müller, W. (2000) 'Vocational secondary education: Where diversion and where safety net?', *European Societies*, 2, 29–50.

Shildrick, T. and MacDonald, R. (2006) 'In defence of subculture: Young people, leisure and social divisions', *Journal of Youth Studies*, 9, 125–41.

Shiokura, Y. (2002) *Hikikomoru Wakamono-tachi (Withdrawing Young People).* Toyko: Asahi-shinbunsha.

Shoemaker, D.J. (1990) *Theories of Delinquency. An Examination of Explanations of Delinquent Behaviour*, 2nd edition. Oxford: Oxford University Press.

Shover, N. (1985) *Ageing Criminals.* London: Sage.

Singh, S., Darroch, J.E., Frost, J.J. and the Study Team (2001) 'Socioeconomic disadvantage and adolescent women's sexual and reproductive behaviour: The case of five developed countries', *Family Planning Perspectives*, 33, 251–8.

Sivarajasingam, V., Shepherd, J.P. and Matthews, K. (2003) 'Effect of urban closed circuit television on assault injury and violence detection', *Injury Prevention*, 9, 312–16.

Skilbeck, M. and Connell, H. (2000) *Access and Equity in Higher Education: An International Perspective on Issues and Strategies.* Dublin: Higher Education Authority.

Smith, D.J. (1995) 'Youth crime and conduct disorders. Trends, patterns and causal explanations', in M. Rutter and D.J. Smith (eds) *Psychological Disorders in Young People. Time Trends and their Causes.* Chichester: Wiley.

Smith, D.J. and Blackwood, D.H.R. (2004) 'Depression in young adults', *Advances in Psychiatric Treatment*, 10, 4–12.

Smith, D.J. and Rutter, M. (1995) 'Time trends in psychosocial disorders of youth', in M. Rutter and D.J. Smith (eds) *Psychological Disorders in Young People. Time Trends and their Causes.* Chichester: Wiley.

Smithers, A. and Robinson, P. (1989) *Increasing Participation in Higher Education*. London: British Petroleum Educational Service.

Social Exclusion Unit (SEU) (1999) *Teenage Pregnancy*. London: The Stationery Office.

Sonenstein, F.L., Pleck, J.H. and Ku, L.C. (1989) 'Sexual activity, condom use and AIDS awareness among adolescent males', *Family Planning Perspectives*, 21, 152–8.

South, N. (1994) 'Drugs. Control, crime and criminological studies', in M. Maguire, R. Morgan and R. Reiner (eds) *The Oxford Handbook of Criminology*. Oxford: Clarendon.

Spilsbury, M., Hoskins, M., Ashton, D.N. and Maguire, M.J. (1987) 'A note on trade union membership patterns of young people', *British Journal of Industrial Relations*, 25, 267–74.

Sport England (2000) *Sports Participation and Ethnicity in England*. London: Sport England.

Springhall, J. (1986) *Coming of Age. Adolescence in Britain 1860–1960*. Dublin: Gill and Macmillan.

Stewart, F. (1992) 'The adolescent as consumer', in J.C. Coleman and C. Warren-Anderson (eds) *Youth and Policy in the 1990s. The Way Forward*. London: Routledge.

Stimson, G. (1987) 'The war on heroin. British policy and the international trade in illicit drugs', in N. Dorn and N. South (eds) *A Land Fit for Heroin*. London: Macmillian.

Stradling, R. (1977) *The Political Awareness of School Leavers*. London: Hansard Society.

Summerfield, C. and Gill, B. (eds) (2005) *Social Trends, No.35*. London: Office for National Statistics.

Sunday Times (2005) 'The Fire next door', 13 November.

Surridge, P. and Raffe, D. (1995) *The Participation of 16–19 Year Olds in Education and Training. Recent Trends*. CES Briefing Paper No.1. Edinburgh: University of Edinburgh.

Sutherland, E.H. (1949) *Principles of Criminology*. Chicago: Lippincott.

Sweeting, H. (1995) 'Reversals of fortune? Sex differences in health in childhood and adolescence', *Social Science Medicine*, 40, 77–90.

Tajfel, H. and Turner, J.C. (1979) 'An integrative theory of intergroup conflict', in W.G. Austin and S. Worchel (eds) *The Social Psychology of Intergroup Relations*. Monterey, CA: Brooks-Cole.

Tarling, R. (1982) *Unemployment and Crime*. Research Bulletin No.14. London: Home Office.

Taylor, I. (1996) 'Fear of crime, urban fortunes and suburban social movements. Some reflections from Manchester'. *Sociology*, 30, 317–37.

Thompson, S.H., Corwin, S.J. and Sargent, R.S. (1997) 'Ideal body size beliefs and weight concerns in fourth grade children', *International Journal of Eating Disorders*, 21, 279–84.

Thomson, R., Holland, J., McGrellis, S., Bell, R., Henderson, S. and Sharpe, S. (2004) 'Inventing adulthoods: A biographical approach to understanding youth citizenship', *The Sociological Review*, 52, 218–39.

Thorpe, K. and Ruparel, C. (2005) 'Reporting and recording crime', in S. Nicholas, D. Povey, A. Walker and C. Kershaw (eds) *Crime in England and Wales 2004/2005*. London: Home Office.

Tomal, A. (1999) 'Determinants of teenage birth rates as an unpooled sample: Age matters for socioeconomic predictors', *American Journal of Economics and Sociology*, 58, 57–69.

Tomlinson, A. (1990) (ed.) *Consumption, Identity and Style*. London: Routledge.

Torsheim, T., Currie, C., Boyce, W., Kalnins, I., Overpeck, M. and Haugland, S. (2004) 'Material deprivation and self-rated health: A multilevel study of adolescents from 22 European and North American countries', *Social Science and Medicine*, 59, 1–12.

Touraine, A. (1985) 'An introduction to the study of social movements', *Social Research*, 52, 749–87.

Townsend, P. and Davidson, N. (1982) *Inequalities in Health. The Black Report*. Harmondsworth: Penguin.

Traene, B., Stigum, H., Hassoun, J. and Zanrtedechi, E. (2003) 'Pre-sexual alcohol consumption and use of condoms: A European cross-cultural study', *Culture, Health and Sexuality*, 5, 439–54.

Trost, J. (1999) 'LAT relationships now and in the future', in K. Matthijs (ed) *The Family: Contemporary Perspectives and Challenges*. Leuven: Leuvan University Press.

Trust for America's Health (2004) *F as in Fat: How Obesity Policies are Failing in America*. Washington, DC: Trust for America's Health.

United Nations Economic Commission for Europe (2003) *Trends in Europe and North America: The Statistical Yearbook of the Economic Commission for Europe*. Geneva: United Nations.

United States Conference of Mayors (2005) *Hunger and Homelessness Survey: A Status Report on Hunger and Homelessness in America's Cities*. http://www.usmayors.org/uscm/hungersurvey/2004/onlinereport/HungerandhomelessnessReport2004.pdf (accessed 3 May 2006).

US Conference of Mayors (1997) *A Status Report on Youth Curfews in America's Cities: A 347-City Survey*. http://www.usmayors.org/uscm/news/publications/curfew.htm (accessed 31 August 2005).

US Department of Justice (2005) *Bureau of Justice Statistics Bulletin: Prisoners in 2004*. Washington DC: US Department of Justice.

van Kesteren, J., Mathew, P. and Nieuwbeerta, P. (2001) *Criminal Victimisation in Seventeen Industrialised Countries: Key Findings from the 2000 International Crime Victims Survey*. The Hague: Wetenschappelijk Onderzoek – en Documentatiecentrum.

Viner, R.M. and Cole, T.J. (2006) 'Who changes body mass between adolescence and adulthood? Factors predicting change in BMI between 16 and 30 years in the 1970 British birth cohort', *International Journal of Obesity*. Advance online publication www.nature.com/ijo/journal/vaop/ncurrent/abs/0803183a.html (accessed 8 August 2006).

Vossensteyn, H. (1999) 'Where in Europe would people like to study? The affordability of higher education in nine Western European countries', *Higher Education*, 37, 159–76.

Vromen, A. (2003) 'Traversing time and gender: Australian young people's participation', *Journal of Youth Studies*, 6, 277–95.

Wadsworth, M.E.J. and Maclean, M. (1986) 'Parents divorce and children's life chances', *Children and Youth Services Review*, 8, 145–59.

Waites, M. (2005) *The Age of Consent: Young People, Sexuality and Citizenship*. London: Palgrave/Macmillan.

Waiton, S. (2006) The construction of the 'social problem' of antisocial behaviour and the institutionalisation of vulnerability. Unpublished PhD thesis, University of Glasgow.

Wakeling, P. (2005) 'La noblesse d'etat anglaise? Social class and progression to post-graduate study', *British Journal of Sociology of Education*, 26, 505–22.

Walkerdine, V., Lucey, H. and Melody, J. (2001) *Growing Up Girl: Psychosocial Explorations of Gender and Class*. London: Palgrave.

Wallace, C. (1987) *For Richer for Poorer. Growing Up In and Out of Work*. London: Tavistock.

Wallace, C. (2003) 'Introduction: Youth and politics', *Journal of Youth Studies*, 6, 243–5.

Waller, P.J. (1981) 'The riots in Toxteth, Liverpool. A survey', *New Community*, IX: 344–53.

Ward, R.A. and Spitze, G. (1992) 'Consequences of parent-adult child coresidence. A review and research agenda', *Journal of Family Issues*, 13, 553–72.

Warr, P. (1987) *Unemployment and Mental Health*. Oxford: Oxford University Press.

Warren, C.W., Santelli, J.S., Everett, S.A., Kann, L., Collins, J.L., Cassell, C., Morris, L. and Kolbe, L.J. (1998) 'Sexual behavior among US high school students, 1990–1995', *Family Planning Perspectives*, 30, 170–200.

Wasoff, F. and Morrison, A. (2005) 'Family formation and dissolution in Europe: Scotland in a European context', Research Findings No. 56/2005. Edinburgh: Scottish Executive.

Watson, I., Buchanan, J., Cambell, I. and Briggs, C. (2003) *Fragmented Futures: New Challenges for Working Life*. Sydney: The Federation Press.

West, P. (1988) 'Inequalities? Social class differentials in health in British youth', *Social Science Medicine*, 27, 291–6.

West, P. (1997) 'Health inequalities in the early years: is there equalisation in youth?', *Social Science and Medicine*, 44, 833–58.

West, P. and Sweeting, H. (1996) 'Nae job, nae future. Young people and health in a context of unemployment', *Health and Social Care in the Community*, 4, 50–62.

West, P. and Sweeting, H. (2003) 'Fifteen, female and stressed: Changing patterns of psychological stress over time', *Journal of Child Psychology and Psychiatry*, 44, 399–411.

Westwood, S. (1984) *All Day Every Day. Factory and Family in the Making of Women's Lives*. London: Pluto.

White, C., Bruce, S. and Ritchie, J. (2000) *Young People's Politics: Political Interest and Engagement Amongst 14 to 24 Year-olds*. York: York Publishing.

White, L. (1994) 'Coresidence and leaving home. Young adults and their parents', *Annual Review of Sociology*, 20, 81–102.

White, M. and McRae, S. (1989) *Young Adults and Long Term Unemployment*. London: Policy Studies Institute.

White, R. and Wyn, J. (2004) *Youth and Society: Exploring The Social Dimensions of Youth*. Melbourne: Oxford University Press.

Widdicombe, S. and Woffitt, R. (1995) *The Language of Youth Subcultures. Social Identity and Action*. London: Harvester Wheatsheaf.

Wight, D. (1993) 'Constraint or cognition? Factors affecting young men's practice of safer heterosexual sex', in P. Aggleton, P. Davies and G. Hart (eds) *AIDS. Facing the Second Decade*. London: Falmer.

Williamson, H. (2004) *The Milltown Boys Revisited*. London: Berg.

Williamson, J. (2005) Youth unemployment in Australia: emerging findings from a three year research and advocacy project. Paper presented to 'Transitions and Risk: New directions in social policy' conference, University of Melbourne, 23–25 February.

Willis, P. (1977) *Learning to Labour*. Farnbourgh: Saxon House.

Willis, P. (1990) *Common Culture*. Buckingham: Open University Press.

Wolff, M., Rutten, P. and Bayers, A. (1992) *Where We Stand*. New York: Bantam Books.

Woodroffe, C., Glickman, M., Barker, M. and Power, C. (1993) *Children, Teenagers and Health. Key Data*. Buckingham: Open University Press.

Wotherspoon, T. (2004) *The Sociology of Education in Canada: Critical Perspectives*, 2nd edition. Toronto and Oxford: Oxford University Press.

Wright, E.O. (1985) *Classes*. London: Verso.

Wyn, J. and White, R. (1997) *Rethinking Youth*. Sydney: Allen and Unwin. www.prisonstudies.org (accessed 3 November 2005).

Yeandle, S. (2003) 'The international context', in P. Alcock, C. Beatty, S. Fothergill, R. MacMillan and S. Yeandle (eds) *Work to Welfare: How Men Become Detached from the Labour Market*. Cambridge: Cambridge University Press.

Young, C.M. (1984) *Leaving Home and Returning Home. A Demographic Study of Young Adults in Australia*, Australian Family Research Conference Proceedings, Canberra, 1: 53–76.

Young, C.M. (1987) *Young People Leaving Home in Australia: The Trend Towards Independence*. Australian Family Formation Project Monograph, No.9. Canberra: Australian Family Formation Project.

Young, C.M. (1989) 'The effect of children returning home on the precision of the timing of the leaving-home stage', in E. Grebenik, C. Hohn and R. Mackensen (eds) *Later Phases of the Family Life Cycle. Demographic Aspects*. Oxford: Clarendon.

Young, J. (1971) *The Drugtakers. The Social Meaning of Drug Use*. London: Paladin.

Zeijl, E., du Bois Reymond, M. and Poel, Y. te (2001) 'Young adolescents' leisure patterns', *Society and Leisure*, 24, 379–402.

Author Index

Index